❧ The Well-Made Book

DANIEL BERKELEY UPDIKE
(*From a study by Rudolph Ruzicka*, 1930)

The Well-Made Book

ESSAYS & LECTURES
by Daniel Berkeley Updike

Edited by *William S. Peterson*

𝔐ark 𝔅atty, 𝔓ublisher
2002

LIBRARY OF CONGRESS CATALOGING-IN-PUBLICATION DATA:
Updike, Daniel Berkeley, 1860-1941.
The well-made book : essays & lectures / by Daniel Berkeley Updike ;
edited by William S. Peterson.-- 1st ed.
p. cm.
Includes bibliographical references and index.
ISBN 0-9715687-4-X (alk. paper)
1. Printing--History. 2. Printing--United States--History. 3. Fine
books--History. 4. Merrymount Press--History. I. Peterson, William S.
II. Title.
Z124 .U63 2002
686.2--dc21
2002011114

Printed and bound in the United States of America

First Edition
10 9 8 7 6 5 4 3 2 1

ISBN: 0-9715687-4-X Hardcover Edition
ISBN: 0-9715687-7-4 Special Edition

Mark Batty, Publisher LLC
6050 Boulevard East, Suite 2H
West New York, NJ 07093

www.markbattypublisher.com

Contents

Illustrations

Introduction

DANIEL BERKELEY UPDIKE (1860–1941), born into an old Rhode Island family ("I only know New England, where we have, as a family, pottered about within a radius of 70 miles for the last 300 years!" he remarked in a letter to Stanley Morison, 9 May 1924), displayed a strongly regional character in both his printing and his personal life. Like many descendants of the first colonial families, he harbored ambivalent feelings toward his forebears. Of course there were undeniable advantages in being the son and grandson of prominent Rhode Island politicians and in bearing the name *Berkeley* because an ancestor had become friendly with the Bishop of Cloyne during his stay in the American colonies. Yet one senses that at moments Updike, a strangely troubled and lonely man, found his distinguished lineage something of a burden. Like Thomas Hardy (in "Night in the Old House"), he could, in his darker hours, imagine himself "lingering and languishing here, | A pale late plant of [our] once strong stock."

Though Updike prided himself on coming from a long line of Anglicans, there was an unmistakably Puritanical streak in his character: "a New England Conscience" was how he grimly described it. The name of his Merrymount Press alludes to a short story by Hawthorne about one Thomas Morton, a rebellious colonist who defied his Puritan neighbors by setting up a Maypole and engaging in conspicuous revelry. Updike claimed that he regarded "Morton's Maypole as a symbol of work done cheerfully and well; of happiness found in work-a-day things; of a high aim and pleasure in trying to attain it"; and he adopted *Merrymount*, Morton's estate, as the emblem of his Press and the *Maypole* as his first printer's device [*Fig.* 1]. But this cheer-

OPTIMUM VIX SATIS

MERRYMOUNT

D. B. UPDIKE, DECORATIVE PRINTING AND BOOKMAKING, AT
THE SIGN OF THE MAYPOLE, THE MERRYMOUNT PRESS, NUMBER
SIX BEACON ST., AND NUMBER SEVEN TREMONT PLACE, BOSTON

1   Updike's first printer's device at the Merrymount Press.

ful interpretation, which ignores the darker undercurrents of Hawthorne's tale, is deliberately misleading, for Updike, as we know from his own testimony, approached work more in the spirit of Morton's Puritan enemies than in the mood of calculated frivolity that prevailed at the first Merrymount. His typographical labors at the Merrymount Press were sober and strenuous, prompted by a strong (dare one say Calvinistic?) sense of duty.

Naturally there was another side of Updike's personality, less obvious perhaps to strangers, which can sometimes be discerned in his writings: he was a man of considerable wit and charm, a wonderful story-teller, an amusing dinner companion, an erudite and cosmopolitan personality. In his more relaxed moments, he displayed a talent for unexpectedly acerbic remarks about his famous contemporaries. After reading a description by T. M. Cleland of Bertram Grosvenor Goodhue's heavily medievalized home, for instance, Updike commented to Cleland (4 June 1906): "I was greatly amused at your account of your visit and I thought the phrase about the monastery quite a masterpiece. It all seems so obsolete and Nurembergian to me—I mean that point of view—something to have had—like mumps." And his hilarious comparison of Bruce Rogers' lectern Bible with the privilege of spitting on a railroad platform (printed in this volume for the first time) reveals an uninhibited Updike seldom disclosed except to his most intimate friends.

Nevertheless, it cannot be denied that the dominant tone of Updike's life and work was one of rigorous self-discipline. What he sought to avoid in his books (as he wrote to Stanley Morison, 8 March 1937) was "sloppy exhibitionism"; what he aimed at was "ordered severity." These phrases offer us, in highly abbreviated form, a summary of Updike's typographical career, for he launched the Merrymount Press in Boston in 1893, at the very height of a private-press mania induced by the example of William Morris's Kelmscott Press, yet Updike, working at the epicenter of this feverish atmosphere, gradually discovered his own distinctive printing style. New England in the final decade of the nineteenth century was awash with pseudo-antique typography, bad imitations of Morris's types and ornaments, and an indiscriminate enthusiasm for *quaint* books and periodicals. At a fairly sophisticated level, the anglophilic Boston publishing house of Copeland & Day was popularizing the Morrisian manner in very close replicas of the Kelmscott books; at a more vulgar level, Elbert Hubbard, in nearby upstate New York, was churning out shoddy publications in heavy, ugly types at his vaguely fraudulent crafts community known as the *Roycrofters*. It is a tribute to Updike's independence of mind that he was able to rise above such unwholesome examples.

Updike, however, was not wholly untouched by this *sloppy exhibitionism* (to use his own phrase). In the early years of the Merrymount Press he publicly described himself as a specialist in *decorative printing*, a term that during the 1890s implied, without much subtlety, the use of Morris-style ornaments and illustrations. For the *Altar Book* (1896), Updike sought unsuccessfully to borrow Morris's own types and evidently hoped that Sir Edward Burne-Jones, illustrator of many of the Kelmscott books, might also furnish some wood-engravings.[1] Despite its reliance upon mainly American resources, the *Altar Book* [*Fig.* 2] was the most ambitious, clever, overpowering imitation of the Kelmscott Press model ever created—in either Britain or America. Then, having nearly out-Morrised Morris, Updike turned in other directions for typographical inspiration. Hence his wry remark to Cleland about neogothicism being a sort of childhood disease. When Updike came into his prime as a printer and book-designer—that is to say, during the early decades of the twentieth century—he regarded Morris as a distant memory.

But what Updike specifically rejected was Morris's medieval obsessions. The essays and lectures collected in this volume demonstrate that Updike never forgot Morris's subtler lesson—that a book could only be satisfactory if typography, ornaments, and illustrations were fully in harmony with each other. The books printed and designed at the Merrymount Press demonstrated (as few other books at the time did) that it was possible to follow the inspiring example of Morris without imitating his personal mannerisms.

It is significant that Updike, in describing his aspirations as a printer, speaks of *the well-made book*, whereas Morris, in 1893, had delivered a lecture on *the ideal book*. Morris began with this definition: "By the Ideal Book, I suppose we are to understand a book not limited by commercial exigencies of price: we can do what we like with it, according to what its nature, as a book, demands of Art. But we may conclude, I think, that its matter will limit us somewhat; a work on differential calculus, a medical work, a dictionary, a collection of statesman's speeches, of a treatise on manures, such books, though they might be handsome and well-printed, would scarcely receive ornament with the same exuberance as a volume of lyrical poems, or a standard classic, or such like."[2] Updike, to my knowledge, never turned his attention to manures, but he did boast that he had once created an advertising brochure for muffins *that actually sold muffins*. Morris's ironic list of books that would not lend themselves to distinguished typographical treatment—dictionaries, reference works, technical manuals, etc.—actually comes amusingly close to a description of many of the titles printed at the Merrymount Press. Morris's *ideal book* is a rarified creature, limited to *belletristic* texts that are thought to be suitable for elaborate illustration and ornamentation; it excludes the vast majority of books that we normally read and use.

Updike's *well-made book*, on the other hand, is a comprehensive ideal that embraces the most familiar, unglamorous publication. Updike believed that any piece of printed matter—including, presumably, even advertisements for muffins—could be improved by careful design and execution. There is no doubt that Updike assimilated certain ideas (and perhaps prejudices) from the private-press world of Morris: he deliberately worked with a limited range of typefaces (Morris had only three at the Kelmscott Press), he cherished the smallness of the Merrymount Press, and he resisted the use of composing machines until the 1920s. But early in his career Updike realized that he could only survive as a *commercial* printer by satisfying the actual needs of his varied customers. Though he printed from time to time exactly the kinds of books that Morris himself admired—collections of poems and literary essays, historical narratives with a charming antiquarian flavor, significant religious texts—the Merrymount Press kept itself afloat financially by producing useful books of the sort that Morris simply ignored: catalogues, reports of cultural and educational institutions, parish and local histories, sermons, lectures, memorial tributes. (And, it should be added, the Press also did a vast amount of ephemeral job-printing that has never been identified by any bibliographer.) Updike, whose own typographical aspirations had been nurtured initially by the arts-and-crafts fervor of Boston in the 1890s, displayed in later years a contempt for enthusiastic *amateurs* of printing; he liked to remind such creatures that printing was a serious craft that required a tough-minded realism in order to bring the ideals of good typography into the market-place.

To be fair to William Morris, it must be said that he followed his definition of *the ideal book* with the proviso that "a book quite un-ornamented can look actually and positively beautiful,"[3] and his own later commercially published books were handsomely but simply printed at the Chiswick Press. But, at least in the extravagant volumes issued by the Kelmscott Press, his insistence upon proprietary typefaces and lavish illustrations and ornaments provided little useful guidance to young admirers like Updike. Morris resisted any kind of normal textual apparatus in the Kelmscott books, not only

S·ATHANASIVS·DOCTOR
S·CHRYSOSTOMVS·DOCTOR
S·AVGVSTINVS·DOCTOR
S·HIERONYMVS·DOCTOR

EASTER·DAY. THE COLLECT.

ALMIGHTY God, who through thine only-begotten Son Jesus Christ hast overcome death, and opened unto us the gate of everlasting life; We humbly beseech thee that, as by thy special grace preventing us thou dost put into our minds good desires, so by thy continual help we may bring the same to good effect; through Jesus Christ our Lord, who liveth and reigneth with thee and the Holy Ghost ever, one God, world without end. Amen.

THE EPISTLE. Col. iii. 1.

IF ye then be risen with Christ, seek those things which are above, where Christ sitteth on the right hand of God. Set your affection on things above, not on things on the earth. For ye are dead, and your life is hid with Christ in God. When Christ, who is our life, shall appear, then shall ye also appear with him in glory. Mortify therefore your members which are upon the earth; fornication, uncleanness, inordinate affection, evil concupiscence, and covetousness, which is idolatry: for which things' sake the wrath of God cometh on the children of disobedience: in the which ye also walked some time, when ye lived in them.

THE GOSPEL. St. John xx. 1.

THE first day of the week cometh Mary Magdalene early, when it was yet dark, unto the sepulchre, and seeth the stone taken away from the sepulchre. Then she runneth, and cometh to Simon Peter, and to the other disciple, whom Jesus loved, and saith unto them, They have taken away the Lord out of the sepulchre, and we know not where they have laid him. Peter therefore went forth, and that other disciple, and came to the sepulchre. So they ran both together: and the other disciple did outrun Peter, and came first to the sepulchre.

S·MATTHAEVS·EVAN
S·MARCVS·EVANGE
S·LVCAS·EVANGEL
S·IOANNES·EVA

BEATA·MARIA·VIRGO
S·MARIA·CLEOPHAE
S·MARIA·MAGDALENE

2   *The Altar Book* (Merrymount Press, 1896).

because he wanted the texts to speak for themselves but also because, as F. S. Ellis acknowledged, his types had no companion italic and small caps fonts. In other words, Morris, by his own choice, was equipped to do only the least complicated varieties of typesetting (poetry and prose in a single type size and usually in a single column); one can, of course, see this as a part of Morris's attempt at radical simplification, but the practical consequence was that he had to restrict himself to typographically undemanding texts, with even simple footnotes beyond his capacity. For Updike, by contrast, the challenges of complex typography were always a source of keen pleasure. He liked to remind his readers that the most apparently dull text, such as a dictionary or catalogue, may actually provide much more interesting problems for the designer than the greatest novel or group of poems would. The literary interest of a text is not identical to its typographical interest.

If, therefore, we wish to take the measure of Updike the printer and book-designer, it is probably misleading to seek comparisons in the enclosed sphere of the private presses, though that is undoubtedly where Updike's roots are to be discovered. The more appropriate analogy would perhaps be the Chiswick Press, which had been responsible for an important typographical revival in mid-Victorian England (and which, incidentally, gave Morris his introduction to the mysteries of printing). The Chiswick Press printed probably the best nineteenth-century English books before Morris, but, like the Merrymount Press, it did so under ordinary commercial conditions and constraints, using types and other materials that (except for Mary Byfield's engravings) were readily available to any printer at the time. Or, if one prefers a more modern example, Francis Meynell's Nonesuch Press, founded in London in 1923, also followed this pattern: Meynell did not even do his own composition or presswork but instead *outsourced it* (as we would say today); to put it another way, he functioned purely as a book-designer, not as a printer—Updike himself had unsuccessfully tried to do this in the early 1890s—but, like Updike, Meynell imported the elevated standards of the private-press world into the very different territory of commercial printing and publishing. Updike's great achievement was to mediate between the apparently incompatible values of Kelmscott Press idealism and the more profit-driven world of ordinary printing.

Updike followed Morris's example in at least one other important respect: he wrote and lectured brilliantly about his craft, making clear the connections between printing and the broader concerns of society. Largely self-educated, Updike brought to bear upon typographical matters an impressive erudition and breadth of intellectual interests. He recognized that the printing of books, apparently a mechanical operation carried on by modest artisans, is in fact a cultural microcosm that reveals much about the human mind and spirit. Mysteriously, the arrangement of patterns of ink on paper can tell us a great deal about the civilization that produced those books, and, even more strangely, it can disclose to us the personality of the craftsman who created the artifacts we are examining. As Updike remarked, the style of the printed page is ultimately an expression of the character of the man (or woman) who designed and printed it, and one cannot doubt that the *ordered severity* of an Updike book displays a mind that finds a profoundly spiritual harmony in the rational, orderly disposition of beautiful abstract symbols upon a sheet of white paper.

A brief comment on the design of this book. It is dangerous to follow too closely in the footsteps of a great designer, but I have tried to make the present volume conform, at least broadly, to Updike's standards. The proportions of the margins and the spacing between words and lines are approximately what he himself used. Since Martin Hutner has demonstrated statistically that Caslon Old Face was overwhelmingly Updike's first choice for the books that he printed,[4] I was delighted to discover, just as I was planning this collection of Updike's writings, that Justin Howes had produced an exact digital replica of Caslon's original types. I adopted it unhesitatingly, and I am confident that Updike himself would have been equally pleased by it.

Notes

1. Updike's letter to William Morris, dated August 1893, is printed in a booklet published by the Huntington Library, *Daniel Berkeley Updike to William Morris* (San Marino, Calif., 1968); the fact that Updike intended to approach Burne-Jones was disclosed in a paper read by Philip Weimerskirch at the annual conference of the American Printing History Association in St. Louis, October 2001.

2. *Ideal Book*, p. 67.

3. *Ibid.*

4. Martin Hutner, *The Merrymount Press: An Exhibition on the Occasion of the* 100th *Anniversary of the Founding of the Press* (Cambridge, Mass.: Houghton Library; New York: Grolier Club, 1993), p. 75. Updike's three favorite faces were Caslon (used in 467 books and pamphlets printed at the Merrymount Press), Scotch Roman (190), and Oxford (122).

Textual Note

THIS volume is a collection of Daniel Berkeley Updike's essays, lectures, book reviews, and ephemeral writings about book-related matters; it excludes, however, his *Printing Types* (first published in 1922 and still in print) and various essays on other subjects. Bringing together this material produces, I think, a surprisingly full and comprehensive body of writings on bibliophilic topics, though there are undoubtedly still some undiscovered pieces in periodicals and archival collections.

I have retained Updike's own notes (indicated by "DBU" in brackets), and I have added a few of my own, but I have resisted the temptation to annotate too heavily, especially in identifying the wide range of Updike's quotations. (Updike was a master of the apt reference, and to annotate every citation of another's words would produce an exceptionally cumbersome textual apparatus.) Many of Updike's original illustrations are reproduced, and I have added a few others that seem appropriate or helpful.

In almost every instance the texts below are are based upon the last version supervised by Updike for the press. (I have indicated the few exceptions to this rule in the notes following the chapters or selections, and I have also recorded there any previous publication of the pieces.) Fortunately, Updike was a meticulously careful copy-editor and proof-reader, and this means that his miscellaneous writings—particularly the things he prepared for publication in *In the Day's Work* (1924) and *Some Aspects of Printing Old and New* (1941)—require very little alteration by an editor, but of course he had far less control over the texts of essays in journals or in books published by others. These latter I have attempted to "un-house-style" by making them conform to his usual stylistic practices.

Readers will notice that Updike's spelling is unusual: it is primarily British (though his punctuation is American), and it shifts slightly through the years. I have nearly always retained his spellings of names of persons and places (except for obvious errors), though they are sometimes nonstandard, but I have normalized the names in the index. I have capitalized words like *Lintotype* and *Monotype*, and I have employed italics more consistently for titles of books and journals than Updike did. The few stylistic alterations I have made, mainly for the sake of consistency, are, I hope, more or less the changes that Updike himself would have introduced had he prepared these writings for publication in a single volume.

I have included a few representative advertising brochures for the Merrymount Press, but they are merely samples of a much larger body of material. The longer essays and lectures are grouped in several broad thematic categories; the shorter ones are arranged chronologically.

SOURCES AND ABBREVIATIONS

The following sources are cited from time to time in this book, and in some cases they are referred to by the abbreviated title in brackets. The sources of individual pieces by Updike reprinted below are indicated in the endnotes following each of them.

Beilenson, Peter, ed. *Updike: American Printer and His Merrymount Press.* New York: American Institute of Graphic Arts, 1947. [Beilenson]

Lathem, Edward Connery, ed. *Rudolph Ruzicka: Speaking Reminiscently.* New York: Grolier Club, 1986.

Lathem, Edward Connery, and Elizabeth French Lathem, eds. *D.B.U. and R.R.: Selected Abstracts from Correspondence between Daniel Berkeley Updike and Rudolph Ruzicka, 1908– 1914.* New York: American Printing History Association,

[1998]. [Updike–Ruzicka correspondence]

McKitterick, David, ed. *Stanley Morison and D. B. Updike: Selected Correspondence*. New York: Moretus Press, 1979.

Morris, William. *The Ideal Book: Essays and Lectures on the Arts of the Book*, ed. William S. Peterson. Berkeley and Los Angeles: University of California Press, 1982. [*Ideal Book.*]

Updike, Daniel Berkeley. *In the Day's Work*. Cambridge, Mass.: Harvard University Press, 1924. [*In the Day's Work*]

———. *Printing Types: Their History, Forms, and Use. A Study in Survivals*. 2 vols. 2nd ed. Cambridge, Mass.: Harvard University Press, 1951. [*Printing Types*]

———. *Some Aspects of Printing Old and New*. New Haven: William Edwin Rudge, 1941. [*Some Aspects of Printing*]

Updike Collection, Providence Public Library, Providence, R.I. [Updike Collection]

ACKNOWLEDGMENTS

I must record a special debt of gratitude to four persons: Philip Weimerskirch (Curator of the Updike Collection and of Special Collections at the Providence Public Library), who furnished much advice and information and gave important assistance in supplying illustrations; Martin Hutner, the leading authority on Updike's life and career, who answered questions, sent me photocopies of two talks by Updike at the Grolier Club, and lent items from his own Updike collection for use as illustrations; Jane Rodgers Siegel and The Rare Books and Manuscript Library, Columbia University, for the use of items from the collections as illustrations; and Justin Howes (proprietor of H. W. Caslon and Company Ltd. and creator of the digital Caslon fonts used in this book), who generously designed two liturgical symbols for one of the essays and supplied beta versions of Caslon's Greek and black-letter.

The Providence Public Library and the Grolier Club have given me permission to publish several Updike typescripts.

Others who have assisted in various ways include Mark Batty, Lissa Dodington, Donald Farren, Kimball Higgs, Sylvia W. Holton, Mark Samuels Lasner, and Fernando Peña.

 General

A FEW WORDS ABOUT PRINTING, BOOK-MAKING, AND THEIR ALLIED ARTS: BEING A SHORT DESCRIPTION OF SOME OF THE WORK DONE BY MR. BERKELEY UPDIKE, AT NUMBER SIX BEACON STREET, BOSTON, MASSACHUSETTS

MONG the arts and crafts in which persons of taste and cultivation have been increasingly interested during the past few years is that of printing, and design as applied thereto. The modern tendency to specialize the different portions of all work has been nowhere more apparent than in the printer's art, so that to-day the compositor no longer sets the styles of typography, but simply works under the direction of those who have made style in printing a special study. In other words, there are arising on every side, workers whose place is not that of the man by whom a printer's work is used, nor of the printer himself, but of one, who, by a knowledge of the requirements of clients on the one hand, and the abilities of the printer on the other, is able to produce a better result than either could do alone. This little preface answers, to a certain extent, a question that is often asked as to the precise place which one holds in relation to printer and public. Mr. Updike has

3   *A Few Words about Printing, Book-making, and Their Allied Arts* (Merrymount Press brochure, 1894)

On the Planning of Printing

"IT must of necessity be," said Sir Joshua Reynolds, "that even works of genius, like every other effect, as they must have their cause, must also have their rules; it cannot be by chance that excellencies are produced with any constancy or any certainty, for this is not the nature of chance: but the rules by which men of extraordinary parts—and such as are called men of genius—work, are either such as they discover by their own peculiar observations, or of such a nice texture as not easily to admit being expressed in words. Unsubstantial, however, as these rules may seem, and difficult as it may be to convey them in writing, they are still seen and felt in the mind of the artist; and he works from them with as much certainty as if they were embodied upon paper. It is true these refined principles cannot always be made palpable, as the more gross rules of art; yet it does not follow but that the mind may be put in such a train that it still perceives by a kind of scientific sense that propriety which words . . . can but very feebly suggest."

Sir Joshua said this in regard to painting, in his case surely the work of genius; but if we substitute for the word "genius" the word "art," we have a quotation which is applicable even to the task of designing satisfactory pieces of typography. Although rules for designing suitable printing may seem unsubstantial and difficult to convey in words, it is still true that they are seen and felt in the mind of the worker. They are illusive rules, and yet none the less a man works from them with as much certainty as if they were set down on paper. It is because they are so illusive that many persons believe that, in designing printing, there are no rules at all; because they commonly think of rules as matters of precise measurement and definite proportion. As a matter of fact, the best rules for planning work are general rules, and rules for the mind rather than for the hand—no less real because applying to what may be called, in a sense, a spiritual matter. So in properly laying out printing (which is nothing more than successfully designing it for a given object) it is necessary to have a certain mental equipment, which is, to tell the truth, where most designers of printing fail. Having said this, I may divide the subject into three parts: the first of which treats of the apparatus with which we work; the second, of the requirements of the persons for whom we work; and the third, of those principles on which we plan our work; or, to put it more simply, the classification of our material, our relations with customers, and how to plan the printing they ask us to do.

I. ARRANGEMENT OF "SPECIMEN-BOOKS"

The specimens of the type which a printing-office possesses should be arranged in orderly and convenient fashion so that the time of the man who is planning the printing may not be wasted. There is no need of going to the expense of printing elaborate volumes to show our types. A blank book in which proofs of type are pasted will do very well, or a "loose-leaf" folder is better still, as it permits additions in proper sequence. The same passage (either in Latin or English) may be used throughout the volume to show types for book-pages and the comparative amount of matter which can be set in various sizes of type. For instance, in a Caslon series the first type may be the smallest size shown; a passage of ten or twelve lines may be set in four ways, solid, and leaded with 1-point, 2-point, and 3-point leads. On the same page an alphabet of capitals, small capitals, swash letters, ligatured letters, and all the "peculiar sorts" used with that particular fount should be displayed, and the amount of type available for use should be stated. In the specimen-book arranged by the late Theodore De Vinne for the De Vinne Press, not only capitals, small capitals, lowercase, and italic in the fount were shown, but also numbers, accented letters, mathematical signs, signs of the zodiac, and every peculiar sort were displayed; and the foundry in which the type was cast was also mentioned.[1]

The four variously leaded paragraphs just spoken of might occupy two facing pages. The next two facing pages would be devoted to italic of the same size, similarly leaded. Then would come the next larger size of roman in the same series with its italic, and so on, up to Great Primer or 18-point, which would probably be the largest size of type used for a book-page. In any size above Great Primer, a few lines of roman and italic type with the alphabet and special characters could occupy a page by themselves.

Transitional types treated in a like manner would come next; then modified old styles; and finally the modern faces. Special faces such as Bodoni, Garamond, or French old style, could be arranged in the same way. These might be followed by black-letters and scripts. After each series a table of graded sizes of its capital letters should be exhibited—from the smallest size of capitals to the largest, "small capitals" being inserted in their proper place, so that the variety of sizes of capitals available may be seen at a glance. By placing small tabs on the edge of the page at which each new type-family begins, marked with a number or name, much time would be saved in turning to founts one wished to look at.

Ornamental alphabets, ornaments, etc., may occupy a second division or another volume of the same size bound in another colour. In this second part, alphabets could be arranged in series, by sizes; or according to styles. Typographical "flowers" should be grouped according to size or style or arranged according to date of issue. In the specimen-book of Briquet, published at Paris in 1757 [*Fig.* 4], such ornaments are displayed very ingeniously. Each "flower" is numbered; a single one is first shown, and is followed by the same "flower" arranged in rows to show the effect if used as a border. Next

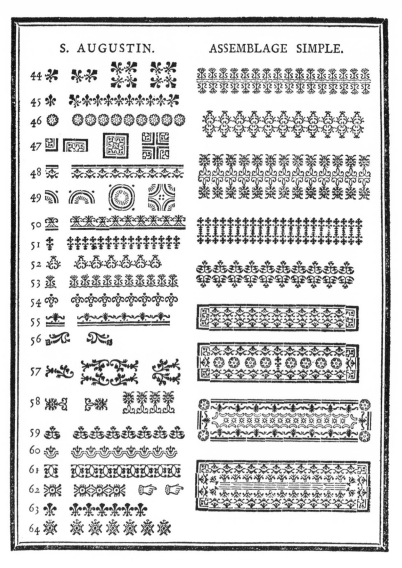

4   Briquet's *Épreuve des Caractères* (Paris, 1757) [reduced].

the "flower" is shown in various combinations—back to back, in two rows together, one running in the ordinary way and the other upside down, etc. A great many effective and ingenious patterns may be made from the same ornament placed in different positions, and still greater variety can be had by combining two ornaments, as a study of old specimen-books will show.

Some pages at the end of this division may be reserved for the miscellaneous type ornaments which slowly accumulate in every printing-house.

It may be said that this seems a practical plan for the man who lays out the printing, but that such a book would not be attractive to a customer choosing type. But why let a customer make a choice of type? As Fournier said, "men who pride themselves most on knowing about books, are often very much embarrassed when it comes to giving an exact idea of the kind of type in which these books are printed; ordinarily they are at a loss for the names of the types; sometimes they miscall them, but ordinarily they employ inexact expressions—saying that such a book is printed in large or small type, which only gives a vague, indeterminate idea, and means nothing at all." And once upon a time there was an author who returned his proofs, with the message that he hoped the type would be larger when the book was printed! But by the time a customer has stated what he thinks he wants (for he does not always end by wanting what he at first thinks he does), the designer has formed an idea of the range of types which it is best to use. If a customer insists that he must see the type to be used, one or two types—either of which is suitable—may be shown him. There is something to be learned, here, from the old trick of allowing a person to choose a card from a pack, and telling him what that card will be before he looks at it. If well done, the trick never fails, because the man who is selecting the card does not really select it, but has a certain card dealt into his hand. I believe a customer should be treated in much the same way, with this difference: that instead of allowing him to think he is selecting one among fifty-two cards, I should give him (and tell him I was giving him) but four cards to choose from—all aces of different suits! In this way a customer would certainly exercise a choice, but it would only be a choice of the four best kinds of the same thing! No one wishes to fool a customer, but it is equally unfair to permit him to fool himself. He should get what he is paying for: the best knowledge the printer possesses.

II. RELATIONS WITH CUSTOMERS

Thus we have suddenly arrived at the relation of the printer to his customers. Cardinal Newman speaks somewhere of the need of practising an "economy in imparting religious truth." This being interpreted signifies to keep back something; and has its authority in certain rather "unevangelical" passages in the New Testament, to the effect that it is at times wise to give out only as much truth as the hearer is able to bear. This is usually the part of wisdom in a printer's treatment of a customer. He cannot be told everything; in fact, he can only be told (advantageously to himself) what it is good for him to know! Anglo-Saxons detest this kind of reasoning, because they say that it appears shifty and untruthful; but what they really subconsciously dislike is the principle of authority inherent in it. As a race we resent experts—though all Americans, and no doubt some English, secretly believe that they are experts themselves! So, though printers often act on some such idea, they do not fancy calling it an "economy in imparting truth." One may hold back information, but it is bad form to admit to yourself that you do, or to hold the theory that it may be defensibly done. Such people agree in principle with George III when he said, "Shakespeare often wrote sad stuff, but one must not say so."

As customers fall into many different classes, they have to be met in many different ways. They certainly sometimes bring difficult typographical problems to the printer, for which they suggest or dictate ridiculous solutions. But a printer cannot be of use to typography by dismissing their views and them. His part is to lead them into the more excellent way, by showing them what can be done to improve their work and what cannot, and by explaining the reason why. Thus he can avoid needlessly annoying a "client," and encourage him not only to have this particular piece of work printed well, but to have more work printed better; for most people will use good types if they can only be made to see the reason of their goodness. I remember once being obliged to print, for a personage who dealt in muffins, a circular which was to show their excellence; and to this end he showed me an announcement printed in coloured ink from horrid types, on brown note-paper, with a "hemstitched" perforated edge, as a model for what was to be done. This circular he had secured from the establishment of a milliner. His mind worked in this way: that as an expensive hat was advertised by a circular adorned with perforations, and this hat cost one hundred times more than a muffin, a circular adapted for the hat must be many times better than the ordinary method of muffin advertising! I explained that there was a suitable and even ideal way of advertising muffins as well as hats, and that to advertise a muffin as one would a hat might very likely mislead the public about its digestibility! We ended by making an advertisement which I thought pretty, and he said was extremely so, *and it sold the muffins!* What more could you ask? Thus it is a part of wisdom, though not, alas, always of inclination, to try to teach a customer—to lead and not drive him. But there are times when, if a customer insists on employing some bad, freaky types in cheap, tawdry display of colour, you are right in telling him that he must have his work done elsewhere.

That amusing person, Lady Mary Wortley Montagu, in a letter to her daughter, Lady Bute, said that "people commonly educate their children as they build their houses, according to some plan they think beautiful, without considering whether it is suitable for the purpose for which they are designed. Almost all girls of quality are educated as if they were to be great ladies. You should teach yours to confine their desires to probabilities." And this is just as true of printing as of education or house-building, and, I am told, is a useful idea when marrying off a daughter.

But customers seldom see that the essential thing in all printing is that it be suitable for the purpose for which it is designed, and printers have not based their practice on any such sensible rule. If printers had more of a standard and a stiffer one, both about the types they employ and the way in which they use them, printing would be better. The printer, if he has no standard, *must* allow the customer to dictate his own wishes about types. He is defenseless, no matter how indefensible typographically the customer's ideas may be. In fixed opinions of what types are good and what are bad, the average printer has been a most spiritless individual. His long-suffering has become a tradition, and for him to assert that there are things typographically which he will not do, has the expectedness of the much talked-of (but seldom seen) turning worm! Clergymen, businessmen, landscape architects, school teachers, and contractors all have what they call "ideas" about types and their arrangement, and make no bones about telling the printer what they are. Yet these people are profoundly ignorant of typography. If the printer had an educated standard in typography, he could show them that they were so. But he has nothing to suggest. He is not leading, but following; if he takes any other position, it is troublesome to him and he is misunderstood by his public. Pained surprise is upon the faces of friends; annoyed resistance is shown by the customer. "Prudential reasons" are suggested by uncles, "kindness" by aunts, "horse-sense" by business acquaintances. The printer who sticks to a standard is usually supposed to be arbitrary, autocratic, wilful, conceited, and generally toplofty. Now, he may be all this, but he is not of necessity so; and as a matter of fact, he is sometimes as weary of his standard as any customer can be. There is, however, a standard. It can be held to, though not without trouble. The lack of it has reduced much modern printing to what it is.

These are some of the difficulties we meet with in dealing with people who know little about printing and, to some extent, admit it. But there is a second class who are worse: those who take a superior tone about it and are very sure that they know the printer's inmost thoughts. To prove this they use an inaccurate semi-technical jargon which has taught me the wisdom of never trying to talk in the terms of another person's trade—I do not deal in architectural terms before an architect, though I may inflict them on my defenseless doctor! To the mind of this second class there are two kinds of work that a press may do, differentiated by the terms "artistic" and "commercial"— terms very carelessly and very currently used. It is often said (as if it were a compliment) that such and such a printer does not do commercial work, but only artistic. One may say that he endeavours to do *good* work, if that is "artistic"; and he *sells* it, so it is after all "commercial." The rejoinder is, "But I mean printing of a commercial character, i.e. used in business"—the inference being that such printing cannot be "artistic" (poor, overworked word!), which, thank God, is often the case! The real difficulty lies in what is meant by artistic printing. To my mind it means: printing as exactly and agreeably suited as possible to the object for which it is to be used—commercial printing being just as capable of possessing this excellence as any other variety. But most people, if they stopped to analyse, would find that they really meant by "artistic printing" something queer, dear, and not well adapted to daily use, delivered later than expected; and by "commercial," something commonplace, cheap, nasty, and done in a hurry. The truth is that the best presses do but one kind of work, which is neither solely commercial nor artistic, but both, i.e. good. Then again, in the mind of the class of customers of whom I speak, literary interest is confused with problems of handicraft. A mere circular or an advertisement, they say, cannot be interesting to arrange. One can never make such persons understand that it is not the matter to be printed, but the problem of design presented by that matter, which is interesting to a printer. An edition of Dante may be a great bore to execute, and offer no very difficult problem; while one may be exceedingly amused and interested by a circular about tea! To see this requires the professional point of view, and does not support the lazy generalizations of the amiable amateur. He will continue to call printing "very artistic" and "only commercial," and rather fancy that he commends himself to a printer by so doing.

Perhaps it may be said that in old times there was not such a variety of types as there is now, or so many kinds of work to be done. This is true. But it is quite easy to restrict the repertoire of types in any office to *good types* and to permit their use only in legitimate ways. The earliest printers were often learned men, and yet perhaps their contemporaries thought that they took themselves too seriously. But what they took seriously was not themselves, but their work. They were educated enough and independent enough to hold to certain ideals. If Aldus had watered down his manner of printing and continually varied his types to suit other people's views, he would never have been heard of. None the less, the heads of contemporary Italian uncles and aunts were sadly shaken, perhaps, and friends of the family were seriously distressed. We remember the types and books of Aldus still; but the names of these "wise and prudent" are forgotten.

III. SOME PRINCIPLES IN PLANNING PRINTING

The man who has to plan or lay out a piece of printing should pause a few moments before he attacks his problem, and his plan is best made alone in a quiet room (from which examples of other people's work are banished) wherein is a large table, and on it nothing but the manuscript of the work to be arranged and a book of specimens of types. Supposing the work to be planned is a book: give thought not only to what the book is about and to the author from whom the work emanates, but to the public for whom it is intended, and to its trade conditions; and in this light examine the manuscript from beginning to end. By the time the designer has done this, some mental picture of what seems a good typographic form for the work will present itself; and his "job" is to express this image in terms of type. "The prophetic eye of taste" (wrote the poet Gray), "when it plants a seedling, already sits under the shadow of it, and enjoys the effect it will have from every point of view that lies in the prospect." So it must be with the designer of printing: he should be able to visualize the effect of his work in its finished form before a single type is set.

Furthermore, in planning this book one must think of its purpose, of its convenience to the reader for that purpose— and remember, also, any requirements as to uniformity with other books or other series. The plan must also provide for illustrations, if such there are to be, and determine how they are to be rendered; for these have a distinct relation to type, which must in some way be made to harmonize with them. Finally, there is the question of limitation of expense, and the price at which the book is to sell, which will give some idea of how much can be spent upon it. All this has to be thought out. And after that we may proceed to choose the type which we think will best suit the above requirements.

Having done this, take from the manuscript those pages which give (1) a solid mass of text; (2) tabular or unusual matter; and (3) quotations or poetry. The page of solid matter, already mentally designed, being the norm, one can then judge how successfully this imaginary page will permit the introduction of those various features which the unusual pages demand. Some of those latter features may require a modification of the imaginary normal page. But if the imaginary page, with these exceptions in view, is successfully designed, it can be set up. If this preliminary work is conscientiously done, that which results from it will be good, because so well adapted for its purpose as to appear inevitable. The result will give the same sense of satisfaction that a well-made glove or a good tennis racket produces. These principles apply to everything that is printed: to an edition of Aristotle, to a choral book for a cathedral, to the circular for a pottery or a sale of handkerchiefs, to the label for a pot of jam.

There is a passage in the *Architecture* of Vitruvius that may serve as a text for printers who forget that the adaptation of a thing for its purpose is half its charm. Speaking of winter dining-rooms, he says that "neither paintings on grand subjects, nor delicacy of decoration in the cornice work of the vaultings, is a serviceable kind of design, because they are spoiled by the smoke from the fire and the constant soot from the lamps." "In these rooms," he adds, "there should be panels above the dadoes, worked in black, and polished with yellow ochre, or vermilion blocks interposed between them." And he goes on in the same practical strain to recommend the Greek method of making floors of a porous material, so that at dinner parties whatever is poured out of cups, "no sooner falls than it dries up, and the servants who wait there do not catch cold from that kind of floor although they may go barefoot." Vitruvius makes, as all good craftsmen do, the necessities of the case the factors of his choice of decoration and material. Indeed, the limitations of a piece of work are often a help to him who plans it. "Any designer is assisted, though also limited, by conditions of construction as well as by art considerations," says a recent writer. "A thorough knowledge and acknowledgement of these conditions will enable the designer, no matter in what material he works, to make the most of his opportunities; and the recognition of his limitations should prove a help rather than a hindrance to him. The architect is limited in the size, site, and cost of his building. The designer is restricted to the use of a certain number of colours for his carpet, and is compelled to recognize the conditions of its manufacture. The artist must plan the positions, form the colour of the features of interest in his picture. In fact, none of them are absolutely free in their work. If they recognize their limitations, they know that there are things they may do, and things which they cannot do; and the success or failure of their efforts will be largely influenced by their acceptance of the conditions under which they work."

Bearing in mind these limitations, and also Morris's three propositions: "First, that a page should be clear and easy to read; second, the types well designed; and third, the margins in due proportion to the page of letter"; and that "furthermore, in a book the effect of headlines, the size of type in relation to the size of page, spacing between words, leading, style of typeface, title-page, and decorations have all to be thought of"—we have the problem before us.[2]

If our books are to be purely retrospective volumes, reprints in the Gothic style, Renaissance style, or the French eighteenth-century manner, that call for close study of books of the period, there is little opportunity to go wrong, if enough time and thought be devoted to the problem. But the important characteristics of a given style are not always those which at first glance appear to be so. Consider an Aldine book. In reproducing one, many printers would lose sight of the fact that the characteristic points of the Aldine edition were as much Aldus's use of small roman capitals combined with a slightly larger italic, as his use of italic for the text of an entire volume. The particular point which needs emphasis in planning reproductive work is that the study of old models must be minute—not alone in the type used, but in all details of its management.

But nine times out of ten a printer's work is to design pages for modern books. It is not enough that such a book should be legible because set in good type, clearly arranged, and sharply printed. Over and above this, there is a suitability which is as important, and which constitutes the charm of typography. Of course no piece of printing is good for anything which is not legible. Yet granted this, it may still be a failure if it breaks down along the parallel lines of literary and artistic suitability. A prayer-book may be printed in a type which is readable, but which is so out of tune with liturgical work that no person who wanted a prayer-book would buy it. You could not sell *Punch*, however well printed, in black-letter; not because black-letter is not in itself a good type-form, but because it is not appropriate nor the kind we like in illustrated humorous periodicals. So while a book must be easily read, it must also be printed in a manner suitable for its purpose—attractive to the cultivated through the mind, as well as to the ignorant through the eye. Thus a modern book is often difficult to plan successfully because it involves a personal view of the question, and there is no explicit guide in designing work of this sort. The designer can succeed only by his ability and taste in taking advantage of the factors in the problem which are pointing out how the book is to be designed. Each piece of printing has a still, small voice of its own if we can but hear it. To listen to it saves taking many "false routes."

The subject-matter of a book should, as has been suggested, furnish a clue to its appropriate treatment. If you are to design a modern book like Vernon Lee's *Studies of the Eighteenth Century in Italy*, you will not produce a suitable or agreeable effect if you use black-letter headlines or a modern German aesthetic roman type for its text, both of which connote an entirely different order of ideas. Give a slight suggestion of an eighteenth-century Italian volume to your modern book by introducing into it a few characteristic eighteenth-century Italian type-forms or methods of arrangement, which can be adapted without affectation to the work of today. The Italian eighteenth-century book should not be copied, but it should be suggested. On the other hand, if you plan a book in such modern fashion that it recalls nothing of the eighteenth century, but might as well be *Stormonth's Dictionary* as far as charm goes, you have not made as good a scheme as you can with the material at hand. Lack of practicality is the most serious fault; but lack of suitability or appropriateness is still a fault, and one which the intelligent typographer must know how to overcome. The two horses must be driven together!

There is, too, the tendency to strive for undue originality. Now originality is all very well, but it must be an improvement on what is less original, and therefore more commonly used. I have often, when travelling, been tempted to go where scarcely any one else had been, because it seemed rather an original thing to do, and interesting (at least, to me) to tell about afterward. When I got to my destination I usually found that the reason the trip was not popular was because it was not in the least worth while to have taken it! The same is true in typography. Most experiments, wise and otherwise, have already been tried, and the sure way—which is not very original now—is on the whole the best way, unless it can be so much improved that its utility can be recognized at once. If it seems commonplace, it is often so because it is so much the best—merely common-sense!

It was said of Congreve that "his nice scholarship had taught him the burden of association which time had laid upon this word or that. He used the language of his own day like a master, because he was anchored securely to a knowledge of the past." A man, to become a master of typography, should have this same anchorage. His typography should be allusive, and his originality should consist in perceiving opportunities for allusiveness when most printers would not. A modern book should show that the man who planned it has a knowledge of old styles, but never allows this knowledge to impair suitability for today's purpose. No matter what book is to be planned, you must always ask these questions: What is it to be used for? Where is it to be used? By whom is it to be used? What is the most suitable, practical, simple, orderly, and

[17]

historical method of producing it?—questions of universal ap-plication, with answers capable of endless variation. The result of such well-laid plans should be typography which is good for what it is meant to be, yet decorative too.

For ephemeral printing—circulars, prospectuses, etc.—we have to follow the principles laid down in planning books, except that we may treat the printing more fancifully and lightly. There, more than ever, we can hear the voice of the work speaking to us, if we are willing to listen. If we are printing a syllabus of studies, we must think of the age of the person by whom the studies are pursued. If it is a lesson-book for children, the type should be larger, and its various features more clearly defined, than if intended for mature persons. In all works of education, where the aim in view is the most lucid possible statement, the typography should be of a transparent nature, i.e. which attracts no attention to itself and is merely a vehicle to convey the words of the printed page to the reader's mind. If a title-page used in educational printing permits of a slightly decorative treatment, the kind of institution which presents the work must be kept in mind. If it is a seminary for clergy, it might have an ecclesiastical look; if a school of com-merce, it should have a strictly business-like appearance. If it is a literary society, an old-style type may be used; whereas for the school of commerce it would be better to employ a modern-face type. But for the religious seminary, school of commerce, or literary society, it is always possible to employ a type which is thoroughly good; the pages may be well proportioned and well imposed; the type well spaced and properly leaded; the impression clear and nervous. When the work is done, if it ful-fils its purposes in the most suitable manner, it will have "that note of rightness which, evasive, indescribable, and intangible, nevertheless clearly marks off the work of a craftsman from that of a hack."

One can only plan successfully these smaller pieces of work by considering minutely what they are meant to accomplish.

Let us take a menu. What questions would be uppermost in one's mind in planning that? The first that would occur to me would be the hour of the meal and where it was to be served. Was it to be by day or night? If by day, by artificial light or not? The colour of the card and the size of type would be somewhat dependent on this. Was there any particular scheme of colour in the decorations of the table? Because my menu must either match or at least not be discordant with it. Was it to be a big table with ample room for each guest, or a small one? Was the menu to be laid on a napkin or to stand upright? That would dictate my choice of size; for a menu is an incident, not a feature, at a dinner, and should not be so large as to be in the way if laid down, nor so big as to knock over glasses and fall into one's plate if it is to stand. Decide all these little points in the light of "What is the thing used for? Where is it to be used? By whom is it to be used? What is the most suitable, practical, simple, orderly, and historical method of producing it?" For even menus have a history, and were first used in the household of the Duke of Brunswick at Ratisbon in the first half of the sixteenth century. By consulting some of the French books which have been written on this and allied subjects, you will find out "a number of things."

Some one brings a programme for a *musicale* to be printed. Here, again, you must know the hour; it must be printed on a single sheet of paper or upon a card; it must not have a printed border close to the margin; it must be in fairly large type. Why? Because the light makes a difference in the colour of paper and ink to be used; because a programme of more than one page rustles when turned over; because the ink may spoil light gloves if it is too near the edge and is much handled; and because all ages and kinds of eyes are to read it. If it is too long a concert for a programme on one page, then one can use a soft or unsized paper, so that it will not "rattle " when turned. And as to the style of the thing, "the world is all before you where to choose." What is the music to be played? old or modern,

French or English, sacred or secular, serious or gay? There are all sorts of sources to be consulted for the appropriate decorations for these varied classes of music.

Again: a service for the consecration of a bishop is to be printed. Now, in the Roman Catholic or Anglican communions, the canon of the Mass or consecration of the Holy Eucharist is the most solemn moment of the service, which must not be disturbed by turning leaves. So one would print all that part of the office on two facing pages and let the liturgical matter before and after come as it would. For a Protestant order of service, where there is no celebration of the sacrament, it is sufficient that the "turnovers" do not come in the middle of prayers, if the prayers are printed in full. About liturgical printing there are many other points to be kept in mind. I merely mention this as one of them.

Every piece of work is different, yet each is governed by common-sense illuminated by imagination. Projeȼt yourself into the situation of the user. What does he need? How does he feel? Where is he? If your design satisfies his feelings, needs, and situation, you have produced printing which is suitable for its purpose.

But customers will not notice all these fine points, one may say. There is no reason why they should—they are not printers! But it is distinȼtly the printer's job and what he is paid for, to help the success of the occasion by making his small part in it as perfeȼt as he can. If he does, in time people will come to him for such printing, because they will say his work is "so right." So it is very much the printer's business to see that as Jack comes home from the musical party he doesn't say to Jill, "Did you hear what a noise the turning of the programmes made in the middle of that solo?" Nor that she replies, "No, but that silly decorated border spoiled a perfeȼtly good pair of white gloves."

Style, said Sir Walter Raleigh, is an index to persons. "Write, and after you have attained to some control over the instrument, you write yourself down whether you will or no. There is no vice, however unconscious, no virtue, however shy, no touch of meanness or of generosity in your character, that will not pass on to the paper." This is as true of printing as it is of writing. If you have anything in you, good or bad, you will translate it into the printed work for which you are responsible. In printing, as in literary composition, by expressing yourself (to use Raleigh's words) you "anticipate the day of judgment and furnish the recording angel with the material."

Having refined our taste by a knowledge of standards, and regarding our work in the light of what is needed to-day, it remains to acquire the one thing needful: that personal touch, that personal note, which shall make our work different from other men's work. The most dangerous moment for an ambitious designer of printing is that when, having learned something of styles of type and ways of arranging them, he begins to put his schemes into actual form. His ideas do not at first come easily. He is either obsessed by the number of things he has learned—like a young architect who tries to express in his first commission all he has ever been taught at the École des Beaux Arts; or he wonders what "the other man" is doing. A pair of horse's blinders would be useful just then! But this will pass. "There is a time in every man's education," says Emerson, "when he arrives at the conviction that imitation is suicide; that he must take himself for better, for worse, as his portion; that no kernel of nourishing corn can come to him but through his toil bestowed on that plot of ground which is given to him to till." For when he begins thus to toil and to till, he releases for the first time that personal element which is "himself," and which is so much the best thing he has to put into his work! The same problem in the design of printing is seen differently by every pair of eyes and every mind behind them, and all one can suggest is the background against which, the material with which, and the principles by which, your personality must "make good." Plan your work sincerely and

[21]

simply, and by and by you will arrive at a way of your own. Follow this way persistently, and inevitably it will make your work personal—so personal that it will not alone differ from the work of the crowd, but from that of any printer on the face of the earth!

Notes

PUBLISHED: *The Fleuron*, No. 2 (1924): 13–27 (where the essay is dated November 1923); *In the Day's Work*, pp. 3–37. Excerpts were also reprinted under the title "The Planning of Good Printing" in *American Printer* 78 (20 April 1924): 25–27.

Updike, in a letter to Stanley Morison, 21 March 1924, complained about "the vulgar and horrible appearance of 'The Planning of Printing' when it came to be put in type. But I am now considerably set up by Mr. Pollard having—possibly to fill space, and not knowing what else to say—called it 'a little masterpiece'! The Boston 'Transcript' wrote an article on the subject (which I send you) and of course, picked out the particular part of the paper which was specially idiotic without the context and which, of all things in it, I should least wish quoted. . . . Mr. Pottinger seems to feel that the article should have been preserved for the Harvard University Press to publish in a little book, but I personally think it was much better to leave it as we have, and I am glad if people like it better than I do."

1. This was an occasional feature of earlier specimen-books. In the specimen-book of Pierres of Paris of 1785, and the little specimen issued for the Temple Printing Office (J. Moyes), London, 1876, the name of the founder immediately follows the name of the type displayed. [DBU]

2. William Morris, "The Ideal Book" (a lecture delivered in 1893), reprinted in *The Ideal Book*, p. 68.

Style in the Use of Type

AMONG the illustrations common to books on typography there is a familiar plate which is an admirable lesson to the modern printer—that showing the 1486 specimen sheet of Erhard Ratdolt of Venice and Augsburg, which exhibits the types that Ratdolt had in his office and with which he made his books.[1] There are ten sizes of black-letter, three sizes of roman type, and one size of Greek, and with these and the use of handsome initials he produced beautiful effects. The books printed from this limited collection of types were beautiful because the types were so in themselves and because the very limitations of his material produced a restraint and harmony that gave the work style. Today, no printing-house would dare to confine itself to such a small equipment.

Again, the cases of books exhibited in the King's Library at the British Museum have long seemed to me among the most valuable of courses in typographic education. And the contents of those cases especially which contain the Italian books are educative in the particular of style beyond the others. In fact, to digress a little, no man, I think, can study this splendid collection without recognizing the preëminent excellence of Italian work in the fifteenth and early years of the sixteenth centuries. There is about it a sanity, a lucidity, and a severity which excels the work of other nationalities. One thing about these books is most apparent: that they are related to the book as we know it today, which the black-letter books are not. The latter speak of a time which is to the modern man largely an archaeological curiosity. For as a writer on the Renaissance has said, "the rest of Europe was free either to repel or else partly or wholly to accept the mighty impulse which came forth from Italy. Where the latter was the case we may as well be spared the complaints over the early decay of mediaeval faith and civilization. Had these been strong enough to hold their ground, they would be alive to this day. If those elegiac natures which long to see them return, could pass but one hour in the midst of them, they would gasp to be back in modern air." And this is true not alone of thought but of life, of the arts and of the trades. I am aware that this is not palatable to those admirers of Ruskin (if anybody reads him nowadays) who accustom themselves to alluding to "the foul torrent of the Renaissance," but who forget that Mr. Ruskin's books were printed in a kind of type which the Renaissance was the first to give! But this is a digression.

The books which had great style and elegance were not, it appears, necessarily dependent upon archaic treatment for these qualities; and are related to books as we today know them, more intimately than any that preceded them. From this I should state as an axiom that a book in order to possess style need not be archaic. This self-evident truth is expressed only for the benefit of persons who, possessing more knowledge than judgment, have worked as if they thought otherwise.

Another quality that makes for style is simplicity; and here again the Italian books have much to teach us. They were strictly simple, depending only on beautiful type, good paper, and a well-proportioned type-page to produce a very elegant result. Any one can place a great red decorated initial upon a page to dazzle the beholder into a momentary liking for the effect. But to produce an agreeable and pleasing page simply by proportion of margins, type, etc., is a matter which requires study, experience, and taste. It appears, therefore, that, as some of the most beautiful books are without decoration, style does not depend upon decoration, but rather on proportion and simplicity.

While to my mind the Italian books of the Renaissance

possess the highest qualities of style that the world has seen, I believe it possible to attain much of the same quality in almost any manner that a man may choose to adopt. In this connection one should mention William Morris's work, which possessed great distinction and style. One may agree or disagree with the conclusions he arrived at as to which books were the most beautiful models in printing, but he taught mightily by the body of colour and unity of effect which his beautiful pages display. He understood the style in which he worked, its capabilities and its disabilities. He made use even of its disabilities in a way that was decorative.

I have said that distinction of manner is happily not confined to Italian books, nor to the school of Mr. Morris. Nor is it confined to any one set of people. The worker who saw the value of simplicity, proportion, and colour has existed at various times in all countries. We find these qualities in much beautiful sixteenth-century French work—that of the Estiennes, for example—and in some of the earliest German work, terrible as certain periods have been in Germany. But if it is the fashion for the Anglo-Saxon to smile self-complacently at some of the Continental printing of the present day, it must be remembered that English printing, which now stands (in my opinion) at the head of typographic achievement, has never been so before. In fact, English printing has not furnished interesting or valuable object lessons in style until within the last hundred and fifty years, and in this statement—which I should hesitate, perhaps, to make unsupported—I am glad to find myself borne out by Mr. Alfred Pollard, who remarks: "It is quite easy to be struck with the inferiority of English books and their accessories, such as bindings and illustrations, to those produced on the Continent. To compare the books printed by Caxton with the best work of his German or Italian contemporaries, to compare the books bound for Henry, Prince of Wales, with those bound for the Kings of France, to try to find even a dozen English books printed before 1640 with woodcuts (not imported from abroad) of any real artistic merit—if any one is anxious to reinforce his national modesty, here are three very efficacious methods of doing it. . . . And if I am asked at what period English printing has attained that occasional primacy which I have claimed for our exponents of all the bookish arts, I would boldly say that it possesses it at the present day."

Again, "manner" may be used with charm, and by this I mean a local and characteristic variant of a real style, which has come to have a literary and historical association of its own. What we call colonial (or Georgian) printing is nothing more than a rendering (often an overstatement) of certain features of seventeenth- and eighteenth-century English printing. It is well adapted for old-fashioned reprints, or for commercial work intended to describe or to sell old-fashioned wares, though it is often used as having in itself a beauty which renders it independent of its fitness. The "colonist," could he see the baskets of flowers magnified to the dimensions of giant chapbook illustrations, would disown any part in such obstreperous decoration. The average ornamentation of such books was not of this *genre* at all, but was rather timid in effect. Yet such colonial typography sometimes possesses style. But it must be remembered that style, being dependent on proportion and simplicity, is more readily to be found in work whose mannerisms are less marked and where there is less decoration. With the quaint features and decorations of "colonial " printing suppressed, there is very little left of it. The excellence of any given style seems to consist in its power to exist apart from such things, and thus the better the style, the less dependent it is on earmarks or whimsicality.

But there must sometimes be decoration, and here of course enters the element of individual taste. Here again early Italian and French books show that, with a little well-chosen decoration,— just enough to give an air of careful luxury,—the greatest elegance of effect can be arrived at. In all the schools of ornament, again, there is special work which, through its grace and reserve, possesses this same happy quality of style and elegance. In many modern books there are ornamental title-pages which have this quality to a very high degree—instances where the introduction of a very little good ornament seems to shed over the whole book in which it is employed a light of luxury and grace. The early printers, in many of their beautiful marks, grasped this idea. With a very plain, simple title-page there was yet one spot of decoration, graceful in outline, rich in colour. Badly conceived ornamentation and the *abuse of good ornament* have become so general that one is tempted sometimes to think that the art of decoration is the art of leaving things out! Finally, if all work reflects the life of the day in which it is undertaken, today's restless and complex life may be reflected in our work, which, in its lack of simplicity and repose, may be but an echo of the time. Possibly, the tasteless exaggeration, and the desire to excel our neighbour in startling effects which we see exemplified in some American printing, may be traced to certain evil qualities in American life. But, on the other hand, the interest in varying styles of work and the open-minded acceptance of them for the printer's purposes is a happy feature of industrial endeavour today, and one, too, which is characteristic of our epoch and country. It would be idle to expect in the art of printing that concerted harmony which we do not find in architecture, in painting, or in literature. We must recognize this lack of concert, whether we like it or not. Instead of wishing it otherwise, it is better to accept it, and make the best of it.

To conclude, style in printing does not permanently reside in any one manner of work, but in those principles on which almost all manners of work may be based. We have to be thankful that of late things are turning in the direction of greater simplicity, greater reserve, and less decoration. And as the printer is more and more deprived of adventitious aids, he will find himself face to face with those fundamental principles of style which have marked the work of the great printers of the past; as they must the work of those to come.

Notes

PUBLISHED: "Style in the Composition of Type," *Handicraft* (Boston) 1 (May 1902): 48–55; *In the Day's Work*, pp. 41–50.

1. Updike reproduces two portions of the specimen in *Printing Types*, 2nd ed. (Cambridge, Mass.: Harvard University Press, 1937), 1:76, 79.

The Seven Champions of Typography

THERE was once upon a time a curate, whose cast of thought ran to symbolism, and who became so fascinated by the mystical meanings of the number seven, that one day, being called upon unexpectedly to preach, he inflicted on his congregation all that he could for the moment remember of seven-fold numbers occurring in the Old and New Testaments—the days of creation, the gifts of the Spirit, the seven churches of Asia, etc.; but like many extempore speakers before and since, he suddenly became confused and ended his phrase precipitately with the surprising words, "And we all remember, dear brethren, that there were seven apostles—plus five!"

When I entitled this paper The Seven Champions of Typography I had in mind (being a lay person) the seven champions of Christendom, the seven wonders of the world, the seven seas, stars, deadly sins, liberal arts, and some other "sevens." But on counting up my champions, I was disconcerted to discover that there were but six—thus (like the curate) finding myself suddenly at sixes and sevens in more senses than one. Yet why spoil a good title for a mere detail! That royal and unpleasant spinster called Good Queen Bess or the Virgin Queen—who appears according to the best modern authorities to have been neither—is said to have considered a lie to be merely an intellectual way of getting over a difficulty. Perhaps so: but, even then, remembering the precept of St. Francis de Sales, "Little things for little people," we have our little scruples. So I propose to make my title good by adding to six Champions of Typography—Spacing, Leading, Indentation, Ink, Paper, and Imposition—one more—the most important

[29]

of all, without which (as is alleged of charity) the rest profiteth nothing. That Seventh Champion, dear Reader, is *You*. And it all depends on how seriously you take the following pages, whether my title turns out to be truth or falsehood! I assume for it no further responsibility.

No matter how admirably we plan our work, nor how fine in design are the types we select, its appearance when printed depends on good composition,—the combination of type into words, the arrangement of words in lines, and the assemblage of lines to make pages. And composition falls into three divisions, spacing, leading, and proper indentation—all factors in the effect of a type-page. Furthermore, the successful presentation of our printing depends upon three things more—ink, colour of paper, and proper imposition on that paper. On these six points—for I shall not bore the reader and myself by continuing the "champion" nomenclature—the successful effect of our plans for printing and the use of good type-forms must rely.

I. Spacing is a term used in connection with composition to describe the space between the words in a line of type, or the lateral distance of one word from another. It plays an extremely important part in composition. Everybody knows that there must be space between words, but the problem for the printer is its proper adjustment. This is effected by the discriminating use of spaces of different thickness, just as leading—the proper adjustment of space between lines—requires the intelligent use of leads.

The spaces between words in a line should be apparently uniform. If they were *exactly* uniform, they would not seem so to the eye; more space being required between two ascending lowercase letters such as "l," which may end one word and begin another (as in "medical libraries"), than between a "y" and an "a" (as in "any author"). "In good printing," said

William Morris, in his paper on "Printing" in *Arts and Crafts Essays*, "the spaces between the words should be as near as possible equal (it is impossible that they should be quite equal except in lines of poetry); modern printers understand this, but it is only practised in the very best establishments. But another point which they should attend to they almost always disregard; this is the tendency to the formation of ugly meandering white lines or 'rivers' in the page, a blemish which can be nearly, though not wholly, avoided by care and forethought, the desirable thing being 'the breaking of the line' as in bonding masonry or brickwork, thus:

The general *solidity* of a page is much to be sought for: modern printers generally overdo the 'whites' in the spacing, a defect probably forced on them by the characterless quality of the letters. For where these are boldly and carefully designed, and each letter is thoroughly individual in form, the words may be set much closer together, without loss of clearness. No definite rules, however, except the avoidance of 'rivers'[1] and excess of white, can be given for the spacing, which requires the constant exercise of judgment and taste on the part of the printer."[2] On looking at the page of Mr. Morris's essay about proper spacing, we find the enemy has sown tares in the field, for in derision of Mr. Morris's own theories, a large white "river" runs across the very phrase in which he deplores them! The book was issued under the auspices of the London Society of Arts and Crafts—an example of how much easier it is to tell people that work should be done "so that our commonest things are beautiful," than it is to put the precept into practice!

While I cannot agree with much that has been said about the folly of close spacing and pages of type set solid (i.e. without leading), as if it were merely an affected return to archaic methods and a perverse desire to make books unreadable, some modern printers, in their efforts to obtain "colour" in a page, have undoubtedly forgotten that the spacing of a line must be sufficient to make a distinct separation between words and one sufficient to be *readily* apparent to the eye. A good test of spacing is to hold a printed page upside down, when, the sense of the words not being caught, the eye more readily perceives whether the spacing of the page is even or not.

An old and rather ignorant prejudice against the breaking of words makes against good spacing. It is better not to break words if one can help it, but often they must be broken, if good spacing is to be maintained. Many printers who may be willing to break single words consider that two consecutive lines should not end with hyphens; but hyphens at the end of two, three, or even four successive lines, while undesirable, are not so ugly as matter unevenly spaced to avoid them.[3] The problem is to space evenly in spite of these difficulties. Then again bad spacing may often be the result of corrections. Sometimes replacing one letter by another makes no change in the proper spacing of a line; but when words are replaced by longer or shorter ones, or when whole phrases are inserted, serious difficulties occur. Useless and expensive changes are often ordered by an author because he does not know the tedious process by which they are effected, or realize that the substitution of one word for another may necessitate carrying over words or parts of words for several lines. Yet if, to avoid expense, this is not done, the result is uneven, and therefore bad, spacing.

The principles of good spacing which have been stated are of equal application to machine-set type. If by the use of type-setting machines printers cannot follow this "counsel of perfection," it would appear to show that, as yet, the best hand composition is better.

II. The excessive indentation of paragraphs, and em width spaces between sentences, are usually unnecessary. In an early printed book the paragraphs were indented to allow a paragraph mark to be put in by hand. Often the paragraph marks were never filled in, and this led to the discovery that the eye could pick out beginnings of paragraphs by blanks almost as well as by paragraph marks. While a paragraph mark preserved more or less the desirable regularity of outline of the page, whereas a blank space broke it, for clearness it was necessary that it should be broken; but not to such an extent as it often is by modern indentation.

Again, the conventional use of an em quad at the beginning of a new sentence is unnecessary and makes "holes" in the composition of pages. In most cases, the same spacing used between other words in the line, together with the period at the end of one sentence and the capital letter at the beginning of the next, make a sufficient break.

III. Leading is to lines what spacing is to words; and the introduction of leads between lines of type has a great deal to do with the effect of a page. Type set solid is usually hard to read, and slight leading improves its legibility. When to lead and how much to lead is a matter of taste and judgment. For with the same type the colour of a page can be increased or decreased by its leading. Nor does every type demand the same amount of leading. Black-letter, although in early times occasionally leaded for purposes of manuscript interlineation, should normally never be leaded, and should be closely spaced: for leading of black-letter makes a "striped" page; open spacing, a page full of holes. On the other hand, light faces of roman type almost always look better leaded, and sometimes require slightly open spacing. So it will be seen that the effect of printed pages often depends on leading and spacing as well as on the face of type employed. The leading of the same kind of type in a given book should be uniform throughout. There is no more wretched product in typography than a book in which, for reasons of economy or convenience, pages which should have the same leading or the same size of type throughout are set with less leading or in a smaller type to "get the matter in."

An unbroken type-page when held at a little distance should make a perfectly defined block of even tint. This impression on paper of a definite parallelogram which is practically uniform in tone is a chief factor in the beauty of a printed book. Early books were remarkable for the even colour of their pages, and that is one reason that they give the eye a sense of satisfaction. This was arrived at by the use of types which were masculine in design and fairly uniform in weight of line, set solid, and close spaced. "Experience proves," says Day, "that the eye is best satisfied by a tolerably uniform distribution of the letters, Roman, Gothic, or whatever their character, over it [the page], so that they give at first sight the impression of a fairly even surface, distinguished from the surrounding surface (that is, the margin) more by a difference of tint than by any appreciable letter-forms within the mass."[4]

What about machine composition and typefaces for machine-work, some one may ask? To answer this very proper question I must make a digression. The introduction of a Linotype or Monotype into a printing-office is open to no objection, provided the machine is operated with the same care that is taken with the best hand-setting, in which case the cost is often, I fear, much the same as if set by hand; for the proper justification of the lines of type reduces the rapidity of their product. Usually machines have not been carefully worked, and to judge them by their ordinary product is not fair. Then again machines can be desirably employed only in printing-houses which have enough work of the kind that can be *well done* upon such machines. They cannot always readily or quickly perform certain sorts of composition, in spite of the ingenious exhibits of this sort of type-setting which are shown as specimens of their work.

The collection of matrices from which types are cast, on both Linotype and Monotype machines, has been, until lately, unworthy of their pretensions, and it is difficult to see on what principle such a variety of mean types, differing so slightly from one another, were for many years "the only wear." Nowadays they are enormously improved, and the best of them have been used for book-work with marked success.

On the other hand, it is absurd to be prejudiced by a machine or machine-work because it is mechanical; the results obtained are what really count. Some ultraconservative men are (or have been) foolish enough to shy at new inventions in machinery—for type-setting, for instance. They feel that somehow a "modern spirit " is in the machinery, and that in some sly and malign way it will defeat artistic excellence! This is quite childish. The problem is to determine how work can be done best. If for some typography the old method (incidentally endeared to the lover of early printing by historical associations) produces a better result than a modern machine, then the old method may be adhered to. If a modern machine does other classes of printing better and quicker than the old method and more conveniently for the workmen, it is to be adopted. The tendency about us, it is true, is to glorify speed, without paying attention to the details of the result. "This machine," says the seller, "can turn out so many ems per hour"; but one must regard only *how many ems properly set up* such a machine can turn out, and not be beguiled by speed, which is an attribute of excellence in automobiles, but not the sole question in type-setting! To judge between the sentimentalist who believes that all virtue resides in the hand, and the commercialist who thinks that salvation is obtained by a machine, is not easy. I prefer good machine work to bad hand work and vice versa. If one is as good as the other,—incidentally I have my doubts,—I take the quickest and cheapest. But I quote without comment the statement of a distinguished colleague—whose name is withheld for what we are nowadays pleased to call prudential reasons—"The machine is like a jungle animal, more or less obedient under the whip, but always a wild animal."

IV. To show good type-setting (whether set by machine

or by hand) to advantage, the inking of a page must be even. Composition, no matter how careful, is dependent on good ink and the right amount of it. The letters in a printed page, if not well inked, show, when examined through a magnifying glass, little specks of white through the black, and the effect of the type, as a whole, is lifeless and faded. The result of using too much ink is so obvious that it is needless to say anything about it.

Furthermore, ink must be black. A great deal of the so-called black ink used in modern books has a brown, green, pink, or blue tinge. If a good black ink is compared with inks commonly employed, it will be found that there is little that is really black. It is cheaper to make ink of materials that give it disagreeable tinges than to use the proper ingredients. But no page will be effective or lively except when printed in pure black ink.

V. Though ink must be black, paper should not always be white. The somewhat irregular Caslon type (and some "period" and transitional types) appears much more agreeably when printed on a slightly rough paper of a cream tint. Caslon's types in his day were printed on wet paper, which thickened their lines and roughened the paper, so that we get more nearly the effect that he meant them to have when we print them on toned, rough paper. If smooth white paper is used for old style types, it exposes their slight crudities of form in a disagreeable way, and accents too much the shape of individual letters. This is understood by some type-founders, who for that reason often display their old style types on toned paper. Many people prefer a smooth and pure white paper (or think they do) because they look at the paper alone, and do not realize that its colour makes any difference in the effect of printing. Some of the lighter modern-faced types look well on a paper that is nearly white; for they are more clean cut, more regular in shape, and have not the irregularities which such a paper reveals. For these types the paper should *look* white.

There are, fortunately, few absolutely white printing papers.

VI. And finally, there is imposition. A page of type, however well set, well spaced, well inked, and printed on suitable paper, may be a complete failure unless well "imposed." "It is no less effective than it is logical," says Morris, "to consider two pages of the open book as one area on which to plant, as it were, two columns of print. A very considerable reduction of the inner margins, as compared with the outer and the upper and lower, has this effect; and it is perhaps the most satisfactory way of imposing the page—if only the binder were to be depended upon. Unless the folding of the sheets is perfect, the two patches of print do not range, and the closer they come together the more obtrusive is the fault; it is not so easily detected when there is a broad space of white between." A well-imposed page, which is to show off the type properly, must have margins widest at the bottom, narrower at the outside, narrower still at the top, and narrowest of all on the inside. If type-pages are imposed in the centre of a paper page, the margins appear less at the bottom than at the top, and the combined inside margins of pages thus imposed, in an open book seem so wide that the print appears to be falling out of it! I believe that there are various *formulae* that are intended to effect perfect imposition; but they are not infallible in their results.

To sum up, therefore, pages of type—however fine in design—must be carefully spaced, tastefully leaded, moderately indented, thoroughly inked, printed on paper suited to their design, and properly imposed. Neglect one of these requirements, and the result is failure. But—and it is the eternal "but" of the half-hearted printer—why should one adopt a style of printing which involves much more labour and little more return? The answer is that these simple but laborious requirements have always been met in the best printing; and that all this is merely typographical truth. It would be easier, no doubt, to believe that there is something wrong about the idea. But there isn't.

Nor is there anything that is new in all this; for in principle it would be admitted by most printers. Yet what men often mean when they talk of principles is a mere theory of conduct upon which they have never acted. The theory becomes a principle only when practised. And thus it depends on *You* whether you will be the Seventh Champion of good typography or not. Perhaps you may find it easier to be a deserter. If so, like the dwindling company of little nigger boys in the old song,

"And then there were Six!"

Notes

PUBLISHED: *In the Day's Work*, pp. 53–70.
1. "Dog's teeth," or as Moxon called them, "pigeon-holes." [DBU]
2. Morris, "Printing" (1893), reprinted in *The Ideal Book*, pp. 63–64.
3. Entire books have been printed without a single broken word. An example of this is Marcellin Brun's *Manuel pratique et abrégé de la Typographie française*—the first edition printed by Didot père et fils at Paris in 1825, and the second by Vroom of Brussels in 1826. The latter is a 12mo volume of two hundred and forty pages, and is set in 8-point type, with notes in a still smaller size. [DBU]
4. Day's *Lettering in Ornament*, London, 1902, p. 20. [DBU]

The Essentials of a Well-Made Book

IN this paper I propose to treat as briefly as I can the essential processes involved in constructing a well-made book. They consist in: the preparation of copy, choice of type and of type ornaments, format, typesetting or composition, proof-reading, make-up, imposition and margins, paper as it affects type, presswork, and binding. Now, before treating the processes I want to define typography. It is (to quote my friend Stanley Morison[1]) "the craft of rightly disposing printing material in accordance with a specific purpose; of so arranging the letters, distributing the space and controlling the type as to aid to the maximum the reader's comprehension of the text. Typography is the efficient means to an essentially utilitarian and only accidentally aesthetic end." That statement straightens out many misapprehensions. Morison furthermore discourages the "arty" practitioner by adding, "Enjoyment of patterns is rarely the reader's chief aim." The conclusion we arrive at from this is that it is the object of a book to be a transparent medium between the words of its writer and the mind of its reader. This dictates the chief factors to be dealt with. "To make a thoroughly good book," said De Vinne, "out of a lot of jumbled manuscript; to select a type appropriate to the subject; to determine its size so that it shall be in fit proportion to the margin; to correctly determine by graduated size of type, the relative importance of extracts, letters, poetry, notes, preface, appendix, index, etc.; to use paper, bindings, and lining papers so that they will be suitable to the print; to space lines neatly; to regulate blanks properly, so that any reader can see at a glance that the whole book is the work of a disciplined hand and an educated taste, and that proper subordination has been maintained in all the little details, from the space between the words to the margins around the page; these, I think, call for more of skill, more of experience, than are to be shown in the most difficult pieces of ornamental typography." No doubt experience taught this to Mr. De Vinne and it ultimately teaches us that no book that by its type or method of type arrangement places a barrier between the words of the writer and the mind of the reader is a well-designed volume. "The reader does not want to see the printer but to hear the writer."

The first thing essential to a well-made book is the preparation of its manuscript, or, as it is called in printing-houses, its "copy" for the printer. The manuscript, in absolutely complete form, should either be presented in double-spaced type-script or written in a legible hand in black ink, on one side of the sheet of paper only. Carbon or mimeographed copies from the original should not be submitted. The sheets should be of uniform size ($8\frac{1}{2}$×11 inches being suggested) and ample margins allowed at top, bottom, and sides. The manuscript, including all preliminary matter, should be sent to the printer numbered consecutively throughout, and delivered flat, not rolled, and very thin, slippery sheets are to be avoided. If clippings from newspapers or other printed matter are inserted in the manuscript they should be pasted solidly on the sheet where they belong, and not attached with pins or clips. Each new chapter should begin at the top of a sheet. The author should always retain a duplicate copy of his manuscript for reference or in case of accident.

For the printer type-script is preferable to handwriting, though a type-script from dictation is not likely to be so carefully expressed as if written by hand and then typed. The reason is that writing being a tiresome performance, the author, as he goes along, sometimes finds that a word or two will bear the burden of a longer phrase. By this literal *vis inertiae* his style is improved by being made more concise. But, oddly enough, manuscript prepared in longhand, when transcribed on a typewriter at once appears to call for considerable improvement, and a new crop of verbal corrections spring up not evident in the written form. When this type-script is put into type a second revision is generally necessary. The reiterated use of the same word or the same phrase, buried in handwritten "copy" and but dimly discernible in type-script, when in print—stares at the astonished author who with all his care is confronted with the use of "perhaps" or "doubtless" four times on the same page. This is, partly, because a page of type includes more matter than a page of handwriting or type-script and hence unconscious repetition, which in these mediums extends over several pages, may by typographic condensation appear on the same page when in type. So the author never finds his proofs quite as perfect as inexperience has led him to expect.

Compositors' errors are usually due to four causes: misreading the manuscript, failure of memory, muscular errors, and what is called a "foul case"—types being in the wrong compartments of a type-case.

Misreading the manuscript and a "foul case" require no explanation. Failure of memory often comes about because a compositor, when working, reads over a few words of manuscript and tries to keep them in mind until they are set in type. Sometimes he substitutes unintentionally a word that sounds like, or is similar in sense to, that in the manuscript. Muscular errors come from fatigue, causing the hand-compositor to pick up the wrong letter, just as a man strikes the wrong key on the keyboard of a composing machine. Many compositors' errors, that seldom get further than the proof-reader, are exceedingly amusing. To show how easy it is to make them, take the frequently quoted phrase with which Chapter I of the *Contrat Social* begins: "Man is born free, and is everywhere in chains." Drop the *s*, rearrange *a*, *i*, and comma, and we find a phrase as surprising to us as it would have been to Rousseau: "Man is born free and is, everywhere in China." The sense is not always changed by these mistakes, however ridiculous their effect. "Blessed is he who remembereth the poor and seedy" is an instance of that.

We now consider the choice of type. The first thing to do is to look over the range of available types and select those which do not give the reader any sense of discomfort or exhibit undue peculiarity of design. That all the types which meet that requirement are equally suitable for a given book is not, however, true. Among the standard types there are variations that make some better than others for a given task. In so far as that is so, so far we have an instance of what has been recently called "allusive typography," the invention of which in late years has been attributed to me. Allusive typography is, however, no invention of mine, for such typographic usage occurs throughout the whole history of printing.[2] Originally, black-letter was generally associated with sacred, and roman type with profane, literature. Printers in their "specimen sheets" and books for a long period followed this custom, black-letter displaying the Lord's Prayer or legal enactments and roman the time-worn passage from Cicero's oration against Cataline. The second Caslon's eighteenth-century specimen of learned types uses the opening verses of St. John's Gospel for passages in Greek and the beginning of Genesis to show his Hebrew characters. All these were examples of allusive typography, a grand term for simple appropriateness. The most familiar examples of this use of type appropriate to its subject in the nineteenth century were Pickering's famous editions printed by Whittingham at the Chiswick Press [*Fig. 5*] and those of the Imprimerie Fick at Geneva. In our day the Nonesuch editions and many of the books designed by Mr. Bruce Rogers furnish examples of it.

In short, certain subject-matter, to the educated man, connotes certain ideas, and these are best represented by certain typographical forms. The more delicate the designer's perception of this, the more likely he is successfully to practise appropriate typography. To illustrate this—no one who knew

I. THE TEMPLE

The Dedication.

Lord, my firſt fruits preſent themſelves to thee ;
Yet not mine neither : for from thee they came,
And muſt return. Accept of them and me,
And make us ſtrive, who ſhall ſing beſt thy name.
  Turn their eyes hither, who ſhall make a gain
  Theirs, who ſhall hurt themſelves or me, refrain.

1. The Church-porch.

Perirrhanterium.

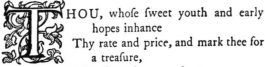HOU, whoſe ſweet youth and early
      hopes inhance
      Thy rate and price, and mark thee for
      a treaſure,
Hearken unto a Verſer, who may chance
Ryme thee to good, and make a bait of pleaſure .
  A verſe may finde him, who a ſermon flies,
  And turn delight into a ſacrifice.

Beware of luſt ; it doth pollute and foul
Whom God in Baptiſme waſht with his own blood
It blots thy leſſon written in thy ſoul ;
The holy lines cannot be underſtood.
  How dare thoſe eyes upon a Bible look,
  Much leſſe towards God, whoſe luſt is all their book!

5   George Herbert, *The Temple* (London:
William Pickering, 1850).

much about William Morris would set the *Arts and Crafts Essays* in a type modeled after those cut by Giambattista Bodoni of Parma. This is not because Bodoni's types are not good of their kind, but because they were not the kind that Morris liked. In fact, Morris said some very nasty and unjust things about Bodoni's types and books.[3] Had Bodoni lived to see Morris's books he would probably have thought them unspeakably uncouth and barbaric! Both men were masters of typography, but they were trying to do the same thing in ways diametrically opposite. It is now the fashion to decry Morris, just as in Morris's time it was the fashion to decry Bodoni. But in the long run Bodoni's books may survive Morris's because they can be easily read and Morris's cannot. Per contra, those who enjoy "patterns" will prefer Morris's books which today seem "dated."

The general public is ignorant of these variations of type design—so ignorant that, for the most part, it will like an appropriate type without knowing why. The so-called taste of the public is seldom led by intelligent preference. It is needless, therefore, for the printer to worry about what the public will think, for if he makes a sound book an intelligent public will like it and know why, and the unintelligent will accept it anyhow; but in producing a volume, the more the printer knows of printing, literature, history, art, science, the better his product will be. He will see opportunities for typographical effects of which his less educated brother is unaware. Given six different designs of type to work from, one of the six will stand out as most appropriate, though all six may be excellent types of their kind. There are a certain number of types which by eccentricity or unfamiliarity of shape are automatically discarded. The uncompromising character of the forms of letters does not permit the designer of a type alphabet to take undue liberties. Letters cannot be pulled about at will for each must retain the elements which make an *m* and an *a* definitely recognizable as these characters. If this is not so, such type faces are useless.

The Essentials of a Well-Made Book

How is a man to arrive at a right selection of types? The answer is, by a mixture of knowledge and taste. This knowledge must come from a trained mind and experience. Where is the taste to come from? It may as well be admitted that some persons have no taste at all, but such persons would not be likely to try to produce a well-made book or know one when they saw it. Most men who go into printing have some sort of taste and a few an almost impeccable taste—which is a gift of the gods. It seems to me that a right taste is cultivated in printing, as in other forms of endeavour, by knowing what has been done in the past and what has been so esteemed that it has lived. If a man examines masterpieces of printing closely, he will begin to see why they were thought masterpieces and in what the mastery lay. He will perceive that all great printing possesses certain qualities in common, that these qualities may be transferable in some slight degree to his own problems, and then he will find himself braced and stimulated into clearer, simpler views of what he can make out of his task. When he sees the books that have delighted all generations and begins to comprehend why they were great pieces of typography, he is beginning to train his taste. It is a process which once begun is fed from a thousand sources and need never end.

The subject of the book has indicated what its type ought to be. The size of paper chosen must now be considered. Very large types on a small format or very small types on a large format are equally undesirable. Then again we have to know the kind of reader for whom the book is printed. Various reports have been made by learned societies on the legibility of type for children, persons of average age, and old people. It has been generally agreed that for adults type smaller than 10 point cannot easily be read and that 11 point and 12 point are the smallest sizes agreeable to the eye for text. Some years ago a report was sent out by a reputable university on the legibility of types. Its conclusions were surprising, and it was not clear how they were arrived at, but at last I discovered that the legibility tests had been performed with characters exhibited at an arbitrary distance. The investigators (possibly confused by uncomfortable experiences with the oculist), mistook visibility for legibility, and forgot that a book is held at only a number of inches from the eye, and that legibility of type for reading is only ascertained by placing type at the distance at which a book would normally be held. Furthermore, the length of line for easy reading should be thought out. No line longer than 30 picas or 5 inches is desirable, for if longer it tires the eye. But if longer lines are required, more leading is necessary than in short lines—just how much depends on judgment and experiment, the kind of type employed and also the kind of reader for which the book is intended.

Whatever size of type or type-page is adopted, allowance must be made for quotations or letters or poetry occurring in the text to be set in a smaller type; notes, that must be smaller still, yet readable; a preface, generally in larger type than the text; an appendix, in type the size of the quotations, and then an index. If the original type selected is too large, all the subordinate types will also be too large; if the normal type-page employs a type too small, the subsidiary portions of the book will, if in proper proportions, be too small to read comfortably.

An adjunct of type, which, even more than type itself, requires knowledge to use properly, are type ornaments. Their use goes far back in the history of printing, and to anyone familiar with them, their date and origin can be readily detected. As early as 1479 two varieties of type ornament in various combinations appear in the Verona *Aesopus* printed by Giovanni and Alberto Alvise, a copy of which is in the Huntington Library at San Marino. The Frankfort specimen of Sabon and Berner of 1592 shows various combinations of type ornaments. Some used by the Elzevirs were rather sturdy in design and colour, harmonizing with the type and style of composition affected by that family in their books. William

Caslon produced a very serviceable series of these ornaments admirably adapted, in the way they were designed, to print well and accord nicely with his type. Baskerville produced a number of these, which, while somewhat anaemic, were in rendering suitable for his more delicate printing. The Bodoni types, so brilliant and sharp in effect, were accompanied by an enormous number of ornaments in all conceivable sizes, harmonious both in line and in spirit with his typography. In England in the early years of the last century fat black types became fashionable and their accompanying type ornaments also went into mourning. In short, these little ornaments like the types that they were meant to decorate always reflected the taste of the times.

Of late we have seen ingenious arrangements of these ornaments or type units to make pictures. That was a very old diversion and was common in France, Germany, Austria, Italy, and Spain. The British never tried this on so grand a scale as elsewhere, but at the end of the eighteenth century "the ingenious Mr. Hazard of Bath," as he was called, made some pretty and amusing arrangements of English type ornaments. In our own day the late Frederic Warde arranged elaborate designs for the Lanston Monotype Corporation, and so has Mr. Bruce Rogers in his work.

Many type ornaments are good, most are good for something, but not all the good ones are good for everything. In short, to use intelligently these typographic "flowers," as they are called, requires knowledge of the dates of their first appearance, and the types with which it was intended they should harmonize, and in some cases their appropriateness in design. To build up typographical ornaments into a picture— save for men with taste and talent—is a dangerous business. For the average printer it is safer to use them "allusively" rather than "literally." Carried too far, ingenuity replaces taste, and the results resemble sad specimens of Victorian wool-work.

Composition is the term used for combining moveable

types into words. To effect this, so that it shall be easy to read and pleasing to the eye, is dependent largely on two processes being efficiently done: i.e., spacing, which regulates the space between words, and leading, which regulates the space between lines. Spacing, to present a good effect, should appear to be equal between words in a line; leading should be uniform throughout a page, the amount of leading being proportionate to the style and size of type and length of line. When the page is completed it should present at a distance an even parallelogram of gray on a white field. If it is carelessly spaced holes appear in the mass of gray. If the page is leaded too much it will appear striped; if too little, of solid colour which makes reading difficult. Proper spacing is, therefore, dependent on care in a process largely mechanical; proper leading is more a matter of taste and judgment. A good way to test the evenness in colour of a mass of type is to turn the page upside down, when the eye, no longer able to read the text, readily perceives the "colour" of the page. Irregular spacing is often caused by the desire to avoid the division of words, but I prefer frequent division to uneven spacing.

In making corrections in type already set, an author should know how type is set. He will then realize how much labour is entailed in making trifling and often unnecessary corrections, if added words occupy more space or less than words struck out. To insert two words of eight letters each to take the place of one word of three letters may mean the resetting of several of the lines of type following the line in which the correction was made. To insert a whole new sentence, unless it contains as many letters (spaces between words being counted as letters) as that which it replaces, may necessitate the resetting of a long paragraph or even a whole page, if the type has been made up into pages. Corrections in *page proofs* are especially undesirable as extensive additions may demand the rearrangement of page after page, until the end of a chapter is reached. If enough new matter is inserted to make an extra page it will necessitate the alteration of every following page number and possibly require the change in position of all subsequent headlines as well. Thus the cost of "author's corrections" is often enormously increased by ignorance on the part of writers of the disarrangement of type that slight corrections may involve, of the time taken in making them, and of what it costs to do so.

When the type is first set it is generally shown in long strips called galley proofs. It is then given to the proof-reader to whom it is read by a copy-holder. Divergences from the manuscript or copy, broken letters, defective punctuation, et cetera are marked for correction by the compositor. The proof-reader also calls the author's attention to doubtful points relating to construction of sentences, errors of statement, repetition, inconsistencies of capitalization, and like matters. Each of the latter queries bears an interrogation mark. If the correction is accepted by the author the interrogation mark is crossed out, signifying that the suggested change is to be made. When the author returns the galley proof to the printer, he effects the desired corrections and makes the type up into pages.

Doing this is called "make-up." It consists not only in dividing the types hitherto shown in galley proofs into lengths which represent the amount of space a page of type will occupy, but also in adding the running-title of the book and the page number. The dimensions of the type-page are governed in part by the format decided on for the book; whether quarto, 12mo, 16mo, or what not. The format, too, may often be dictated to the printer by the fact that a particular paper is of a size always kept in stock by paper-makers. These "stock sizes," as they are called, are more economical than unusual sizes, which involve either special making of paper or cutting down paper from stock sizes in a way that involves waste. Proofs in page-form are then sent to the author for final approval. If returned approved, the pages are ready to go to press, if the book is to be printed from type; or to be locked up for foundry if it is to be electrotyped and printed from plates.

Type-pages are placed in forms and printed so that when a sheet comprising 8, 16, 32, or 64 pages is folded, the type-pages not only follow in proper order, but are in proper relation to the paper page. This arrangement of type-pages is called imposition; and imposition determines the margins of a book. To arrive at proper margins is a delicate business—so delicate that a poorly printed book with proper margins will look better than a well-printed book with margins badly proportioned. There are various formulas for obtaining correct margins. The general rule is that the inside margin should be the narrowest, the top margin wider, the outside margins wider still and the tail margin widest of all.

I speak of paper only in so far as its quality and finish affect type. As a general rule, old style types show to best advantage on toned papers, slightly rough in texture, and the more modeled types, the vogue for which was introduced by Baskerville, require a paper of a higher finish, which he too employed. In this use he was followed, to even a greater degree, by Bodoni and the Didots, who also affected whiter paper, though not the pure white paper that came into fashion later. The reason that old style types, as a rule, look better on a rough, toned paper is that, their design being in general more irregular and less finished in detail than later founts, such papers veil these slight crudities. If printed on a smooth white paper these irregularities become too obvious. A more finished form of letter does not require this assistance and its delicate lines, which are lost in impression on rough paper, show to advantage on a smoother surface. An important detail to be considered is the grain of the paper, which must in a well-made book run the right way—with the height of the book and not the width. If this is not the case, the book will not open as it should and the pages of the finished book are not agreeably flexible to the hand.

Presswork is that part in the production of a printed book which consists in the impression of the type on paper. It is necessary that this impression should be even over the entire printed sheet which usually involves adding to it here or reducing it there. The process employed to effect this is called "makeready." It is accomplished by pasting thin sheets of paper on a "spot" or "overlay" sheet, placed just under the top sheet on the cylinder or platen of the press. When a form contains cuts which are below the standard type-height, thin sheets of paper are pasted on the bottom of such blocks to bring them to the correct "height-to-paper." This is called an "underlay." When this evening-up process is completed, the pressman turns his attention to the inking necessary to produce the desired density of colour on the printed sheet. Once the colour of the page, i.e., the amount of ink that displays the type to advantage without grayness or over-inking, is decided on, the requirements of good presswork make it needful to keep all subsequent pages of an even, firm colour, according exactly in this respect with the first approved form or "colour sheet." Some pressmen are clever about this, but in most cases the first sheet of each form as it comes from the press must be inspected and made to conform to the approved colour sheet. The result should be that in looking over the finished volume, its pages appear to be uniformly even in colour from beginning to end. If not, a form of 32 pages when folded might bring pages clearly varying in colour opposite each other.

Now that the book is set up and printed, the sheets must go to the binder. He must be told exactly how the book is to be bound, the number of folded sheets or signatures in it, how the plates, if any, are to be placed, what the end papers are to be and the kind of binding desired. A badly folded book will ruin the effect of the most carefully printed page. In short, every process, all through the making of a book, has to be perpetually watched. Even so, mistakes creep in and when the book is finished one can almost always see how it might have been bettered. "Life is all a weariness," sang the poet, but the amateur who printed his verse observed casually that a slight mistake had crept into that line, though he added, he "guessed that nobody would notice it." Asked what the error was, he said brightly, "Oh, just an *m* instead of an *n* in weariness." With the printer's best efforts a book is often a very weary mess indeed!

I am aware, too, that these descriptions have not been entertaining reading, and there is a certain appositeness in this. Many of these processes *are* as tiresome to perform as they are to read about, but they have to be done. If these specifications are not regarded and these requirements are neglected, your sin will find you out—not only at the end of the job, but when it is half finished. It is then too late to do much about it, but weep or curse according to the gravity of the error, your part in it, and your particular temperament. In short, a book must be planned from the start so that it is fool-proof and the original scheme must somehow support the regulations and specifications I have named, troublesome as they are. A visitor to a farm I have in Vermont told me that in trying to get there, he thrice lost his way. On the last attempt to find the right lane, he met a boy whom he asked, "Is this the road to Mr. Updike's farm?" The boy said, "Yes." "Is it a good road?" he asked. The boy said, "No." "Well," said the man, "I suppose it's a passable road?" "It's the road you'll have to pass over," said the boy, and walked off.

There is a very definite satisfaction in planning successfully a well-made book. But to the average man who loves books, or the beginner in designing them, there is a considerable misapprehension and confused thinking about the kind of pleasure one gets in constructing them. To quote my own words, "The attitudes of mind of a professional and of an amateur about printing—as in most forms of creative endeavour—are quite different. The onlooker supposes the printer to enjoy doing what he enjoys seeing and to be bored by what bores him; and he also believes that the feeling of a man who does a piece of work successfully is 'joy,' when it is mostly relief. The *problem* is what interests all but beginners in typography. Its solution may be, and often is, moderately exciting; although if the problem is successfully solved no one perceives that it has existed. Because all persons who work realize this, it is easier for one worker to talk to another, however dissimilar their occupations may be, than it is to talk with (or to be talked to by) an admirer of one's own class of work, whose likes or dislikes are often based on quite the wrong reasons." Printers, too, suffer from well-meaning amateurs who artlessly propose to enter the trade at the top rather than start at the bottom. Too much is thought about beauty; too little about the knowledge, skill, and mechanical drudgery necessary to attain it. Printing is not to be considered as an art but as a trade, even though it has frontiers on the arts, and I have noticed—as I have said elsewhere—that those who practise it as a trade in private are most likely to talk about it as an art in public. But it is a trade that takes all that man has to give—no less.

"What makes printing good," says Mr. Holbrook Jackson, "is neither the ritualism of handicraft nor the methodism of the machine, but the accordance of the design with the wishes of the reader who wants to get down to the business of reading. Good printing is readable printing, and no print is readable that is not simple, direct, plain, and inclining towards austerity. Printing is not a thing in itself like a picture, admitting the maximum of personal expression, but part of a tool called a book; a bridge between writer and reader. It should contain nothing to impede that traffic. Graciousness, friendliness, even dignity should be there, but always unobtrusively. Self-effacement is the etiquette of the good printer."

Notes

PUBLISHED: *Some Aspects of Printing*, pp. 23–40.

Delivered as a lecture at Harvard University and Pasadena, Calif., 1940. Updike's self-deprecating remark about the lecture was that "it is a matter with which I am too familiar to find it very interesting to write about, and that is why I have probably been unable to make it very interesting to anyone else" ("Foreword," *Some Aspects of Printing*, p. 2).

1. Updike is quoting from Stanley Morison's celebrated essay "First Principles of Typography," which appeared in the seventh number of *The Fleuron* (1930) and was later reprinted as a pamphlet.

2. Morison to Geoffrey Keynes, 14 June 1924: "I wish the point had been made that Pickering was the first to design books in an eclectico–antiquarian spirit: I mean that he was the first to go back to the XVIth century Venice & Lyons for inspiration. Before his time the development of the book shows no instance of atavism. If I am right Pickering is the tribal chief of the Morris–Ricketts–Rogers school" (Nicolas Barker, *Stanley Morison* [London: Macmillan, 1972], p. 156).

3. "It was reserved for the founders of the later eighteenth century to produce letters which are *positively* ugly, and which, it may be added, are dazzling and unpleasant to the eye owing to the clumsy thickening and vulgar thinning of the lines. . . . The Italian, Bodoni, and the Frenchman, Didot, were the leaders in this luckless change . . ." (Morris, "Printing" (1893), reprinted in *The Ideal Book*, p. 62).

The Place of the Educated Man
in the Printing Industry

IN treating the place of the educated man in the printing industry, I have not called printing a trade intentionally, lest I might unduly discourage my readers. I have not termed it an art, lest that might unduly attract and mislead them. Printing is a trade, but it can be practised in the spirit of an art and in rare cases made one. But industry covers both these varieties of endeavour. It is a more modest term, since an industry merely requires the industrious, be he workman or artist.

It has been my fortune or—to speak more accurately—my lot, for many years past, to be interviewed by young men and young women who desired, or thought they desired, to engage in this kind of work. This experience has led me to separate these applicants into three main classes. The first class is the easiest to deal with because their approach to the problem is extremely simple. If untrained, such persons are willing to take any job, however rudimentary, that a printing-house has to offer. They would be equally willing to be trained to drive a grocery cart or serve at a lunch-counter. The reason for this is *first*, that the applicant has to earn some money—I do not say a living, for he could scarcely live on what he at first earns; *second*, because he does not know what he wants to do and has no particular predilection for any form of labour. This is a predicament not unknown to young men more fortunately placed. The untrained lad is, therefore, easily disposed of. If he is faithful and shows ability, after some years he may become a trained workman. He seldom gets further than that. The skilled workman offers no problem at all when he applies

for a position. He is hired or not according to the requirements of the employer at that particular moment. Neither the
unskilled boy nor the trained man has, in most cases, much
education—usually little more than a high school can give;
nor is more education—though desirable—necessary. On the
other hand, in technical skill the untrained boy may become,
or the skilled workman is, far ahead of those who fall into the
second class of applicants for places.

This second class may be divided into two groups. The first
group is made up of older lads and young men. They have had a
little experience in printing of an amateur kind—just enough
to make them feel that this experience is in the nature of an
asset, and perhaps an equipment for the place for which they
apply. This is seldom so. They confuse dabbling with types
on a school paper, an ability to spell, and some love of reading,
with the possession of knowledge sufficient to produce creditable pieces of typography. They are more difficult to deal with
because they approach the problem from an impractical and
slightly romantic angle. Having decided that what they know
is valuable to them, they are a good deal disconcerted to find
that it does not appear valuable to you. Their reasoning is often
peculiar. I remember a young woman who interviewed me at
considerable length about obtaining a position. She wished to
learn the steps necessary to set up a press of her own. When I
asked her if she knew anything whatever about printing, she
frankly said, "No." Her reasons for deciding to enter my establishment were as follows: she was, it appeared, a poetess. Using
letters, which she informed me composed words, she considered printing was directly connected with poetry, which she
stated was also composed of words. Having absorbed what I
could teach her, she could then set up her own shop and by
printing her own poems she would (as she phrased it) "escape
the humiliation of having them refused by a publisher!" Another applicant of the same sex paused in her remarks to ask
a question. Had I, in completing a beautiful piece of work,

ever experienced "craftsman's ecstasy"? I assured her that I had never suffered an attack of that nature, and I was even ignorant of the symptoms or character of such a seizure. She explained that when one had completed a really beautiful example of typography, it was by no means unusual to fall into a trance—apparently swooning (possibly with surprise) at the success of one's efforts. Such, she said, was craftsman's ecstasy! When I laid no claim to any such emotional crises, she appeared disappointed, and shortly departed. She seemed to feel (like the young persons in *Gentlemen Prefer Blondes*, who saw women working in "the Central of Europe"), "this is no country for we girls." Another enquirer, a man this time, desired a position, because he was so fond of literature and he thought, too, that it would be interesting and exciting to meet authors! And one learned compositor, for a short time a member of our force, was so addicted to philosophy that he kept a copy of Kant on his desk. The result was that one or two strange and entirely irrelevant terms crept into a town report, so we had to get rid of him. There is an easy technique in dealing with individuals of this group. It is to allow them to tell you, as fully as they desire, what you can do for them. You then ask, "And what can you do for me?" Generally the interview does not last much longer.

The second group in this class, consisting of persons who want positions in a printing-office, is the most interesting. It is also the most difficult class to deal with. It comprises, usually, men who have had the advantages of an education and a different and more solid background than those of whom I have been speaking. They come from families with the cultural tradition common to educated people. A number of them are seriously interested in literature and may have already tried their hand at writing. Some of them love books not only for what they contain but have opinions about their physical appearance. Others have leanings toward book-collecting and bibliographical activities. Accordingly, it is most natural for them to be interested not merely in books as books, but in their making. They are inclined to think that to have a hand in their production is tinged with literary and artistic pleasure. In short, loving books, they believe that this love will give them proficiency—possibly a modest preeminence—above their fellows in the printing industry. The latter may, alas, love books less, but know better how to make them!

The difficulty with these ideas, which as far as they go are praiseworthy, is this—that no account is taken of the mechanical proficiency, the knowledge and skill, which are necessary for a real mastery of typography. Such men are—very naturally I think—unwilling to undergo, for the length of time necessary to accomplish anything, a thorough mechanical training. They cannot, however, direct others without it. They do not want to be compositors or pressmen. Proof-reading also requires some knowledge of mechanical processes, wide general information, and a long apprenticeship. To add to the difficulty, many of them, because better educated, are also apt to feel, as I have just said, a certain superiority to the workman who, by greater experience and concentration, is technically ahead of them. The real objective of such men is to be what is called an executive—to direct the production of what they do not in any practical fashion know how to produce. Of course any such direction is bound to be fatally defective for it lacks a knowledge of the elementary principles of practical typography and any grasp of what can and cannot be done because of mechanical and economic reasons. How can such men with the interest and knowledge they already have about printing and their love of good books make themselves useful?

Such men can be of great use to printing—and the best printing—by making its encouragement and support their avocation. Such lovers of well-printed books and of sound typography can become effective patrons of what has been called one of "the servant or applied arts." By giving good printers work, by buying well-made books, by discouraging and declining to purchase poor work, by gifts to learned presses, they can help printing as an art and cultivate their own taste. "The great majority of men are in a sense artists," wrote George Leigh-Mallory, "some are active and creative, and some participate passively. No doubt those who create differ in some way fundamentally from those who do not create; but they hold this artistic impulse in common: all alike desire expression for the emotional side of their nature. . . . Not only those who perform are artists, but also those who are moved by the performance. Artists, in this sense, are not distinguished by the power of expressing emotion, but the power of feeling that emotional experience out of which Art is made." So, without making printing a vocation, there is yet a field for those whose equipment is defective but who still have an opportunity to show their practical interest in good printing. Under the rubric of a university press I have something to say later on this point.

There is, however, a third class who still feel that they wish to connect themselves in an active way with the printing industry. They ask, "What am I to do? What is the next step for me?" The answer is, "Go to a technical or trade school and familiarize yourself with all the processes involved in printing a book. After these are learned, when you ask for a position in a printing-house you will have something to offer. You will know to some extent how to direct others." This is a hard saying. To ask an educated man to pass long days in a trade school is like expecting a man enthusiastic over walking to take a course in shoemaking. He asks himself, "Am I, after years at school and college, to begin all over again? Can't I find something to do in which I can utilize what education I have? Must I wander off into a by-path where I shall find few, if any, of my present associates?" These are valid questions. If such a man gives up the idea of devoting himself to printing, he is not necessarily wrong.

Yet there are those who can, and are willing to, undergo

this further training and do not consider it drudgery. They are determined to enter this particular branch of endeavour. I have still to remind them that printing is an occupation in which to succeed involves unending and meticulous care for detail, and where failure in any one point ruins the whole. In making each book, a wise choice of type must be made; a quality of paper suitable for that type must be selected; the type must be properly set; the page of type correctly proportioned and properly imposed on the paper; the presswork even in colour. How these are accomplished are things a man must know. And then there is the proof-reading, about which care and knowledge are vital. This must be scholarly, careful, and speedy; it involves correctness in spelling and grammar, familiarity with historical allusions, and accuracy of quotations in English and other languages—and also among other things an eye for broken letters, wrong founts, and uniform length of page. Though such a man need not be a proof-reader he must know how proof should be read, and he must know, too, what one may reasonably require of those who are proof-readers. He must know what can best be done by machinery and what can best be done by hand. He must know the amount of work that workmen can reasonably be expected to perform. He must be prepared to print rubbish with the care appropriate to a masterpiece. He must suffer fools gladly, and not be impatient when customers call spacing leading, and margins borders. In an age when mass production is the aim and money is the yardstick, he must be willing to keep up the standard of product—to consider quality above quantity. Lastly, he must be content with profits less than those gained by mediocre success in most kinds of business.

The rewards of these efforts will consist merely in the personal satisfaction he gets in doing what interests him and in expressing himself typographically. That does not seem much of a reward. Is the satisfaction sufficiently great? Has he anything of value to express? If the answer is "yes," then I can assure him that the printing industry has enormous need of just such as he. There is a real place for educated men in it, for in such a vocation one can't know too much. One will die learning, though that is what we all have to do. Really, the question is not whether the industry wants the educated man, but whether the educated man can be found who wants to go into it.

My readers may well ask why I ever embarked on such an adventure myself. I can but reply in Dr. Johnson's words, "Ignorance, pure ignorance." Had I known its difficulties beforehand, I should never have had the courage to try to surmount them. Through the training the printing trade has given me, I have learned much, but I shall always regret not having had an education which obliges one to learn many things one does not *want* to know. A man may, by pursuing some particular branch of knowledge that interests him, become, in a narrow sense, cultivated, yet this is a lop-sided sort of development. That it is so can be readily detected by the broadly educated person. I have had to undergo a long and needlessly difficult training because I was never taught how to learn, and, in particular, because no one ever took the trouble to tell me the things I am telling you in these pages.

Perhaps for the educated man this form of livelihood must choose him—he must as a revivalist would say, "feel the Call." Otherwise it is a dubious adventure, all the more if one is not obliged to undertake it. Poussin was once asked by a young Italian nobleman, who painted but fairly well, what was the chief thing needed to assure his success. Poussin replied, "The necessity to do it." Compulsions are a great help in work and for those who are not prodded by necessity, something must be found to take its place. That something is *a compelling desire to do a particular thing.* The printing industry has through five hundred years compelled the labour, interest, and devotion of some scholarly and educated men. Their times needed them. It is truer today than it was then that there is a place as employing printers for educated men, especially those with university training. They should bring to their work disciplined minds, larger views, a general knowledge, which are rare among printers today. For such a person is always something of an idealist and the higher ranges of American industry starve for want of such idealism.

A Latin inscription on the Cloth Hall of Leipzig reads *Res severa verum gaudium.* Hard work and serious purpose must actuate the educated man if he desires to pursue a course which will bring him what seems to me success in the industry of printing. It may even make him a success to himself, which is the truest success of all.

ℕotes

PUBLISHED: *Print* 2, no. 1 (1942): 1–10; *Some Aspects of Printing*, pp. 50–59.

Delivered as a lecture at Harvard University and Pasadena, Calif., 1940. Updike remarked that it "comes from many years of experience and is truer than anyone who is not an employing printer can realize" ("Foreword," *Some Aspects of Printing*, p. 2).

Updike to Morison, 30 September 1941: "The paper you speak of was part of five or six which are collected in a book called 'Some Aspects of Printing—Old and New.' It was not the best one, in my judgment. People seem to like the book, but to me nothing matters much any more in the way of frowns or smiles of the public." There are also some references to the lecture in the Updike–Ruzicka correspondence, pp. 148–49.

❧ Historical

Quod cū audiſſet dauid:deſcendit in
preſidiū.Philiſtijm autem venientes
diffuſſi ſunt in valle raphaim.Et cō=
ſuluit dauid dūm dicens.Si aſcendā
ad philiſtijm·et ſi dabis eos ī manu
mea? Et dixit dūs ad dauid. Aſcende:
q̄a tradens dabo philiſtijm in manu
tua.Venit ergo dauid ad baalphara=
ſim:et percuſſit eos ibi et dixit.Diuiſit
dūs inimicos meos corā me:ſicut di=
uidunt̄ aque.Propterea vocatū ē no=
men locï illi⁹ baalpharaſim.Et reliq̄=
runt ibi ſculptilia ſua:q̄ tulit dauid et
viri eī⁹. Et addiderunt adhuc philiſti=
im ut aſcenderent:et diffuſſi ſūt ī valle
raphaim.Cōſuluit autē dauid dūm.
Si aſcendā cōtra philiſteos:⁊ tradaſ
eos in manus meas?Qui rūdit. Nō
aſcendas cōtra eos ſed gira poſt tergū
corū:⁊ venies ad eos exaduſo pirorū.
Et cū audieris ſonitū clamoris gra=
dientis ī cacumīe piror̄ tūc inibis pliū:
q̄a tūc egredietr̄ dūs āte facie tuā: ut p=

6   Type of Gutenberg's 42-line Bible (Mainz, *c.* 1455)

Gutenberg and His Relation to Printers Today

WHEN I was a little boy, school books usually included an anecdote about Aristides, who, you may remember, was exiled from Athens. The reason for this exile was—as one voter artlessly said to Aristides himself—that the Athenians, or this particular Athenian, had become tired of hearing Aristides called "The Just." In this five-hundredth year since (what is somewhat inaccurately called) the invention of printing by Gutenberg, I suspect that there are other printers besides myself who are tired of hearing his praises sung. The reason for this can be easily explained. It is not because Gutenberg is unworthy of praise, but because the kind of praise to which he is entitled has not been made at all clear. The extravagant laudation he has received has made him appear not alone as the first inventor of moveable type, which incidentally he was not, but as a disseminator of knowledge itself and in a sense an apostle of beauty. It is forgotten that the knowledge which his invention did in the long run disseminate was already extant, and was the legacy which antiquity and Gutenberg's more immediate predecessors had left to his generation. We have no well-grounded reason to think that the spread of knowledge particularly interested Gutenberg. What engrossed him was his invention and the perfecting of it. While like many idealists he was a man of taste, the conscious intention to achieve beauty in his printing was not at first predominant in his programme, though it finally became so. Because his real eminence as a mechanical genius has been so confused by unwarranted claims and with the results of his invention, many of us are a bit weary of hearing about Gutenberg, who seems a mythical figure, rather forbidding, very remote from us, and because remote not particularly interesting. Yet he has a close relation to printers today, and I propose to indicate what that relation is.

The story of Gutenberg's life in detail, I have no intention of telling. It can be found in numberless books. In this brief paper I confine myself to the nature of his invention, his aim in making it, and his relation to us now.

Gutenberg, it must be remembered, belonged to an important and highly placed family of goldsmiths in Mainz. His familiarity with working in metal gave him facility and experience in the use of it and this led to his experiments with metal types; much as William Caslon's training in metal engraving fitted him for type-cutting. I have said that Gutenberg was not the inventor of moveable types. Nor was he. They had been made by the Chinese. He was not the inventor of moveable types in Europe, for these appear to have been made in a crude form in Holland before his time. What he did invent were moulds and matrices, by which types could be accurately cast in large quantities. By this he put typecasting on a practical basis. Relief printing, paper, hand engraving, printed books, even moveable types had all been thought of before Gutenberg availed himself of the different experiments of his predecessors and made something which, however it has been improved upon in detail today, has not been improved upon in theory. What he invented, therefore, was the adjustable typemould, by which identical characters could be produced in quantity. This process, carried on in secret, was sufficiently perfected to be shown by 1439, and was given to the world in 1440. This was the nature of Gutenberg's invention. Some of this period of experimentation was spent in the construction of a printing press.

About his aim in making and further perfecting his invention, there are two schools of opinion. One is that he was an inventor with an idea; that he began and ended in trying to make books cheaper in order to get potential profits. According to this view he had no conscious interest in their appearance, except as selling value required similarity to what the user was accustomed.

Another view is that Gutenberg sincerely and consciously worked to imitate the beauty of the manuscripts — witness the elaborately illuminated copies of the Bible — and "in that, he and his associates succeeded only so far as their metallic medium permitted. The materials of the new technique even then forced a departure from the manuscript, a divergence that later became more marked. Then, too, the religious character of the first printed books demanded a respectful and traditional approach in their execution." Of these opinions, the first is the statement of a bibliographer, the second of an artist.

To my mind, Gutenberg did not *at first* see the artistic possibilities which opened out to him later. His earliest tentative experiments in type were of inferior merit, but in his twenty years of labour he aimed more and more to show that a printed book could emulate or even rival fine manuscripts and thus could supplant them by production in quantity at a low price. This was his aim. The result was that ten years after his first experiments he interested a certain Johan Fust who was willing to finance the new project, and about 1450 work was begun on what is known as the 42-line Bible. Like work undertaken by an experimenter who loved to perfect details as he went along, the book did not progress, or progressed so slowly that Fust began to wonder if he would ever get back the money sunk in the scheme. After various quarrels, Gutenberg was made to turn over the types in the printing-office to one of its workmen — Peter Schoeffer. It was under his direction that the Bible was finished in the winter of 1455–1456, though by that time the printing-office had passed out of Gutenberg's hands. He still went on with his work and designed another, smaller and less attractive but more workable type. This was employed in the *Catholicon* of 1460 — a sort of dictionary — and the only book we can safely consider as wholly the work of Gutenberg.

These appear to have been the results of Gutenberg's aims in his own day.

To judge rightly Gutenberg's claim to fame, we must also scrap the idea that he desired or foresaw the later effects of his invention, which would probably have horrified him. We know, what he did not, that printing is an engine for the dissemination of error as well as of truth, and that it has diffused every heresy, religious, political, and social, that since his day has afflicted man. If the spread of knowledge was what he was after, there was no need to take much pains in the models he chose for his type. Truth or falsehood — as we have since learned — can be, and has been, as readily spread — indeed more so — by badly printed books as by fine ones. If the early printers made fine volumes, it was because they comprehended fully, what Gutenberg saw vaguely at first though more clearly later, that their product had to compete commercially with fine manuscripts. Unless a printed book came somewhere near these manuscripts in effect, no purchasers could be found. From the business end of it, the problem of the early printer then was just like yours and mine under similar circumstances now. If I am able before the end of this paper to make you feel this, I shall have brought Gutenberg and his associates down from the clouds and placed them squarely on earth, within hailing distance of a printer today.

For reasons somewhat similar to those which make Gutenberg seem remote, an exhibition of the great landmarks of typography may well be disconcerting to the common or garden printer. Such a man is puzzled by the praise lavished on these great books by book-lovers or artistic amateurs of printing. They use a very different vocabulary from that used in trade and employ terms that may appear to a craftsman inaccurate, obscure, and affected. The viewpoint, and therefore mode of expression, of a working printer and that of the lover of beautiful printing are so entirely different that neither quite understands the other. In short, those who are interested in how the problem presented is solved belong to a different class from those who admire the result of that solution.

To illustrate this let us suppose that a man of taste visits Rome. He is charmed by its fountains and the splendid profusion of gushing, surging water that they offer to the eye. He does not much care how this comes to pass. An hydraulic engineer — or perhaps an Irish plumber on a pious visit *ad limina Apostolorum* — sees these fountains too. His interest lies in how this play of water is effected. To the cultivated amateur the interest lies in what they do; to the engineer or workman the interest also lies in how they do it. A certain emperor once visited the piazza of St. Peter's to see its celebrated fountains: after a few moments, supposing them to be playing in his honour, he observed that the water could now be turned off. The reply was that the order could not be obeyed, for the force that propelled the water was solely gravitational, its supply unlimited. This would perhaps have occurred to a plumber, but it did not occur to the potentate. Both were interested for different reasons, but the emperor had but one source of enjoyment — visual, while the workman had two — visual and intellectual; so the latter had the best of it! This analogy holds good in printing, between the lover of fine books and the man who makes them — one enjoys the end, the other is interested both in the end and the means.

If I could show you in detail how some of the imposing, splendid, but to us seemingly remote pieces of printing came into being, the conditions under which they were produced and the results aimed at in their production, you would probably find that the difficulties and problems they presented were much the same to their printers that they would be to you and to me. Think, for instance, of some splendid examples of early printing, folio volumes, with double columns of type, so even in word spacing and solid in colour of print. These effects were gained by means open *mechanically* to us, but absolutely closed to us today by the changed attitude of present-day readers.

Why closed? Because even spacing and solidity of colour was formerly gained partly by massive type forms now popularly discarded, but chiefly by close and even spacing achieved by endless abbreviations and lack of uniformity in indicating the same word, which was contracted at will by the use of diacritical marks. If more solid composition was attained thereby, the times when these early books were printed allowed this. Readers were then accustomed to these labour-saving expedients in the manuscripts with which they were already familiar. In printing they served no such useful purpose, for it was found easier to spell a word in full than to search for the typographic character indicating its appropriate contraction. Hence they were abandoned. Even when the words were later spelled out the printer was given great latitude in arbitrarily lengthening or shortening the spelling of the same word to suit his convenience. We cannot do this now for the public will not accept a book so printed. In consequence, even spacing is more difficult to accomplish now than it was then. Aldus at Venice, about 1500, thought it a very bright idea to imitate cursive handwriting in his italic type for pocket editions and he had, God only knows how many, variant letters and logotypes to effect this. Like most ill-digested schemes it fell by its own weight and nowadays in normal italic we find scarcely any trace of his elaborate plan. It has taken a long time for printing to escape from the bondage of the manuscript, nor has it yet. In almost every modern book there is still a trace of it, namely, the indention of paragraphs. This, in manuscripts, was filled in by an initial in colour, but in early printed books this blank space was generally left to be filled in by hand or printed in another colour. Today we find that the blank space sufficiently indicates a paragraph and a coloured or black initial is no longer needed for the purpose.

Keeping all this in mind, we come to realize that these early books, so highly respected and valued, so reverentially preserved, presented to the man who printed them the same sort of problem with which you and I have to struggle. There is no reason, accordingly, for the average printer to be bewildered or discouraged by their *apparent* lack of relation to his present-day job. All these books were jobs and all jobs offer problems. We don't see that at once, because we do not know enough about what each particular problem was or how it was solved to make these great pieces of printing human — really and truly related to us. About some of these books we never can know because no documents exist to enlighten us. In a second class, investigation, if we are not too lazy to make it, will tell us a good deal. About some modern monuments of fine printing, we have been told by their makers what the printer's problem was and how that problem was solved.

There is one book in the splendid collection of great examples of typography — "Great Books in Great Editions" — shown here which belongs to the second class — near enough to us to enable us to find out something about it, yet far enough away to seem aloof from present-day interests. It is an edition in four folio volumes of La Fontaine's *Fables* issued in Paris between 1755 and 1759. It is commonly called the Oudry La Fontaine, though the Cochin La Fontaine would just as accurately describe it. The publication of this very fashionable undertaking seems to have been chiefly promoted by C. N. Cochin *fils*, a brilliant personality and a talented engraver, who came of a race of engravers. He was a great favourite at court, and a protégé of Madame de Pompadour, mistress of Louis XV and a woman of considerable perception in matters connected with the fine arts — to which, unfortunately, she added a disastrous taste for meddling in politics. She chose Cochin, Soufflot, and the Abbé Le Blanc (as "coaches" respectively for art, architecture, and antiquities) to accompany her brother, then Monsieur de Vandières, on a famous journey to Italy. This excursion which lasted nearly two years was to fit him, by educating his taste, for the post of *Inspecteur des Batiments du Roi*, for which he was already slated. Cochin maintained close relations with Vandières, later Marquis de Marigny, all his life, and Marigny called Cochin *mes yeux*—for, as he got fat and lazy, no matters of taste were settled without Cochin's advice. It was on their return that the La Fontaine was started with brilliant prospects of success.

Why was the edition known as the Oudry La Fontaine? It was because its most conspicuous feature was the 276 engraved plates, after drawings by the painter Jean Baptiste Oudry. Oudry began his career as a portrait painter, and Peter the Great sat to him on his visit to Paris in 1717 and liked his work so much that Oudry was nearly dragged to Russia with him, and had to go into hiding to escape the journey. Later Oudry turned his attention to still life and pictures of animals. For Louis XV he painted royal hunts and pet dogs. Thus Oudry, too, was a court favourite. Now it happened that Oudry had for a number of years previous made, as an amusement, a quantity of rough pencil and wash sketches based on La Fontaine's *Fables*. These were thrown off with no thought that they would ever be engraved. The collection might have been dispersed if Cochin had not got wind of it and seen its possibilities for use in this edition. These studies were not sufficiently finished to permit engraving, and it was Cochin who touched them up and prepared exact drawings. He also supervised the production of the plates which were engraved by a group of well-known men—LeMire, Choffard, and others, and one by Cochin himself. Whether Cochin improved Oudry's designs remains to be seen. Anyhow Cochin and his associates thought so.

Besides being a painter, Oudry had received in 1734 the appointment of director of the tapestry works at Beauvais (destroyed a few months ago by the *furor Teutonicus*), which supplied coverings for sofas, chairs, screens, and tabourets. Later he was made director of the Gobelin Manufactory. Persons familiar with Beauvais work will recall that La Fontaine's

Fables was a very common subject for tapestry coverings woven there for suites of furniture—after Oudry's designs. He also furnished designs for tapestry hangings, often representing hunting subjects and still life.

The production of this monumental edition was by no means plain sailing. The typography of the first volumes was violently criticised in the *Journal des Sçavans* by an anonymous writer (apparently a type-founder) who seems to have known what he was talking about. A Monsieur de Montenault was the editor and in charge of the typography. The work was published in Paris by Desaint and Saillant and by Durand. It was printed by Charles Antoine Jombert, printer to the crown for works on fortifications. The first two volumes appeared in 1755, the third in 1756, and the final volume in 1759. The care of the typography of this great and extremely "smart" project was shared by a banker named Darcy, Berryer, another protégé of Madame de Pompadour, and Malesherbes, who later defended Louis XVI at his trial. The progress of the work was terribly hampered by the members of this committee, as distinguished in position as they were incompetent in the business they were supposed to oversee. A particularly trying individual was a certain Monsieur Bombarde, pretentious, opinionated, and ignorant, who had to be treated with deference because he partly financed the scheme and because he had important connections in the great world. Malesherbes was a good-natured addle-pate who could never remember what was being discussed. Monsieur Berryer was forever joking. Bombarde agreed with everybody in turn. There were long dissertations as to whether ornamental initials should be one or one and a half times the height of the letters that follow. When these conferences were over, Cochin, Jombert, and the publishers put their heads together and, by deciding what the committee's indecision had left in the air, gave the work a further push towards completion. "Never," said Cochin, "did I hear so much serious talk about nothing. . . . The best of it was that after many conferences at which nothing was decided, we remained and politely made ourselves masters of the edition, or we should never have finished. The humblest printer knew more than they did."

There were other difficulties to be adjusted. At that date wood-engraving had gone out of fashion and was generally considered "gothic," a word then used in the sense of barbaric. The La Fontaine seemed to offer a chance to revive its prestige, by introducing tailpieces and decorations engraved on wood. To make designs for these a flower painter, J. S. Bachelier, director of design at the Royal Porcelain Manufactory at Vincennes, was chosen. These designs were engraved chiefly by Nicolas Le Sueur and Jean Baptiste Michel Papillon *fils*, a relation of Oudry's and an enthusiastic supporter of wood-engraving, about which he wrote a long and rather diffuse treatise. Between them they produced perhaps the most beautifully conceived and executed series of floral decorations to accompany type ever printed from wood-blocks. These were purposely designed in a very open style, splendidly adapted to accord with type printed on rough paper, though the introduction of decorations cut on wood was of questionable taste in a book illustrated by copperplates. These charming wood-engravings seem, however, to have fallen flat. They had not, as Papillon hoped, any effect on the general practice of book-making. A hundred years later they would have been appreciated as the beautiful things that they are. In fact, nowadays, persons of taste think them better and far more interesting than Oudry's pretentious and rather second-rate illustrations.

Was Oudry's work really second-rate? I have a suspicion that his original rough studies had far more life in them than appeared in Cochin's finished drawings; that in Cochin's redrawing he "gentled" the animals, and the wilder they appeared as drawn by Oudry, the tamer they got as redrawn by Cochin! In such work Cochin's delicate and elegant art had no place. Oudry's original designs—still extant—show the practised hand of a master and Cochin by perfecting these designs spoiled them! This, Oudry, who died at Beauvais the year the first volumes came out, fortunately did not live to see. Finally, after interminable discussions and delays the great work was finished. This brief account gives some idea of the heartaches and headaches, the troubles, misunderstandings, and mistakes its production engendered — now forgotten when we look at these important looking volumes.

Now the history of this great La Fontaine is only that of almost all great books. The *Voyage Pittoresque ou Description des Royaumes de Naples et de Sicile* of the Abbé J. C. R. St. Non, with its beautiful colour prints, and one of the finest books of the eighteenth century, ruined its author because he would keep faith with his subscribers. The Plantin Polyglot Bible was never fully paid for by Philip II, who discharged his debt in part by giving Plantin the monopoly of Spanish liturgical printing, a nuisance which the Spanish Church only got rid of in the late eighteenth century. The Paris Polyglot Bible of Le Jay — in ten folio volumes which it took seventeen years to complete — nearly ruined its editor. Its very learned printer, Antoine Vitré, specialist in Oriental languages, bought, by order of Richelieu, for the crown a collection of Oriental types about 1632 from the heirs of a former French ambassador to Constantinople. After interminable legal difficulties and a delay of twenty years the debt was paid, but only through the good offices of the clergy of France. Beaumarchais' three fine editions of Voltaire, printed from Baskerville's types which he bought for that purpose, were made a failure by the French Revolution, which the influence of Voltaire and Beaumarchais did so much to bring about. All these books and all great books have their histories, just like Oudry's La Fontaine.

All the same Oudry's La Fontaine is a monument to French craftsmanship. The edition was produced on a scale and in a manner impossible except in the eighteenth century, or in any country except France. It was characteristic of the reign of Louis XV, a splendid, showy performance—*un livre de parade*—and one of the last of its kind at that period, for public taste was even then turning to smaller books. Now and then we see such attempts today, but they do not ring true. That is because they are not—as this book was—characteristic of their time, and so such modern attempts at the grand manner of printing appear anachronisms. The day of pompous volumes is over. The spread of popular education, a clearer view of what books are meant to accomplish, a more fastidious taste have changed our way of printing. We feel now that the most beautiful book is still intended to be read, and that a very large format forbids this, however clear the typography. From that point of view the Oudry La Fontaine is a failure.

The modern printer's problem is to produce books mechanically well-made, tasteful without pretension, beautiful without eccentricity or sacrifice of legibility. In his work he must be of his day and generation and will be whether he tries to be or not. Such important yet ignorant and ineffective committees, that must be respectfully listened to, as that which teased Cochin and Jombert, have their counterparts now. The stupid moneyed backer who places flattery first and service second is with us still. The enthusiastic amateur, who "adores" books and is "thrilled" by printing, and who in expressing his admiration uses technical terms all wrong—we know him too. And lastly, the well-meaning and distinguished man who, because of his reputation, is chosen to interpret a talent entirely different from his own, and so spoils what he is supposed to improve—he, too, is inflicted on us. Times may differ, books may differ, but the men we have to deal with are much the same. It has been said that the saints were saints because they were cheerful when it was difficult to be cheerful; patient when it was difficult to be patient; they pushed on when they wanted to stand still, kept silent when they wanted to talk, and were agreeable when they wanted to be disagreeable. You and I know how much a printer needs to have some of the qualities of saintliness and what a nuisance it is to have to have them.

You may say, what *has* all this to do with Gutenberg? It has a great deal to do with him. For as I have tried to show you, all the books that I have named were the results of ideals, just as Gutenberg's monumental Bible and *Catholicon* were, though such monuments are built with blood and tears.

We still have to consider the second reason for Gutenberg's greatness. This second reason is his persistence in carrying out an idea and an ideal to the fullest degree of perfection that he could imagine. I doubt if he was an easy man to get on with, to those who wanted quick results or viewed the work from a money-making angle. I doubt if his life could have been a satisfactory or successful affair, as his world counted satisfaction then, or as ours counts it now. To him it was possibly satisfying because, amid all sorts of obstacles, he succeeded in carrying out his ideal. He died in respectable retirement in 1468, but he had lived to see other men enter into his labours, and perhaps an even finer volume than he had made — the Psalter of Fust and Schoeffer — produced by former associates and rivals. Debts, law suits, a breach of promise case, business quarrels, alienation of his types, of his work-shop, his Bible completed by other hands, all this was not very amusing to a man like Gutenberg. Yet it is said that "every thing worth doing is done *in spite of*" and to this Gutenberg would have agreed. The story of his life, if we think of it in simple, homely terms, brings the man nearer to us, not as a great genius, but as an ancient fellow craftsman. If as printers we want to get anything out of his work, and the work of other masters of typography, think of it and look at it, not as the handiwork of a group of remote, idealistic, impractical phantoms, but as that of human, everyday men like ourselves. Unlike most of us, however, they were willing, in spite of the mistakes, disillusions, and disappointments common to us all, to "carry on" to a successful issue. In the history of the printer's craft Gutenberg is one of the most famous of this small class, though not the only one. "Who knows," said Sir Thomas Browne, "whether the best of men be known? or whether there be no more remarkable ones *forgot* than any that stand remembered." We call the fame of Gutenberg immortal. But Sir Thomas reminds us that "only that which hath no beginning may be confident of no end" and that "there is nothing strictly immortal but immortality."

Notes

PUBLISHED: *Some Aspects of Printing*, pp. 5–22.

"The address with which the book opens, on 'Gutenberg and His Relation to Printers Today,' was prepared especially for the printers of Los Angeles and its vicinity, at the pre-view of a splendid exhibition of 'Great Books in Great Editions' held at the Huntington Library. It is an attempt to make Gutenberg a human being and not a remote, almost mythical figure" (Updike, "Foreword," *Some Aspects of Printing*, p. 2). The Huntington exhibition of 1940 was "in commemoration of the 500th anniversary of the invention of printing," according to a revised edition of the catalogue (1966).

Updike to Rudolph Ruzicka, 27 January 1941: "It was delivered before some 50 Printing-House craftsmen, of whom possibly 6 knew what I was trying to point out." Updike to Ruzicka, 6 Feburary 1941: "As I read this paper it sounds rather elementary, and I am not able in my present state of mind to discover whether it is elementary because it is not sufficiently well written, or whether it is elementary because it tells the truth."

Review of Stanley Morison's
'Four Centuries of Fine Printing'

MR. Stanley Morison has already deserved well of the
Republic of Letters—to use a term common to a century in which few other republics existed—for the papers
that he has written on typography and the practical application of his knowledge to its problems. The essay on "Printers'
Flowers and Arabesques" (produced in collaboration with
Mr. Francis Meynell), in the first number of *The Fleuron*, attracted, and deserved, the attention of printers. For although
their theory of the origin of these ornaments had been anticipated some years earlier by an American designer, Mr. W.
A. Dwiggins,[1] their paper so elaborated and documented his
contention as to be in the nature of a discovery. More valuable, and less obvious, was an essay in a succeeding issue of the
same periodical—"Towards an Ideal Type"—which showed
that in Morison we have to do with a man who, by painstaking examination of his subject from unexpected and original
angles, is able to support a novel point of view in a sober and
convincing way. Nor has he stopped there. He has practised
his own precepts. And today both printers and public are,
through him, richer in sound typographic material—both by
type-ornament and founts of type—used so that its method of
utilization is little less valuable than the material itself.

Mr. Morison was, therefore, among the few men fitted to
prepare the book which is the subject of this review. Ever since
its imposing prospectus in folio was issued, I have looked for
the appearance of *Four Centuries of Fine Printing* and its illustrative examples with considerable curiosity, and a rather fearful

[79]

joy at finding my own work among the elect. What had Mr. Morison to say in the prefatory pages laconically described in the prospectus by the words "With text"? What would these examples, exhibiting the development of typographical style in the use of roman letter, disclose? And how was the work to be presented?—questions that may now be answered in the order they proposed themselves to me.

I. THE TEXT

The Introduction that Mr. Morison has supplied to the six hundred examples of the work of presses existing between 1500 and 1914 begins with a definition of what "fine printing" is, and how "fine types" may be described. He then tells us of the origin of the roman letter—by which must be understood both roman and italic—in capitals and lower case; tracing its course through various vicissitudes until it reappears in a modified form in the early Renaissance; at first retaining gothic characteristics, but perfected in Florence about 1440 and adopted in a sloped form by the chancery of the Vatican under Nicholas V. The differentiation is exhibited between the refinements of roman letter in the great fifteenth-century school of Florentine calligraphy, and the less subtle type-forms common to Venetian printing—a differentiation very strongly recognized at that period by bibliophiles. For although great credit is given to Jenson, Mr. Morison believes that the Da Spiras surpassed him in their types, because following more closely Florentine calligraphic traditions; and that Aldus's roman letter, cut by Griffo, in the Da Spira tradition—copied in France and re-introduced into Venice—was the real precursor of what is now called "old style" type. This point he appears to have made for the first time—none the less soundly because supported with ingenuity as well as research. This, with his excursus on the present inadequate terminology of the Renaissance letter, seems to me the most original portion of his Introduction.

[80]

After comment on the early Italian press, we have a description of the passing of its primacy to the French sixteenth-century presses, in which, of course, Tory, De Colines, Estienne, and Garamond are outstanding names. Basle and Frankfort are then surveyed, and the scene of pre-eminent endeavour shifts to Lyons, where the printer De Tournes, the designer Bernard Salomon, and the type-cutter Robert Granjon—also designer of printers' "flowers"—are the prominent figures. Mr. Morison gives a very just survey of the work of Plantin who, he says rightly enough, as a printer has been over-written and over-rated. This is followed by informing passages upon the origin and development of the Imprimerie Royale at Paris; the extraordinarily clever group of men who designed and cut its types during the reigns of Louis XIV, XV, and XVI; and the fashions in French type-design popularized by the Imprimerie and followed outside it, notably by Fournier-le-jeune and other commercial typefounders, who copied the "royal" types, at a distance kept respectful by various fines, penalties, and confiscations. This brings us to Baskerville, of Birmingham, whose influence on Continental printing in general and on Bodoni and Didot in particular, I think Mr. Morison overestimates, though in this many persons agree with him. The author's statement that the finest English printing was produced between 1770 and 1820 will probably horrify the few remaining "Goths" and amuse the increasing horde of Vandals! I confess an admiration for this period, though I had not thought of it as exactly "the golden age of English typography." But perhaps it is!

Bodoni is, of course, amply noticed; the Didots, more cursorily. It may be said, in passing, that it is commonly thought that Didot's types were accepted in France without protest; though as a matter of fact, Anisson, last director of the Imprimerie Royale before the Revolution, would not allow their use in that establishment. But, unfortunately, at the Revolution, Anisson—not the types—perished!

[81]

We are now in modern times, and here Mr. Morison turns to England and surveys the "deliberate archaising movement" which was the distinctive contribution of William Pickering, both in printing and publishing. None before him, he says, "dreamt of returning to the typography of a past age." And with such exceptions as the eighteenth-century imitation of a sixteenth-century edition of *Boccaccio* and a few similar *tours de force*, this is true. But if, in his phrase, we replace the word "typography" by "letter-form," we describe accurately enough precisely what did happen in the earliest Italian employ of roman type. A harking back to old typographic models has continued to the present day, Mr. Morris being, next to Pickering, the great exemplar of its later and more Gothic development. This general tendency has not yet spent its force. And if any comfort can be derived from the observation, the departures in architecture, decoration, and many of the minor arts—among which, for convenience, we include typography—that have been made in the interests of originality, have not been particularly agreeable.

Mr. Morris's work and influence are treated with discrimination, and the printing of the Doves Press, the Oxford University Press, and a few other outstanding English printing-houses, closes the consideration of English work. Then follow a most generous appreciation of the efforts of the Merrymount Press, Boston, and an estimate of Mr. Bruce Rogers' inimitable series of beautifully conceived and executed books. I could wish that some other Americans were included here—such as Mr. Cleland, responsible for some typography and typographic embellishments of distinction, and Mr. Rollins, of the Yale University Press, who has done some excellent work. And there are several other American printers who might well have been represented.

The Introduction closes with a *résumé* of the chief influences observable in Continental typography. Here Mr. Morison introduces (to most of us) the Lyons printer, Louis Perrin, whose

Caractères Agustaux, produced in 1846, were based on roman inscriptional letters; the Ficks, of Geneva, who executed distinguished work with Perrin's material; the Parisian printer, Claye, who had a hand in this revival of older type-forms; and the comparatively recent use by French publishers of the historic founts of the Imprimerie Nationale. Modern German printing is very fairly and generously accorded such praise as it deserves—though not all that it probably desires.

The passage that ends the Introduction admits without evasion the weak spot in today's practice of typography. Modern "fine printing," Mr. Morison tells us, "is an anachronism and will never be singled out by the historian of the future as the representative printing of our period. Nevertheless, it must be admitted that, so much does almost every individual among us assist in the cult of the past that, to provide the mock antique is one of the surest ways to a reputation for fine printing. Yet this seems fundamentally wrong. To some of us it may be more exciting to play with sixteenth-century flowers, and to all of us it is easier to copy old styles than to make a good one of our own. . . . We come back to the question of basic principles. If we are acting against the highest interests of typography by remaining content with resurrected Garamond, Aldus, Jenson, and period usages thereof, what is the next step? We must have new types, new ornaments (perhaps even new conventions of display can be worked out), by the living rather than copies from the illustrious dead; therefore it is proper, indeed necessary, to study the history of printing, not as an end in itself, but as a means, an inspiration, towards the typographical task before us."

This is sound sense, and contains a truth that it is not altogether comfortable or flattering to ourselves to recognize; though after all, today's mock antique will always betray that it is a very 1924 form of "mockery," and may, as such, find favour in the eyes of collectors a hundred years hence. Nevertheless, I agree with Mr. Morison, and am equally in the dark as to precisely what the next step may be in the evolution of type, ornament, and conventions of display. Perhaps one step towards a solution is to change the method in solving such questions—less to assemble together to talk (or be talked to), and more often to go apart to think—to be less stirred by various ancient or modern winds of doctrine—to realize that "the judgments inspired by reaction are as ephemeral as those from which they react"; and above all, to remember that (as Dumas remarked) "all generalizations are false, even this one!" By such reasonable mental behaviour, whatever befalls typography, whether (as seems to me more probable) it will rise in occasional tides of beauty, only again to ebb and fall "in shallows and in miseries"; or whether it will go steadily from strength to strength, no great disaster can befall us. In any case, as Mr. Morison says, "we must study the progressive history of printing as an inspiration to our typographical task." And it is in such books as those to which *Four Centuries* is a guide, that we must study it.

II. THE PLATES

The illustrative plates of printed pages form, of course, the chief features of this book. Of these, sixteen reproduce pages from books of the fifteenth century, all but one being work of Venetian printers—intentionally a scanty exhibit, because the Incunabula have been thoroughly illustrated elsewhere, and pages from them are (like most of the plates that Mr. Morison shows) extremely familiar. They are needed chiefly to show the derivation of, and furnish a point of departure for, the sixteenth-century work, which is shown so fully. Of sixteenth-century printing we have 301 examples, 86 of these being Italian—Florence, Venice, and Rome being the chief cities represented—and numbers 87 to 280 are devoted to French work, divided between Paris and Lyons. For this period the other cities represented are Basle, Frankfort, Lausanne, and Antwerp. Seventeenth-century France has but twelve ex-

amples of books printed at Paris, which seems a scanty showing for that particular hundred years. The eighteenth century,
however, is represented by numbers 324 to 453, and includes
Paris, Madrid, Parma, London, and Birmingham. The nineteenth century is represented in France, England, and Switzerland only; and the twentieth century by a number of examples
taken from French, English, and American books—Holland
and Germany being represented by but two volumes each.
Thus the allotment of reproductions to different countries and
periods is somewhat arbitrary, and though sometimes necessary, is in certain cases surprising. I cannot believe, for instance, that twentieth-century England is fairly represented by
twenty-six numbers, when the United States, in work divided
between but two printers, is represented by forty-eight plates!
This discrepancy is partly accounted for when we consider that
some of the most striking English work of the last twenty-five
years was printed in black-letter. Even so, I am not sure that
the balance is justly held.

Among the books which particularly stand out, either for
their rarity or for interesting founts of type employed, are the
Aldine *Epistole* of Saint Katharine of Siena (6–8), the pages
by Tagliente, Marcolini, and Janiculo (13–22), showing interesting forms of italic, the Torrentino Justinian and Pausanias
(57–60), the work of Blado and the Blado italic (65–81), the
Vatican *Biblia Sacra* (86), De Colines' editions of Oronce Fine
(107–114), the *Horae* of Fezandat and Tory (128–144), the
magnificent pages of Le Royer's edition of Cousin (192–197),
Vascosan's Paschalius (200–205), the delightful *Calendrier* of
De Tournes (231–244) and his New Testament (247–249),
Moreau's calligraphic types (315–318), Le Bé's Hebrew
Grammar (319–320), the Imprimerie Royale *Médailles* (324–
327), some pages from Bulmer's books (448–451), titles from
the Imprimerie de la Republique (454–457), Perrin's *Inscriptions Antiques* (462), the work of Fick of Geneva, interesting for
its period (481–496), some Bensley title-pages (497–498) and

[85]

those of Bulmer (501–502), Bridgett's *Holy Eucharist* (545) and the splendid Oxford *Book of Common Prayer* (546–551).

Some other volumes which are particularly charming as examples of typography are by Torrentino (57), De Colines (103–106) and (115–116), Tory (137–144), Kerver—*Poliphile*—(155–158), Vascosan (164–165), Estienne (174–175), De Tournes—Froissart—(268), the Imprimerie Royale—*Imitation*—(312–314), Barbou–Fournier (376–388), Didot (376–388), Bodoni (408–424), Baskerville (426–429), Edmund Fry (434–437), Pickering and Whittingham (517–530 only), the Oxford University Press (552–557), and Bruce Rogers—particularly numbers 568–595.

When I first glanced through these plates, my sense of direction was lost at certain points; and there also appeared to be many examples of much the same thing—an iteration not so much tiresome as confusing. On examination, I am convinced that what is really lacking is a sufficient critical and explanatory apparatus. The Introduction covers groups of plates, it is true; but we are left in the dark as to the reasons for including the various items in these groups. If, therefore, half-titles could have been inserted before the centuries, and these centuries again subdivided by half-titles bearing the names of countries, there might have been placed upon the back of such half-titles, or on a following page, the contents of the section, with annotations showing just what each plate was intended to convey. Unless one is a very advanced student, one does not always see what Mr. Morison is driving at; and lack of annotation *of each plate* hinders the average reader from easily following the author's idea. Then again, the inclusion of superfluous pages leaves no room for other pages, which might well have been included to show a certain progression. And, too, a more restricted number of examples would have avoided the crowding of too many examples of work on the same page, or the inclusion on one page, or on facing pages, of plates so different in character that they seem to destroy each other. An effort has evidently been made to keep pages from the same printer or in the same general style in groups; but it has not always been possible.

There are also some omissions which I regret; but that is a matter of taste, and such will occur to (and be different for) everybody. I am sorry that, in the Spanish portion, De Sancha's *History of Mexico* is not given a chance, or the magnificent piece of printing by Monfort of Perez Bayer's book on Hebrew–Samaritan coinage. I am also surprised to see that the Foulis of Glasgow have no representation. To Mr. Morison's high appreciation of Bulmer's work, a page from that printer's splendid *History of the River Thames* would have given support. And for a later period, why were the Vale Press types or the Brook type of the Eragny Press omitted? Horne's Florence type also seems to me worth a showing (though the author condemns it), as well as a page from Mr. Horne's famous *Hobby-Horse*.

These are random observations made without method, and undoubtedly there are other lacunæ which will occur to persons more conversant than I am with books printed from 1500 to 1920. As reproductions, some of the plates are wonderful examples of clear, delightful facsimile, which (although somewhat "surfacy," owing to the gelatine process which was used) could scarcely be improved. There are others which should have been thrown out, where the lines are either quite gone or else unduly heavy. In evenness of execution, I do not think the reproductions are up to the standard that such a book should set. And yet I do not know where a better assemblage of examples of work typical of these interesting and neglected periods may be found.

III. THE TYPOGRAPHY

The title-page of the announcement of *Four Centuries* I did not think worthy of the distinguished typography which it introduced. I do not like drawn title-pages for printed books, and this in particular seemed to me a bit "postery" and flamboyant—too much the title-page of a designer, and too little that of a printer. In the final book, however, this is discarded. The present title-page goes to the other extreme in its intentional and apparently consistent—but to my eye unsatisfying—employ of the capitals and lowercase letters in which the Introduction is printed. So refined has it become as to be almost prudish. Even the words that described Miss Mitford's famous turban seem strong for it! 'Tis of the nature of angels, without parts or passions, and seems almost too innocent for the employ of fallen man. But alas, 'tis not so innocent, after all. For its flowery double border—"of daisies pied"?—is made up of lowercase italic *g*'s, perhaps to remind one of that mediæval theory that the chief enjoyment of angels is the love of a joke!

The effect of the text pages, set in type copied from the roman letter cut by Griffo, is admirable; ample and noble—distinguished and sane—happy and unusual combination! This type shows the result of Mr. Morison's contention that capital letters of a fount should be slightly shorter than the tops of the tall ascenders of a lowercase letter—a result both workable from the reader's view-point, and agreeable from the standpoint of a careful designer. This was the letter used by Aldus Manutius in the famous *Hypnerotomachia* of 1499. The adaptation of Antonio Blado's italic—in the design of which the Roman calligrapher, Vicentino, probably had a hand—is even more interesting than Griffo's roman. It is clear, nervous, calligraphic; but legitimately so, and a permanent addition to fine types of a stylistic character—the best italic, of its class, that I know. It is a pleasure to recognize that these two excellent types were designed for and worked on a machine. The light of taste and business sense has been late in dawning on type-design for composing machines. But let bygones be bygones! There is no need of reminding the convert of his original darkness, nor examining too meticulously the precise reasons for his conversion. 'Tis enough that he is numbered with the faithful at last!

But while these great pages of roman type, with their wide margins on which appear notes, or references to plates, printed in italic, are really imposing, they are hard to read: partly because their size necessitates very long lines of type; partly because the type (slightly leaded and more lightly inked in the prospectus) is here set solid, heavily inked, and composed without indentation; and finally because Mr. Morison's style, at times somewhat elaborate, demands more assistance from the type-setting than it obtains. The capitalization, by the way, is not always consistent; else, why "general council," "eastern and western churches," "vatican chancery," on the one hand, and "Oxford Movement," "French Church," "King and his Ministers," on the other? Then "florentine" and "subiaco" and "beneventan" trouble me, but are possibly excused on the ground of being types like "roman" and "italic."

The weak spots of the book, typographically, are the pages allotted to the List of Plates (pp. xxvii–xxix) and the Index to Printers and Publishers (p. 243). Elsewhere the roman and italic founts of the title-page and Introduction have been consistently adhered to. But the List of Plates is set in a small size of old style Caslon arranged in double columns, with headings in the Griffo roman and Blado italic. I cannot understand why the same type was not used throughout the book, nor why, in the List of Plates, the contents of what is now one column of matter were not set to page width. The same feeble combination of Caslon again appears in the triple-column Index to Printers and Publishers. Compare the page of Contents (p. vii), and we see what might easily have been done in the cases just mentioned. The arrangement suggested would have made more pages, 'tis true, but this is not a volume in which the "nicely calculated less or more" is pleasing to gods—or men. 'Tis a penalty of printing in the grand manner, that one must always be grand! But this is only a slight blemish on what is typographically a most splendid volume.

To print well-above all, if one's aim is "fine printing"—there is no short and easy way. 'Tis at best a difficult and elusive business. Each typographical problem is, as Mr. Santayana says of life, a "predicament," out of which each man must extricate himself according to his knowledge. We are told by ascetical writers of the feeling of desolation which is the experience of those who aim at the higher reaches of prayer or of the spiritual life. There is an analogy between this and the paralysing sense of futility and frustration that sometimes overtakes anyone who seeks for an extraordinary degree of perfection in an art, in a profession, or even in a trade—moments when he seems, like the night-encircled castaway in *Moby Dick*, to be merely "holding up an imbecile candle in the heart of almighty forlornness." Faith, hope, and charity that may console the mystic, appear to be less needed in such a minor situation than the antique virtues of patience, prudence, temperance, and fortitude. Yet in both species of endeavour—material or spiritual—there must be a dogged sticking to one's job, in good days and bad days; or—if one likes to put it in the terms of parsons—"final perseverance." It is for those who are willing to toil all the night and catch nothing, that the miracle is performed!

Men who try for excellence, even in printing, are prone, or at least open, to similar desolations. It is good, therefore, to remember that in the history of typography we are compassed about by a great cloud of witnesses. It is as an evidence of this great body of patient effort that the examples of work shown in this book have their highest value. On a less idealistic plane, they are valuable because they exhibit, or should show, the principles on which the work has been executed. And the plates are still respectable (in the eighteenth-century sense of the term), merely as an interesting display of different ways of arranging type. No doubt, some men will acquire *Four Centuries of Printing* as a source-book, where they hope to find answers well enough fitted for the typographic riddles that they are too slovenly or lazy to think out for themselves. To such as are looking for a mere superficial acquaintance with modes of type arrangement, this book is as dangerous as the rules in a locksmith's manual to the morals of a burglar—'twill but serve for his greater damnation! But a man, if he can be made to comprehend the principles that influenced printers to make these examples what they are, and to acquire the kind of knowledge that directed Mr. Morison's choice of them, will get from the book what really most matters; and in years to come may find his own work holding a place in some like collection. "For fine printing," as Mr. Morison reminds us, "certain vital gifts of mind and understanding are required. Only when these are added to a knowledge of the technical processes will there result a piece of design, i.e., a work expressing logic, consistency, and personality. Fine printing may be described as the product of a lively and seasoned intelligence working with carefully chosen type, ink, and paper."

Comparer, c'est comprendre! In such a book as this a man may find the stuff to season his intelligence, to enrich his understanding. It will be an understanding of how to go and do likewise—but not the same. "We cannot overstate our debt to the Past," says Emerson, "but the moment has the supreme claim. The Past is for us; but the sole terms on which it can become ours are its subordination to the Present. Only an inventor knows how to borrow, and every man is or should be an inventor . . . The divine gift is ever the instant life, which receives and uses and creates, and can well bury the old in the omnipotency with which Nature decomposes all her harvest for recomposition."

PUBLISHED: *Fleuron* no. 3 (1924): 107–16.

Morison's book is thus described in the *Fleuron* headnote: "FOUR CENTURIES OF FINE PRINTING. Upwards of six hundred Examples of the Work of Presses established during the Years 1500 to 1914. With an Introductory Text and Index by STANLEY MORISON. London, Ernest Benn, 1924. Folio."

Updike to Morison, 27 October 1924: "As to the review, am really extremely pleased if you think well of it. I took great pains with it, and yet it had to be, as you know, written one hundred miles from any book with the slightest reference to typography, and that made me omit certain things which I should have like to put into it, but which I would not put in because I could not absolutely verify them. I thought the notice, perhaps, a little long—not because the book did not merit it, but because the reader might be bored by the way I said it. The book is important, and I felt that perhaps I did not sufficiently say that it covered a ground which no other book has covered up to now; and probably no book will ever take its place."

1. Dwiggins, "A Primer of Printers' Ornament," *Direct Advertising* 7, no. 3 (1920), reprinted in *Mss. by WAD, Being a Collection of the Writings of Dwiggins on Various Subjects, Some Critical, Some Philosophical, Some Whimsical*, Typophile Chap Books, 17 (New York: The Typophiles, 1947), pp. 101–12.

Some Notes on Liturgical Printing

THE word "liturgy," from which comes the word "liturgical," is derived from the Greek λειτουργία, signifying public worship, but in English its primitive meaning was the service of the Holy Eucharist, sometimes called the Divine Liturgy, because it is a service instituted by Christ Himself. There was, too, a secondary meaning, which has now obscured the original idea; it signified the set formularies for the conduct of divine service in the Christian Church. Liturgiology is the science, if it may so be called, which pertains to liturgies, their construction, peculiarities, forms, and use; and liturgical printing is that branch of typography which has to do with the arrangement and printing of such forms.

To understand liturgical printing as it is now practised, we must know something of its typographic history, for it has retained the marks of that history to the present day. The first liturgical books were, of course, manuscripts, and although in the earliest of these there appear to have been scanty directions for the performance of divine service, when fuller directions came into use the writers had in some fashion to differentiate the words to be said or sung from the accompanying directions as to where, when, and how to say or sing them. The easiest way to show this was to write the words to be said in one colour and the directions in another, the latter sometimes in a smaller letter as well. The words to be said, being of major importance, were written in black, and red was adopted for the directions. These directions, being rubricated, were by a transference of meaning called "rubrics." Apparently the word "rubrics" first appeared as applied to a liturgical book in a Roman breviary *printed* at Venice in 1550; but it occurs in manuscripts of the fourteenth and fifteenth centuries. "*Lege rubrum, si vis intelligere nigrum*," says the adage: "Read the red, if you wish to understand the black."

As early printed books were nothing more than a mechanical imitation of manuscripts, when liturgies came to be printed they followed the arrangement of liturgical manuscripts, with text in black and rubrics in red. The materials used for manuscripts and books differed—manuscripts being usually on vellum, printed books on paper—though even in printed missals vellum was often used for the canon of the Mass, since the pages devoted to this were subject to wear by constant handling.[1] Both in manuscripts and in printed missals, the canon was arranged in considerably larger type than the rest of the book, and the old name given to a large size of black-letter type, "canon," is a reminder of this. A smaller size was called "brevier," which was sometimes used for breviaries. For a very long period black-letter type with rubrication was altogether used for all such books;[2] but later roman type was adopted, with, however, precisely the same rules as to rubrication. A good deal later italic type (invented by Aldus about 1501) was, for economic considerations, employed to represent rubrics, as this avoided the necessity of printing in two colours; and this plan was adopted for inexpensive editions of liturgical books, though sometimes a very small size of roman type was used instead. This, in brief, is the story of the development of liturgical printing.

Indeed, rubrical directions exist in the Bible—for instance, in the Psalms the word *Selah*, which appears to be some sort of musical direction, meaning, probably, an interlude. Whether any difference was made in the characters used for *Selah* in Hebrew manuscripts, I do not know, but it is a fact that the differentiation in the use of type in liturgical printing was not confined to Christian liturgies. In Hebrew modern books of devotion one finds the same thing. Rubrical directions are indicated by the insertion of a Hebrew character in outline,

По не́мъ же ѿпꙋ́ста не быва́етъ, но глаго́летъ і҆ере́й нача́ло:
Блгослове́нъ бг҃ъ на́шъ:

И҆ чте́цъ:

Прїиди́те поклони́мсѧ: И҆ ѱало́мъ р҃г: Блгослови̑
дꙋшѐ моѧ̀ гд҃а, гд҃и бж҃е мо́й:

І҆ере́й же, пред ст҃ы́ми две́рьми ста́въ ѿкрове́нною глабо́ю,
глаго́летъ моли̑твы свѣти́льничныѧ.

Млт҃ва пе́рваѧ:

Гд҃и, ще́дрый и҆ млⷭ҇тивый, долготерпѣли́ве
и҆ многомлⷭ҇тиве, внꙋшѝ млт҃вꙋ на́шꙋ,
и҆ вонмѝ гла́сꙋ моле́нїѧ на́шегѡ, сотвори́ съ
на́ми зна́менїе во бл҃го: наста́ви на́съ на пꙋ́ть
твоѝ, є҆́же ходи́ти во и҆́стинѣ твое́й: возвесели̑
сердца̀ на̑ша, во є҆́же боѧ́тисѧ и҆́мене твоегѡ̀
ст҃а́гѡ. занѐ ве́лїй є҆сѝ ты̀, и҆ творѧ́й чꙋде́са, ты̀
є҆сѝ бг҃ъ є҆ди́нъ, и҆ нѣ́сть подо́бенъ тебѣ̀ въ бозѣ́хъ
гд҃и: си́ленъ въ млⷭ҇ти, и҆ бл҃гъ въ крѣ́пости,
во є҆́же помога́ти, и҆ оу҆тѣша́ти, и҆ спаса́ти всѧ̑
оу҆пова́ющыѧ во и҆́мѧ ст҃о́е твое́.

Ꙗ҆́кѡ подоба́етъ тебѣ̀ всѧ́каѧ сла́ва, че́сть и҆
поклоне́нїе, оц҃ꙋ̀, и҆ сн҃ꙋ, и҆ ст҃о́мꙋ дх҃ꙋ, нн҃ѣ
и҆ при́снѡ, и҆ во вѣ́ки вѣкѡ́въ, а҆ми́нь.

Млт҃ва

7   *Sluzhebnik* (Moscow: The Synod Printing Office, 1894).

or by the use of a small size of the normal Hebrew character. Furthermore, the important sentences or words in the service are indicated by very large type, precisely as in Roman Catholic missals, or by setting certain words in capitals, as in the American *Book of Common Prayer.*³

The earliest Greek Orthodox liturgical book printed in Russia was *Chasovnik*, a book of hours, issued at Moscow in 1565—the second earliest dated volume printed in Russia, the first being an edition of *The Acts of the Apostles* printed in 1564. These books were printed in the Cyrillic character, a letter derived from late Greek capital letters. Liturgical books of the Greek Orthodox Church appeared prior to that date outside of Muscovy, the earliest ones having been printed at the end of the fifteenth century in Poland—at Cracow in 1491. These, too, were printed in "Church Slavonic," using the Cyrillic character.⁴

Two modern books printed at Moscow are good examples of comparatively recent Greek liturgical printing, for under the Soviet régime such books are no longer produced. The first book mentioned is a service book (*Sluzhebnik*) of 1894, and the second (*Trebnik*), of 1906, is of the same nature. Both the *Sluzhebnik* and the *Trebnik* came from the press of the Synod Printing Office (*Sinodalnaya Tipografiya*) of Moscow. These books are printed in red and black, and an illustration of a page in the *Sluzhebnik* volume is reproduced [*Fig. 7*]. Before the Revolution, the Synod Printing Offices of Moscow and of St. Petersburg were the chief printers of Greek Orthodox liturgies and of devotional works generally. Although the Moscow establishment came under the jurisdiction of the Most Holy Synod only in 1721, its history goes back to 1563; as for the St. Petersburg Printing Office, it was active for over two centuries prior to the Revolution, with some intervals.

As far as I have been able to examine the eighteenth-century books used in the services of the Orthodox Church, they are roughly put together and are not very good pieces of typography. But the rubrication in all these books, whether old or new, appears to be governed by the usual rule that words to be said are printed in black, and directions for their use in red, as in Roman Catholic and Anglican rubricated prayer books. When only black is employed, the rubrics are printed in a smaller size of type.

These Greek Orthodox service books are so unfamiliar to most English-speaking people that they have little practical value for the reader, except as showing the universality of certain methods of printing liturgical books.[5]

For liturgical printing, as English-speaking people know it, we have two sources—Roman Catholic liturgical books and the liturgies in use in the Anglican Communion. These differ in some particulars.

The printing of the authorized Roman Catholic books is chiefly in the hands of three publishing houses, Desclée & Cie of Tournai (otherwise known as the Société de St. Jean l'Évangéliste), Pustet of Ratisbon, and the Vatican Press, at Rome, about each of which something should be said.

The brothers Henri and Jules Desclée, who had already built a monastery on their property at Maredsons, Province of Namur, Belgium, founded a printing press in 1882 at Tournai, and under the name Société de St. Jean l'Évangéliste published a series of admirable liturgical works, arranged according to the best liturgical traditions, harmoniously decorated, and technically excellent [*Fig.* 8]. They had a part in the musical printing required in the movement for the reestablishment of the liturgical chant, inaugurated largely through the influence of the Benedictines of Solesmes. Their editions served as the basis of the Vatican edition ordered for universal use by Pius X.

In the Desclées' books the principle that the directions are to be printed in red and all else in black is consistently followed, and headings such as "Introit," "Gradual," "Epistle," or "Gospel," are rubricated, as these are in a sense directions.

Moreover, references to passages in the Old and New Testaments are rubricated, for they are merely guides to the verses quoted and would not be said. For the same reason, apparently, the running headlines describing the contents of the page below appear in red, for they, too, are directions as to the day, hour, or occasion of the service. But for purpose of convenience the headings of each new section on the page are printed in bold black capitals—which, while not absolutely consistent, is convenient for purpose of speedy reference. In these books the "Amen" to prayers is treated as a response—as it actually is—and is preceded by ℞ in red in rubricated editions, and the words of all versicles—short sentences said by the officiant—are preceded by ℣. In the matter of initials there appears to be no fixed rule, and prayers begin with rubricated initials or black initials, as taste directs. I think this is a mistake. Strictly speaking, prayers should have initials in black, for these initials are part of a word to be said, and, moreover, black initials have a better typographical effect. Rubrics in these books have initials in black, which I think also open to exception, for rubrics, except in rare instances, require no initials; but if used, such initials should be rubricated also. A more serious fault is the introduction of gothic initials in prayers printed in roman type. As a whole, however, these books are consistent and careful pieces of typography.

The Pustet family was of Bavarian origin. In the first quarter of the last century Friedrich Pustet, who had been a bookseller, started a printing house at Passau which four years later, in 1826, he transferred to its present location at Ratisbon. Enlarging the establishment and adding a paper mill to the plant, the firm began to print and issue liturgical books in 1845, and later added facilities for the printing of church music. In 1870 the Pustet house was given the style of *Typographus S. R. Congregationis*, and the Vatican authorities have placed in its hands the *editio typica* of all liturgical work. The best books issued by Pustet are excellent, but their product is uneven and

Communio Ps. 109, 3 In splendóribus sanctórum, ex útero ante lucíferum génui te.

Postcommunio

Da nobis, quǽsumus, Dómine Deus noster : ut, qui Nativitátem Dómini nostri Jesu Christi mystériis nos frequentáre gaudémus; dignis conversatiónibus ad ejus mereámur perveníre consórtium : Qui tecum.

✠ Debet Sacerdos, etiam ante sequentes Missas, Confessionem dicere et in fine cujuslibet populo benedicere. In fine autem hujus Missæ et sequentis legit, more solito, Evangelium S. Joannis In princípio.

AD SECUNDAM MISSAM
In Aurora

Statio ad S. Anastasiam

Introitus   Isai. 9, 2 et 6

LUX fulgébit hódie super nos : quia natus est nobis Dóminus : et vocábitur Admirábilis, Deus, Princeps pacis, Pater futúri sǽculi : cujus regni non erit finis. Ps. 92, 1 Dóminus regnávit, decórem indútus est : indútus est Dóminus fortitúdinem, et præcínxit se. ℣. Glória Patri.

Oratio

Da nobis, quǽsumus, omnípotens Deus : ut, qui nova incarnáti Verbi tui luce perfúndimur; hoc in nostro respléndeat ópere, quod per fidem fulget in mente. Per eúmdem Dóminum.

Et fit Commemoratio S. Anastasiæ Mart.

Oratio

Da, quǽsumus, omnípotens Deus : ut qui beátæ Anastásiæ Mártyris tuæ solémnia cólimus; ejus apud te patrocínia sentiámus. Per Dóminum.

Léctio Epístolæ beáti Pauli Apóstoli ad Titum.

Tit. 3, 4-7

Caríssime : Appáruit benígnitas et humánitas Salvatóris nostri Dei : non ex opéribus justítiæ, quæ fécimus nos, sed secúndum suam misericórdiam salvos nos fecit per lavácrum regeneratiónis et renovatiónis Spíritus Sancti, quem effúdit in nos abúnde per Jesum Christum Salvatórem nostrum: ut justificáti grátia ipsíus, herédes simus secúndum spem vitæ ætérnæ : in Christo Jesu Dómino nostro.

Graduale Ps. 117, 26, 27 et 23 Benedíctus qui venit in nómine Dómini : Deus Dóminus, et illúxit nobis. ℣. A Dómino factum est istud : et est mirábile in óculis nostris.

Allelúja, allelúja. ℣. Ps. 92, 1 Dóminus regnávit, decórem índuit : índuit Dóminus fortitúdinem, et præcínxit se virtúte. Allelúja.

✠ Sequéntia sancti Evangélii secúndum Lucam.
Luc. 2, 15-20.

In illo témpore : Pastóres loquebántur ad ínvicem : Transeámus usque Béthlehem, et videámus hoc verbum, quod factum est, quod Dóminus osténdit nobis. Et venérunt festinántes : et invené-

8   *Missale Romanum* (Tournai: Société de St. Jean l'Évangeliste, 1928).

they have been less fortunate in their decorations than the Desclées, whose books show a greater uniform excellence. A disagreeable feature is the use of coloured lithographic frontispieces and pictures, and a later series of these, intended to be more modern in feeling than those they supersede, are no improvement on them. "In the latest Pustet Missal," writes a correspondent learned in these matters,[6] "the *incipit* letter of the text itself is often in colour, usually red. Another characteristic is the introduction into the Canon of certain parts of the varying *Communicantes* and *Hanc igitur* prayers, to obviate turning the page at that important moment of the service. In general, this new Pustet Missal pays attention to the pagination of the prayers."

The Vatican Press (*Tipografia Vaticana*), founded by Pope Sixtus V in 1587, was housed in the palace in the building known as the *Cortile della Stamperia*, and an interesting "specimen" of its types and characters for musical notation—*Indice de Caratteri, . . . esistenti nella Stampa Vaticana, & Camerale*—was published in 1628. Shortly afterward, the Congregation of the Propaganda established a separate printing office for the needs of missions, in which connection it issued, during the seventeenth century, a series of grammar-specimens of its various exotic alphabets, the first of which, *Alphabetum Ibericum*, appeared in 1629. This press later developed into the *Tipografia Polyglotta*. In 1910, Pope Pius X effected an amalgamation of the two, under the name *Tipografia Polyglotta Vaticana*, and arranged a modern and finely equipped plant. The new office prints the usual output of the Curia, especially the *Acta Apostolicae Sedis*, as well as the special choral editions of the liturgical chant, and the typical editions of the missal, breviary, ritual, and other service books.

The Vatican editions of plain song printed in one colour, italic being used for the rubrics, are practical, workmanlike, and handsome; they are well adapted for what they are meant for. "The typical editions of the Vatican Press have the custom of printing the top of the page in red for the title—for example, *Praefatio solemnis in festo Sancti Josephi*, but using black for this same title as a heading for the actual preface itself. Furthermore, in the actual directions, when a text is referred to by name, the text itself is printed in black. For example, 'Dicto Pater Noster et Credo,' the underlined words are in black, the others in red"—precisely the use in rubricated English prayer books. To persons wishing to consult authoritative Roman Catholic liturgical books, the Desclées' publications will serve the purpose best. The books to be looked at are the *Missal*, *Breviary* (in four volumes for the four seasons), *Rituale*, and *Officium Majoris Hebdomadae* (Offices for Holy Week).

For Anglican prayer books the three authorized houses are the University Press, Oxford, the University Press, Cambridge, and the King's Printers. These have in the Anglican Communion much the same authority as the publications of Tournai, Ratisbon, and Rome in the Roman Catholic Church.

The chief of these three houses is the Oxford University Press [*Fig.* 9], which dates from about 1517, though there was a long interruption in its work and it was only in 1585 that it began its present function. Its chief promoters were Robert Dudley, Earl of Leicester; Archbishop Laud, who secured for it a royal charter; Dr. John Fell, Dean of Christ Church, and later Bishop of Oxford; and Edward Hyde, Lord Clarendon. The printing of Bibles and prayer books was secured to the University in 1675, largely through Fell's efforts. Its present equipment numbers some 550 fonts in 150 characters, a foundry, a bindery, a paper mill, etc. It is governed by a body styled "delegates," headed by the vice chancellor. In its prayer books "every attention has been paid to accuracy and excellence of printing and binding, to the provision of editions suited to every purpose and every eyesight, and to the efficient and economical distribution of the books all over the world at low prices. In all these respects a standard has been reached which is unknown in any other kind of printing and pub-

Yea, that thou shalt see thy children's children : and peace upon Israel.

Glory be to the Father, and to the Son : and to the Holy Ghost; As it was in the beginning, is now, and ever shall be : world without end. Amen.

¶ Or this Psalm.

Deus mi-sereatur.
Ps. lxvii.

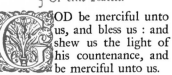

OD be merciful unto us, and bless us : and shew us the light of his countenance, and be merciful unto us.

That thy way may be known upon earth : thy saving health among all nations.

Let the people praise thee, O God : yea, let all the people praise thee.

O let the nations rejoice and be glad : for thou shalt judge the folk righteously, and govern the nations upon earth.

Let the people praise thee, O God : yea, let all the people praise thee.

Then shall the earth bring forth her increase : and God, even our own God, shall give us his blessing.

God shall bless us : and all the ends of the world shall fear him.

Glory be to the Father, and to the Son : and to the Holy Ghost; As it was in the beginning, is now, and ever shall be : world without end. Amen.

¶ The Psalm ended, and the Man and the Woman kneeling before the Lord's Table, the Priest standing at the Table, and turning his face towards them, shall say,

Lord, have mercy upon us.
Answer. Christ, have mercy upon us.
Minister. Lord, have mercy upon us.

UR Father, which art in heaven, Hallowed be thy Name. Thy kingdom come. Thy will be done, in earth as it is in heaven. Give us this day our daily bread. And forgive us our trespasses, As we forgive them that trespass against us. And lead us not into temptation; But deliver us from evil. Amen.

Minister. O Lord, save thy servant, and thy handmaid ;
Answer. Who put their trust in thee.
Minister. O Lord, send them help from thy holy place ;
Answer. And evermore defend them.
Minister. Be unto them a tower of strength,
Answer. From the face of their enemy
Minister. O Lord, hear our prayer.
Answer. And let our cry come unto thee.

E e 2   Minister.

9   *The Book of Common Prayer* (London: Oxford University Press, 1912).

lishing, and which is only made possible by long experience, continuous production, and intensive specialization."[7] Of the hundred editions of the prayer book, the Coronation prayer book of 1902 in octavo and the Fell prayer books are perhaps the best known, but the smaller editions are often exquisite though unobtrusive specimens of printing. Just as the Roman Catholic books of devotion continue to need constant additions through the canonization of new saints, so "the accession of a sovereign makes it necessary to print a large number of cancel sheets, which have to be substituted for the old sheets in all copies held in stock or in the hands of booksellers."[8]

The Cambridge University Press, now four hundred years old, has printed Bibles and prayer books since early in the seventeenth century. Baskerville produced for this press, in the eighteenth century, some prayer books, more remarkable because he printed them than for any merit of their own. Creditable as are the Cambridge books and those issued by the King's Printers, Messrs. Eyre & Spottiswoode, I should recommend the consultation of the Oxford prayer books to students of English liturgical printing.

The Anglican use in printing these official prayer books differs from the Roman use only in minor details, the chief of which is its employment of italic for responses, eliminating the use of ℟ before each response. Italic even in rubricated editions of a prayer book has in Anglican books come to signify something not readily signified otherwise, i.e., a response, as, for instance, the responses to the suffrages in the Litany, and to the versicles in Matins and Evensong, and "Amen" when said by the people [*Fig.* 10]. For the printing of Protestant orders of service this use of italic is desirable, for to the average congregation the ℟ and ℣ would be unknown, but when a response is printed in italic the ℟ mark should be omitted. The rule that italic should never be rubricated still holds. In both Roman and Anglican uses, notes indicating references to the Bible *which are not said* are rubricated. In the folio Oxford prayer books the Collect, Epistle, and Gospel are printed in full measure and, as far as may be, on facing pages, enabling the book to be carried, open, from the "Epistle" to the "Gospel" side of the altar. The quarto prayer books are printed in the traditional double column, which in liturgical books saves space and avoids ragged pages. Both editions are printed from the celebrated types given to the University by Bishop Fell, and are duly rubricated, but are disfigured by the introduction of a ponderous series of seventeenth-century Dutch "bloomers," as that kind of initial letter is called, mixed with free initials, both kinds being rubricated. A better piece of printing is the octavo Coronation prayer book,[9] also from Fell types, issued in 1902—though a bad fault is the rubrication of italic in the catechism. There are also a number of liturgical books issued by Anglican convents, private societies, or persons, which, while having no authority, are interesting pieces of typography.

So far our attention has been given to rituals of liturgical and historic churches. But modern Protestantism is more and more leaning to liturgical forms, either for constant use or for certain occasions. Protestant "orders of service" offer no great difference in typographic treatment from services in the *Book of Common Prayer*, except that they very often introduce the names of those taking part in them, composers of the music, the words of hymns, or anthems that are sung.[10] The prayers, being extempore, cannot be printed, and for that reason these "orders of service" lean toward the form of programmes, and the endeavour should be to avoid this as much as possible. As far as feasible, everything that can be ascertained beforehand should be printed in full, and the names of those taking part in the service should be as inconspicuous as possible and grouped on a separate page. Decoration should be omitted, and, above all, the indiscriminate use of crosses avoided. Further than this it is not possible to give any very detailed directions, as each service is a problem in itself. In general, what is said should be made of the first, and who says it of secondary, importance.

A wise lady of my acquaintance once remarked that although moral laws were clear, simple, and explicit, the cases to which they could be applied in their entirety were few; and she added that this was because the circumstances or situations to which they were applicable were in themselves often confused and complex. I am reminded of this dictum in connection with our subject, for while it seems simple to say that all directions in a liturgy should be rubricated and all else printed in black, along with the understanding of a difference between liturgy and rubrics there must be some knowledge of the particular liturgy in question, *as it is used.* This knowledge demands some further acquaintance with the theological views implied or expressed therein, and I doubt whether a printer unfamiliar with the ritual of the historic communions could acceptably print services for them. Certain theological views lead to certain acts; and these acts have to be expressed by certain words used in certain ways, and these words and ways have to be fostered, or at least not impeded, by the typography that presents them. Nor are rules for rubrication, etc., simple from another point of view: they cannot always be pushed to an absolutely logical conclusion without doing violence to the appearance and convenience of the book when in use. So while such systems are of very general application, there are "exceptional exceptions," and one must know when these are allowable.

The following axioms may be of practical use to persons to whose lot it falls to prepare for printing, or to print, liturgical work.

CONCERNING TYPE

1. Roman initial letters, either free or block, should be used with prayers set in roman; and gothic initials if prayers are set in black-letter.

2. Rubrics at the beginning of an office or service do not re-

The Collects, Epistles, and Gospels

To be used throughout the Year.

¶ The Collect, Epistle, and Gospel, appointed for the Sunday, shall serve all the Week after, where it is not in this Book otherwise ordered.

¶ The Collect appointed for any Sunday or other Feast may be used at the Evening Service of the day before.

ADVENT SEASON.

The First Sunday in Advent.

The Collect.

ALMIGHTY God, give us grace that we may cast away the works of darkness, and put upon us the armour of light, now in the time of this mortal life, in which thy Son Jesus Christ came to visit us in great humility; that in the last day, when he shall come again in his glorious majesty to judge both the quick and the dead, we may rise to the life immortal, through him who liveth and reigneth with thee and the Holy Ghost, now and ever. *Amen.*

¶ This Collect is to be repeated every day, after the other Collects in Advent, until Christmas Day.

The Epistle. Romans xiii. 8.

OWE no man any thing, but to love one another: for he that loveth another hath fulfilled the law. For this, Thou shalt not commit adultery, Thou shalt not kill, Thou shalt not steal, Thou shalt not bear false witness, Thou shalt not covet; and if there be any other commandment, it is briefly comprehended in this saying, namely, Thou shalt love thy neighbour as thyself. Love worketh no ill to his neighbour: therefore love is the fulfilling of the law. And that, knowing the time, that now it is high time to awake

90

10   *The Book of Common Prayer* (printed by the Merrymount Press for the American Episcopal Church, [1930]).

quire initials, the initial occurring in the first prayer following the rubric. But, if used, they should be printed in red.

3. Paragraph marks before rubrics may be printed either in red or black, but when a number of rubrics follow each other, black paragraph marks separate them from one another more clearly. In some Roman Catholic books a black arabic figure is substituted for the paragraph mark, but then only when a considerable number of rubrics follow each other.

4. When it is intended to indicate a versicle and its response, ℣ and ℟ marks should be used in either red or black. But in Protestant services, as these marks are unfamiliar, the words *Minister, People*, etc., may be employed, printed in italic.

5. Italic, being a substitute for rubrication, should never be rubricated.

6. "Amen" when said by the people should be printed in italic in a service printed in one colour, but when said by the clergy only should be printed in roman. Note that in Roman Catholic services the "Amen" is preceded by ℟ in red or black when said by the people.

7. A Maltese cross ✠ is a sign of blessing and should never be used except to denote that the sign of the cross is to be made. Almost the only exception is its use in the singing of the Passion in Holy Week, when it indicates the words of our Lord; or before the printed signature of a bishop.

8. Prayers, psalms, hymns, etc., must be set throughout in the same size of type and with the same leading; and rubrics must follow this rule and be uniform throughout the work.

9. While black-letter may be used for titles or display lines on title-pages, or for running titles, it should never be used for prayers in a liturgy to be publicly used.

10. The use of coloured inks to indicate liturgical seasons (i.e., violet for Lent) is always to be avoided.

CONCERNING ARRANGEMENT

11. A rubric should be on the same page with the prayer, etc., to which it refers, and should be closer to the text following than to the matter preceding it.

12. The breaks caused by the turning of a leaf should occur, if possible, at the end of prayers that are followed by anthems or hymns.

13. "Turnovers" should be avoided during prayers, psalms, or lections. But turnovers during music are less objectionable than during portions of the service which are said or intoned.

14. A versicle should never have its response appear on another page.

15. In Anglican services the canon and the prayers following should always appear on pages facing each other, unless the Roman use is followed of a facing representation of the crucifixion.

16. The traditional form of service books was in double column, probably adopted by calligraphers to save space, and to avoid blanks by short lines on a wide page. For books of private devotion this is allowable. In books for public use, however, a full-page measure is preferable, since it is easier to follow. In the Roman Catholic missal, the canon is probably for this reason sometimes printed full measure, though the remainder of the service is set in double column. This also applies to the arrangement of plain song, which must be set in full measure for the same reason.

Here these notes on liturgical printing end. So little of a practical nature has been written in English on the subject that they may be a slight contribution to a codification of the rules applying to it. In an age when there seem to be more questions than answers, it may be asked what need there is of such minute rules at all. But in this instance there is an answer. It was made by St. Paul when he said to the Church at Corinth, "Let all things be done decently and in order." [11]

Notes

PUBLISHED: *The Dolphin* 2 (1935): 208–19.

Updike to Morison, 30 September 1941: "It is a dry affair, I will send you, however, a typewritten copy of it without the illustrations (which amounted to very little) but of which I will make a note when it goes.... To you it will seem very rudimentary."

1. "In modern times the sheets containing Matins, Evensong, the Litany and Psalter are issued separately for renewing the great and more costly editions of the Prayer Book used by the minister in English churches." Wordsworth and Littlehales, *Old Service Books of the English Church*, p. 268. [DBU]

2. *The Directorium Sacerdotum or Rules called the Pye*, printed in black-letter, unrubricated, was so called because it was all black and white—magpie colours, if black and white may be styled colours. [DBU]

3. The 1928 American *Book of Common Prayer* was designed and printed by Updike: see Ray Nash, "Types for the Standard Prayer Book of 1928," *The Library* 5th ser., 29 (1974): 61–79; and Martin Hutner, *The Making of the Book of Common Prayer of 1928* (New York: Chiswick Book Shop, 1990).

4. For an account of the beginnings of Russian printing—chiefly confined to liturgical or religious books—see a paper in *The Library Quarterly*, Chicago, 1931, vol. 1, no. 3.

I am indebted to Mr. A. Yarmolinsky of the New York Public Library for this reference and for the titles of the two modern books referred to and information regarding them. [DBU]

5. Those interested in the subject should consult *The Greek Liturgies, chiefly from Original Authorities.* Edited by C. A. Swainson. Cambridge, 1884. See chap. i, "Printed Editions of the Greek Liturgies," and chap. ii, "Liturgical Manuscripts."

A very fine book of this sort containing the magnificent liturgies of St. James, St. Basil, and St. Chrysostom, in Greek, with a Latin translation, was printed by Morel of Paris, in 1560, in one colour, from the Royal Greek types, the rubrics in these Greek liturgies being distinguished by a small Greek character justified into the lines of text, and by a tiny italic in the Latin translation. A feature, also, of the Latin versions is the printing of the words *Sacerdos, Diaconus, Populus,* in spaced capitals, above the text, much as if they were speakers in a drama. [DBU]

6. The Rev. John E. Sexton, of St. John's Ecclesiastical Seminary, Brighton, Massachusetts, to whom I am indebted for this and much other information in reference to Roman Catholic Liturgical printing. [DBU]

7. *Some Account of the Oxford University Press*, Oxford, 1926, pp. 65 and 68. [DBU]

8. *Oxford University Press*, p. 68. [DBU]

9. So called because the form for the Coronation of Edward VII is added. [DBU]

There was an aborted attempt to publish an even more ambitious edition of *The Book of Common Prayer* in the Fell types in 1913: see Peter Foden, *The Fell Imperial Quarto Book of Common Prayer: An Account of Its Production* (Risbury, Herefordshire: Whittington Press, 1998).

10. An excellent example of simple liturgical printing for Protestant orders of service is published by the Presbyterian Board of Christian Education (1932), entitled *The Book of Common Worship (revised)*. *Approved by the General Assembly of the Presbyterian Church in the United States of America*. *For Voluntary Use*. In arrangement it is much like the *Book of Common Prayer*, on which it is obviously modeled. [DBU]

11. 1 Corinthians 14:40.

Notes Supplementary to Gough's Memoirs

THE Memoir of Edward Rowe Mores by Richard Gough, the antiquary, which precedes these Notes, first appeared in Nichols' *Bibliotheca Topographica Britannica*, as a preliminary to Mores' *History and Antiquities of Tunstall*, which was the first paper of the collection. It is the chief source of information about him, and all subsequent notices are based upon it, if they are not mere transcripts thereof. But there are passages, chiefly in the notes to Nichols' *Biographical and Literary Anecdotes of William Bowyer,*—whose "apprentice, partner and successor" Nichols was,—in his *Literary Anecdotes of the Eighteenth Century* and *Illustrations of the Literature of the Eighteenth Century*, which as they further describe Mores' interests, explain his activities and illustrate the whimsical characteristics of the man, I have drawn on here.

The connection of Mores with Low Leyton, in which Essex village he passed much of his life, came about through his father, Edward Mores, who had there served as curate to John Strype, the historian. For his paternal relative Mores exhibited considerable piety, and in his *History and Antiquities of Tunstall* in Kent, of which parish the elder Mores was later rector, he devotes some pages to a quite irrelevant account of the buffetings suffered by his patient parent at the hands of a sinister individual named Bannister—whose son's defence of *him*, published somewhat ironically by Nichols as an appendix to Mores' *History*, fills nearly sixteen closely printed quarto pages, abounding in angry and unintentionally amusing passages. From Edward Rowe Mores' picture of the elder Mores, one would suppose him to be a guileless and amiable gentleman who, besides other benevolent activities, rebuilt, in

1712, the rectory-house of Tunstall, at his own expense. But "for the encouragement of those who may be hereafter minded to go and do likewise," says his son, "be it known that the only recompense he met with from his parishioners was a continuous series of abuses, insults, and oppression." Nichols—also a native of Low Leyton and a friend of Mores—tells quite another story. His statements are evidently based on a passage in a letter written to Richard Gough in 1781 by the Reverend William Cole,—the friend of Walpole and Gray,—which runs: "I this week sent for, from Mr. Merrill, the '*Bibliotheca Topographica Britannica*,' and was rather concerned to find Mr. Mores has employed eight or nine pages unnecessarily to inform the world of his father's disputes with his parish; had he been ever so much in the right, it would surely have been more judicious to have let the remembrance of such squabbles die with the authors of them. Yet I am sorry to say, that I am afraid *this gentleman by birth* was also of a litigious and quarrelsome disposition. I am warranted to say so, by a perusal of several of his original Letters to Mr. John Strype the Historian, a man of a quiet, humane and meek disposition, to whom Mr. Edward Mores was curate at Low Leyton in 1739, with whom he had disputes; and from his own Letters, his boisterous and wrangling nature may easily be discerned, and from which it should seem that Mr. Mores was not the neighbour one would wish to live near. I think I discern a spice of the same spirit in the son, whom I once was in company with, being introduced to him by my worthy patron, Browne Willis, esq. But our acquaintance ended in the first visit."

Even in Mores' Oxford years, he managed to attract attention for his learning in extraordinary and out-of-the-way subjects, and by conduct often as eccentric as his interests. Andrew Ducarel, keeper of the archiepiscopal library at Lambeth Palace (which Mores helped him to set in order), in a letter written from Doctor's Commons in 1751 to the Rev. William Cole, says: "Mr. Mores is a young Gentleman of very good Fortune and about 25 year's of Age, educated at Queen's College, Oxford, a very fine Scholar, very good natur'd Man and an excellent English Antiquary,—the Progress he has made in our English Antiquities is amazing and his Discoveries of Antiquities now extant in Oxford, unknown to Tom Hearne and even to the present Antiquaries there, tho' very obvious when he shew'd 'em to them, makes me believe that he will make a very great Figure hereafter.—I will in future Letters give you some Account of those Antiquities, and have the further Satisfaction of having him for a neighbour in The Herald's Office where he has lately taken a House."

It was about the year 1760 that Mores definitely retired to Low Leyton, where he had inherited some property, and where he built a house no less odd than himself. This he called Etlow Place—the plan of which, he said, was that of a house once seen in France. He mystified his friends by appearing in a strange academic costume which he stated was that of a Dominican friar; and called himself "Doctor of Divinity," which he allowed people to fancy was a degree bestowed by the Sorbonne. And the discursive Nichols, after minute investigations and correspondence, which are reported by him at length and are not worth printing here, exclaims, "When, where or how, he came by this degree is extremely unaccountable!" and adds that he had "been assured by a very intimate friend of his, that Mr. Mores received the *honorary* title of D.D. in consequence of a literary favour which he had conferred on some foreign Roman Catholic Ecclesiastics, who wished to repay him by a pecuniary acknowledgement, which he politely declined accepting. Mr. Mores," he continues, "was as ambitious of singularity in religion as in other pursuits; and if he could be said to be a member of any particular church, it was that of Erasmus, whom he endeavoured to imitate. He thought the Latin language peculiarly adapted to devotion, and wished, for the sake of *unity*, that it was universally in use. He composed a creed in it, with a kind of Mass on the death of his wife, of which he printed a few copies, in his own house, under the disguised title of '*Ordinale Quotidianum,* 1685. *Ordo Trigintalis.*'

"Of his daughter's education," writes Nichols, "Mores was particularly careful. From her earliest infancy he talked to her principally in Latin. The gentleman from whom I received this information dined with Mr. Mores when his daughter was not more than two years old. Among other articles they had soup, with which the child had soiled her lip. *Absterge labium,* said the father. The child understood the Latin, and wiped her *upper* lip. *Inferius,* said Mr. Mores, and she did as he meant she should. She was sent to Rouen, for education; but without the least view to her being a Roman Catholic: on the contrary, he was much displeased when he found that she had been perverted."

The establishment in which Mores placed his daughter was undoubtedly the *Maison des Filles Hospitalières de Saint Joseph,* a sisterhood established at Rouen in 1654. Its foundress was Marie Delpech de Lestan, a *protegée* of Anne of Austria, and its object was the education and maintenance of poor orphan girls of respectable family; though from Mores' first letter it appears that children of a better worldly situation were admitted. This work was developed by members of the Brebion family, and seems to have been supported chiefly by them up to 1730. At that period the establishment was situated near the old church of St. Nicaise. Its later history I cannot trace, except that it was in existence in 1774. It undoubtedly shared the fate of all French religious houses at the Revolution. Two curious Latin missives survive, addressed to the superior of the convent by Mores, dated, respectively, *die decollationis S. Joh. Bapt.* (29 August), 1768, and *postridie concept.* (9 December) in the same year; probably to show the reverend mother that he was as erudite in church festivals as she could possibly be! The first letter, "English'd" by Mores himself, is an interesting example of his whimsical yet entertaining style; the second, for the first time translated, follows it.

Notes on Gough's Memoirs

I

To the worshipful Matron the Superior of the Convent of S. Joseph at Rouen, EDWARD-ROWE MORES *greeting:*

WE commit, worshipful Madam, our only daughter to your keeping and management: and the more willingly for that, besides the strict discipline of your house, we understand that none others of our Nation are at present with you.

She is a child of a ready wit, an acute judgement, and of a temper not unamiable; docile and tractable: but, being deprived of her mother (who whilst living was afflicted with almost continual illness) and being too much loved and indulged by me, and entrusted rather beyond what her years might justify, and being in some respects superior to the generality of her age and sex, she refused obedience to all command but mine; who, being busied about many things, had not nor have sufficient leisure to superintend and direct her conduct.

Nevertheless she comes to you, most venerable Matron, from her father's house; brought up and fostered there (and only there) from the first moment of her existence, not transporting with her from any female school of ours (all which I detest and hate) any spot or blemish to your sacred flock; but pure and blameless, and innocent from the corruptions of the world: and I trust that in the same purity and blamelessness and innocence she shall with the blessing of Providence be restored to us again.

Touching works to be performed by a needle, and how far it may be proper for her to be exercised therein, as they are matters out of my knowledge, I leave them to the women who accompany her.—Let them be useful, not trifling; accommodated to the purposes of domestic œconomy.

Touching other works which more properly fall within my direction and judgement—let her be well instructed in the arts of writing, drawing, and arithmetic.

We place her in the upper order of pensioners; not that upon

[115]

that account the reins may be let loose to indolence or idleness, or that the most rigid discipline exerted amongst the nuns of your house and order may in any wise be infringed or relaxed. Though in station she is superior, yet in obsequiousness and duty let her be as the lowest; and though she is lay, let her be as religious. By no means, upon any pretence whatever, let her go into the city, or pass the walls of the convent, or form any acquaintance but with the nuns of your own house. With them let her dine; with them let her sup; and with them let her be a companion; for, having been trained hitherto with grown persons, we would not have her now associated with children. Let her diligently attend the service of the church; matins I mean and vespers. Let her rise early and go to rest early, and with sedulity perform the business allotted to her. And by how much the more, reverend Madam, you shall enforce obedience in these particulars, by so much the more will you rise in our respect and estimation, and claim the tribute of our obligations and thankfulness.

All letters directed by the child to me, and all letters directed by me to her, I wish to pass unopened. As to any others, if any such should be, which I believe not, let them be opened, let them be read, and do with them according to your discretion.

Nearly the same request I am to make as to the books which she brings with her. Let her be permitted to read them in her chamber. Not any of them concern Religion but the Bible.

And having said thus much, most excellent lady, I might commit both you and her to the protection of the Almighty; but I cannot fail to add, that as I, a Divine of another church, have committed my daughter to your care, I must expect the same indulgence and the same fidelity as I myself should show were your daughter committed to my care. Your dictates I should strictly obey, your directions observe in all things. And as we are both devoted to the same service, the glory of God and the salvation of souls, bear in mind the affinity which is betwixt us; and consider me as your brother, even as I consider you as my sister in the Lord. The end we aim at is the same, though the means we use to attain that end in some things differ. May the blessing of God be upon you and your holy house! Amen.

From Leyton in the county of Essex
   the day of the decollation of St. John the Bapt. 1768.

II

To the worshipful Matron the Superior of the Hospitaler Sisters of the Convent of S. Joseph at Rouen, EDWARD-ROWE MORES *greeting:*

I REJOICED exceedingly, and return my heartiest thanks, most distinguished Madam, because, moved by my ardent wishes, you deigned to receive my daughter into your convent, although she was a foreigner, the offspring of a parent whom you did not know.

My delight is increased because the newly arrived guest will lodge in a room near the Superior—by how much the closer her proximity to you should be, reverend Madam, by so much the closer would she be in learning, and in manners, and in every virtue. Living in the midst of so many examples of piety, it is hardly possible that she fall into transgression: nevertheless, as she is an alien, and of a foreign nation, and accustomed to foreign manners, if she waver through ignorance, let her be pardoned for her offence. If she should overstep these bounds, however, and either in your presence or in the presence of another should be more seriously at fault, I pray that I may be informed; nor shall paternal authority be wanting for her correction.

But my joy was somewhat tempered, reverend Madam, by a vain and silly letter (written by a certain religious zealot of our Nation, as I infer) which was repeated to my W———,[1] who is rightly most devoted to you and yours, without your knowledge: for I consider that you and yours are not of the kind who are given to such foolish talk. From this we learn that the young girl has been addressed on the subject of Religion. Assuredly I am distressed, and think it contrary to the pledge made to me, that another should put a sickle in my harvest: I am the more distressed because, believing my daughter to have been committed to the safest trust, I seem to feel that my instructions have been slighted. It was my devout wish that on matters of this kind, which are less adapted to her tender age, there should be unqualified silence, in strict conformity with the injunctions that she should have no association with English people. We ask again the same solemn pledge; we repeat the same injunction. Let me entreat you, reverend Madam, that she be instructed in those things on which we formerly decided. The other matters shall be my care.

Farewell, and (though unknown to you) keep me in affection.

From Leyton in the county of Essex,
Morrow of the conception [B.V.M.] 1768.

The "religious zealot of our Nation," to whom Mores alludes above, may have been a member of either of two ancient English communities in Rouen, one of which we know existed in Mores' day. The first was the *Religieuses Angloises de Sainte Claire*, formerly of Gravelines. Their original convent was the gift of an Englishwoman, and their church, built in 1667, was consecrated by an Irish prelate. The second was that of the *Religieuses de Sainte Brigitte*, a community driven out of England in Elizabeth's reign. This throws light on Mores' injunction that his daughter should have no intercourse with persons of her own nationality while in Rouen. However that may be, the unqualified silence he demanded was not, apparently, obtained; for the daughter, while at the convent it would seem, was received into the Roman Catholic Church. And as is common with ladies, the lady superior had the last word, or at any rate the last laugh, which is still considered desirable even in the holy mirth of ecclesiastical circles!

Mores' antiquarian tastes led him to prepare, or to assist in preparing, books on genealogy, history, and like subjects, although many of such projects he tired of before they were completed. He collected material for a history of Oxford, which was particularly full in relation to his own college, Queen's, the archives of which he arranged and calendared. Of his various essays in parochial history, perhaps the most important was that of Tunstall, in Kent, his father's parish, to which was prefixed the memoir by Gough, already alluded to. The surprising range of Mores' interests may be inferred from the fact that he was one of the first to suggest a society for life insurance; and indeed organized such a company. It is less surprising and equally characteristic that as soon as it became a practical and working affair, he abandoned it!

In typography Mores was always interested and he appears to have set up a private press at Low Leyton. One of his abortive schemes was a new edition of *Typographical Antiquities*, by Joseph Ames,—against whom, by the way, he had some ancient grudge,—for which he left a few notes in manuscript. Mores figures somewhat unfavourably in the episode of Bowyer's gift of Anglo-Saxon types used in the Anglo-Saxon grammar compiled by Elizabeth Elstob—a lady amusingly depicted by Mores in his *Dissertation*. These characters were confided to Mores' care by William Bowyer, the younger, in 1753, for presentation to the University of Oxford, and the letter that Bowyer wrote on this occasion is printed in the *Dissertation*. Bowyer chose Mores to do this, as he was much interested in Saxon studies, and was of Queen's College, the rallying-point of Saxonists at Oxford. "For some reason that does not appear," says Reed, in his account of the Oxford University Foundry, "Rowe Mores, on receipt of the punches and matrices, instead of transmitting them to Oxford, took them to Mr. Caslon's foundery to be repaired and rendered more fit for use. Mr. Caslon having kept them four or five years without touching them, Mr. Bowyer removed them from his custody, and in 1758 entrusted them to Mr. Cottrell, from whom in the same year he received them again, carefully 'fitted up' and ready for use, together with 15 lbs. of letter cast from the matrices. In this condition the whole was again consigned by Mr. Bowyer to Rowe Mores, together with a copy of Miss Elstob's 'Grammar,' for transmission to Oxford. On hearing, two years later, that his gift had never reached the University, he made inquiries of Mores, from whom he received a reply [in 1761] that 'the punches and matrices were very safe at his house,' awaiting an opportunity to be forwarded to their destination. This opportunity does not appear to have occurred for three years longer, when, in October, 1764, the gift was finally deposited at Oxford. Its formal acknowledgement was, however, delayed till August, 1778, exactly a quarter of a century after its presentation.

"The correspondence touching this transaction, amusing as it is, throws a curious light on Rowe Mores' character for exactitude and it is doubtful whether the publication of Mr. Bowyer's first letter in the 'Dissertation,' together with a few flattering compliments, was an adequate atonement for the injury done to that gentleman by the unwarrantable detention of his gift. Nor does the title under which the gift was permitted to appear in the University specimen, suppressing as it does all mention of the real donor's name, and giving the entire honour to the dilatory go-between, reflect any credit on the hero of the transaction. The entry appears thus: *'Characteres Anglo-Saxonici per eruditam foeminam Eliz. Elstob ad fidem codd. mss. delineati: quorum tam instrumentis cusoriis quam matricibus Univ. donari curavit E.R.M. è Collegio Regin.,* A.M. 1753.'"[2] This time it was Mores who laughed last—virtue, as far as Mr. Bowyer was concerned, being its own (and only) reward.

These types do not seem ever to have been used. Their punches and matrices are still in the Oxford University Press.

Mores is particularly important to the student of English typefounding and printing because toward the end of his life he purchased all the older portions of the stock of John James, of Bartholomew Close—a collection inherited from his father, Thomas James[3] (notorious for his trickery of William Ged),[4] and dating from very early times. "Whether any motive besides a pure antiquarian zeal prompted the purchase," says Reed,—or whether he [Mores] held the collection in the capacity of trustee, is not known, but it seems probable he had been intimately acquainted with the foundry and its contents for some time before James's death. He speaks emphatically of it as 'our' foundry, and his disposition of its contents for sale is made with the authority of an absolute proprietor. It does not appear, however, that during the six years of his possession any steps were taken to extend or even continue the old business, which we may assume to have died with its late owner."[5]

From Mores' examination of the material of this foundry he prepared his paper "On English Founders and Founderies," for I think the title *A Dissertation upon English Typographical Founders and Founderies* was given it by Nichols, who added a title-page and notes to the original treatise. Only a few months before Mores' death, he wrote—I quote from Nichols—"the following short billet, dated Leyton, July 22, 1777, the last that Mr. Bowyer received from him, which no doubt had to do with the preparation of his 'Dissertation'":

"DEAR SIR, I am desirous of ascertaining the time at which the bodies received their names, and I think I can do it pretty well. I shall take as a great favour your opinion why English is called English. An additional favour will be the Italian names of the bodies, or a direction where to find them. Another addition, are the names given by other printing nations besides the German, French, English, and Dutch, to be found in books? I could go on with additionals; but I must not be further troublesome."

Mores' *Dissertation* falls into certain divisions. He first mentions the early printers who were their own type-founders,—like Caxton, De Worde, Pynson,—and then considers early and later learned types in what Mores styles "Oriental" and "Occidental" languages. He then takes up type of the "Septentrional" tongues; and after a digression on the names of type and the regular and irregular bodies commonly used in England, returns to the subject of northern types and their derivations. Some pages follow, devoted to "flowered letters" and printers' "flowers." The treatise then considers the early type-founders proper, beginning with those appointed by the Star Chamber decree, and continues with notices of Moxon, the Oxford foundry, Grover, Andrews, Thomas James,—with letters about his search for types in Holland,—Caslon, and Ilive. An account of the foundry of John James—whose establishment included material from nine old English foundries and whose stock Mores bought—follows; with notices of the four authorized founders in Mores' own time—Caslon, Cottrell, Jackson, and Moore—and paragraphs devoted to some less-known—among them, Baskerville. Mores ends his *Dissertation* with (1) a table showing that, with the exception of the four authorized founders and the Oxford foundry, the James collection contains the material of all the old English foundries of which precise knowledge exists, and (2) a synopsis of the "learned" types then extant in England, grouped under languages and, in turn, classed as Orientals, Meridionals, Occidentals, and Septentrionals, with the names of the founders in whose possession they were.

The *Dissertation* is full of picturesque bits and contains an immense amount of curious information imparted in the author's characteristic manner. Why Mores adopted in it such an extraordinary and inconsistent method of abbreviation, I do not know. The lack of capitals at the beginning of all sentences, except those which commence a paragraph, was (I think) an affectation based on classical manuscripts and early printed editions of the classics, which were often arranged in this way.

The number of copies printed of the *Dissertation*, and is-sued with notes by Nichols, is commonly stated as eighty; but a letter written to him by Samuel Paterson in August 1779, casts some doubt on this statement. "I spoke to Mr. Mores[6] this morning," he writes, "and told him I thought . . . a very fair price for the remainder of his Father's Tract on Founders, &c. considering the purchaser had a just title to the profits of his profession; and, if sold at . . . to gentlemen, it was the full worth of it, even to consider it as a curiosity. He consented; and desired only that I would reserve him a few, some eight or ten copies. I judge then you may have about 50. To tell you the truth, I had some thoughts of purchasing the whole myself, and might have had them for a word speaking—for, upon a cursory view, I thought I discovered some oversights, which might be removed, and the tract reprinted with advantage. But, finding that you are of the same opinion, who are so much bet-ter qualified, I have given over all thoughts of it, and will read-ily give you any little assistance in my power. I shall be able to set you right respecting Ged, where Mr. Mores is manifestly wrong. I could give you also a note on Baskerville, to demon-strate that he knew very little of the excellences of Typography, beyond the common productions which are to be found every day in Paternoster Row; and therefore, in a comparative view, might readily conclude he had outstript them all. But is it not astonishing that one so well informed as Mr. Mores should fall into such a blunder as to call Dr. Wilkins, Editor of the 'Cop-tic Testament,' '*Concilia Britannica*,' &c. our Countryman? Dr. Wilkins, it is well known, was a German Swiss."

Paterson, the writer of the above letter, was first a bookseller, and then became an auctioneer of considerable reputation as a bibliographer and cataloguer, and at one time was librarian to Lord Shelburne—afterwards Marquis of Lansdowne. Pater-son's rooms were then in King Street, Covent Garden; and it was he who sold both Mores' collection of types and his pri-vate library. "Few men of this country," says Nichols, "had so much bibliographical knowledge; and perhaps we never had a Bookseller who knew so much of the contents of books generally. . . . If, in his employment of taking Catalogues, he met with a book he had not seen before, which excited his curiosity, or interested his feelings, they must be gratified, and his attendant might amuse himself as he chose. The consequence was, that, on many occasions, Catalogues could be procured only a few hours before the sale commenced."

Mores intended the *Dissertation* as an introduction to a specimen sheet which was to exhibit what his collection contained, or at least the most interesting of the enormous mass of matrices, punches, and types which he had acquired; for James's foundry represented the material of De Worde, Day, Moxon, Walpergen, and all the old founders. This specimen Mores did not live to complete; nor was the close of our antiquary's days, we blush to say, particularly creditable. "Habits of negligence and dissipation" is the phrase used to describe his failings, but their nature—whether he became a victim of Punch or a votary of Judy—history does not relate. At any rate, he fell into an irregular and indolent manner of life, and died in the forty-ninth year of his age because of "a mortification[7] in his leg, which he suffered to reach his vitals, sitting in an arm-chair, while the workmen passed through the room to repair the next. He would not admit physician or nurse; and scarcely his own mother, who constantly resided with him after she had lost an annuity of 100 £. His daughter had been some time married, and was dead; and his son had been sent to Holland for education." The dying, wilful, lonely man ran true to type to the end; and so, not quite fit for hell nor yet for heaven, this odd mortal put on immortality on 28 November 1777. He was buried in Walthamstow Churchyard, and upon his monument were engraved those armorial bearings that were so dear to him in this life, and which (if I am rightly instructed) are singularly unimportant in that which is to come. *Requiescat in pace.*

The printing materials belonging to Mores were disposed of at auction by Paterson on 20 November 1781. His matrices and punches were sold as a separate collection in the summer of 1782. The sale catalogue of the latter is a somewhat puzzling compilation, and, if Paterson put it together, it does him little credit. It covers 120 small octavo pages. Its title-page is reproduced on the following leaf [*Fig.* 11].

In all, 349 lots are recorded. The matrices were placed in boxes named after early printers—Bynneman, De Worde, Wolfe, Cawood, Berthelet, Copland, Pynson—and in "a Press named Caxton filled with drawers containing Punches." In addition, there were "flowers," moulds, and printers' materials. It would appear from the entries as if the matrices were of the period of Bynneman, De Worde, etc.; but although the collection did contain early material, the contents of the boxes had no necessary relation with the names they bore. "Misled by this circumstance," says Reed, "it seems more than likely that Paterson may have enhanced the importance of his lots by dwelling on the fad that one fount was 'De Worde's,' another 'Cawood's,' another 'Pynson's,' and so on. The absurdity of this delusion becomes very apparent when we see the Alexandrian Greek some years later puffed by its purchasers as the veritable production of De Worde (who lived a century before the Alexandrian MS. came to this country), and find Hansard, in 1825, ascribing seven founts of Hebrew and a Pearl Greek to Bynneman."[8]

On the first page of the Specimen proper a Latin paragraph appears—no doubt written by Mores—which may be translated thus:

"Let the scholars who shall chance to examine with critical eyes this specimen of the *James* types not hold us blameworthy if so be that it appears less finished than desirable, especially in the more learned languages: the purpose was to present it most faultless, albeit the makers think they have done enough if, the faults of the press and the other defects disregarded, it

A

CATALOGUE AND SPECIMEN

Of the Large and Extensive

PRINTING-TYPE-FOUNDERY

Of the late ingenious

Mr. JOHN JAMES, Letter-founder,

Formerly of Bartholomew-Close, London, deceafed:

Including feveral other FOUNDERIES,

ENGLISH AND FOREIGN.

Improved by the late Reverend and Learned

EDWARD ROWE MORES, deceafed:

COMPREHENDING

A great Variety of Punches and Matrices of the Hebrew,
Samaritan, Syriac, Arabic, Æthiopic, Alexandrian, Greek,
Roman, Italic, Saxon, Old Englifh, Hibernian, Script,
Secretary, Court-Hand, Mathematical, Mufical,
and other Characters, Flowers, and Ornaments;

Which will be Sold by Auction,

By Mr. PATERSON,

At his Great Room (No. 6), King's-Street, Covent-Garden,
London,

On Wednefday, 5th June, 1782; and the Three following Days.

To begin exactly at 12 o'Clock.

To be viewed on Wednefday, May 29, and to the Time of Sale.

Catalogues, with Specimen of the Types, may be had at the Place
of Sale.
[Price One Shilling.]

11   Title-page of *A Catalogue and Specimen of the Large
and Extensive Printing-type-foundery of the late ingenious Mr.
John James . . . (1782).*

exhibits the form of the letters—great care was exercised; but when the *founder* was idle, the *furnace* was idle, and there was a lack of type cast for removing the blemishes."

The first matrices shown in the Specimen are "Orientals, Hebrew, Biblical," of which there are eighteen lots, running in size from two-line English to nonpareil. The succeeding Oriental matrices are Rabbinical Hebrew (5), Samaritan (2), Syriac (3), Arabic (2), and Aethiopic (2). Then come the Occidentals represented by an English Alexandrian Greek, "copied from the ancient manuscript in the Museum, written in caps," followed by ordinary cursive Greek in sizes from double pica to pearl. Of Gothic founts there is but one set of matrices, of Anglo-Saxon four, and of Anglo-Norman two. The next division is styled Septentrionals—Runic, Court Hand, Union, Scriptorial, Secretary, and Hieroglyphics. The next section is devoted to English (black-letter) types (in all nineteen sets of matrices), a small collection of roman capitals and a very large assemblage of roman and italic matrices, descending in size from canon to diamond. The specimen concludes with six pages of "flowers," some old, but most of Mores' own period. In the list of material, those lots not displayed in the Specimen have a note to that effect, and, to quote a phrase of Mores (used in another connection), "it is not to be doubted, considering the elegance and simplicity of the assortment which we see, that the foundery was as completely furnished with those we see not, and which for that reason we cannot mention."

"What was the result of the sale financially," says Reed, "we cannot ascertain. Of the fate of its various lots we know very little either, except that Dr. Fry secured most of the curious and 'learned' matrices. How far the other foundries of the day, at home and abroad, enriched themselves, or how much of the collection fell into the hands of the coppersmiths, are problems not likely to find solution. With the sale, however, disappeared the last of the old English foundries, and closed a chapter of English typography, which, though not the most glorious, is certainly not the least instructive through which it has passed."⁹

Mores' library was sold by Paterson in August 1779, and its contents are described in a catalogue of 184 pages, the long-winded title of which is also reproduced [*Fig.* 12]. But no title-page could cover the extraordinary literary by-ways exhibited by the library. Classical literature was well represented, and there was a good collection of books on divinity. The topographical history and antiquities of England, and English ecclesiastical and monastic foundations, figured largely both in books and prints. There were volumes on heraldry, travel, civil and common law, liturgies, and a mass of out-of-the-way tractates of every description. The books comprised 2838 items, prints and copperplates 115, and MSS. and miscellaneous belongings 146 lots. The sale lasted over a fortnight.

In the eleventh day's sale, a short section is devoted to books on the history and the art of printing—fewer than one might have expected. A transcript of it is given—in its italic, etc., following the original:

Mentelius *de vera Typographiae Origine*, 4to. Paris. 1650

Seiz *Historica Enarratio de Inventione nobilissimae Artis Typographicae, fig.* 8vo. Harlem. 1741

Hist. of the Origin and Progress of Printing, 8vo. 1770

Psalmanazar's Hist. of Printing, by Palmer, 4to. 1732, *with some few MS. Corrections by* Mr. Mores

Wolfii Monumenta Typographica 2 tom. 8vo. *Hamb.* 1740

Meerman Origines Typographicae, 2 tom. en 1. *c.m.* 4to. *Hag. Com.* 1765

Janssonius ab Almeloveen de Vitis Stephanorum celebrium Typographorum, 8vo. *Amst.* 1683

Spoerlii Introductio in Notitiam insignium Typographicorum, 4to. *Norimb.* 1730

Maittaire *Hist. Typographorum Parisiensium*, 8vo. Lond. 1717
——— *Anales Typographici, cum Indice*, 7 tom. 4to. *Hag.* C 1719–25. *Lond.* 1741

BIBLIOTHECA MORESIANA:

A

CATALOGUE

Of the LARGE and VALUABLE

LIBRARY

OF

PRINTED BOOKS,

Rare old TRACTS, MANUSCRIPTS, PRINTS
and DRAWINGS, COPPER PLATES, fundry AN-
TIQUITIES, PHILOSOPHICAL INSTRUMENTS, and
other CURIOSITIES,

Of that eminent BRITISH ANTIQUARY the late
Rev. and learned

Edward Rowe Mores, F. A. S.
Deceafed ;

Comprehending a very choice Collection relative to the
Topography, Hiftory, Antiquities, Genealogies, Laws,
and ancient Chartulary of Great Britain and Ireland ;
together with a great Variety of fcarce and curious
Books and Tracts in Theological, Philofophical, Mathematical, Claffical, and Critical Learning.

Which will be fold by AUCTION,

By Mr. *PATERSON*,

At his Great Room, No. 6. *King-Street,
Covent-Garden, London,*

On *Monday* the fecond of *Auguft* 1779, and the
Sixteen following Days,

To begin exactly at Twelve o'Clock.

To be viewed on *Wednefday* the 28th of *July*, and
to the Time of Sale.

Catalogues may be had at the Place of Sale,
Price ONE SHILLING.

12   Title-page of *A Catalogue of the Large and
Valuable Library of Printed Books of . . . the late
Rev. and learned Edward Rowe Mores* (1779).

Moxon's *Rules of the three Orders of Print Letters*, 4to. 1676

—— Mechanick Exercises, *with the Art of Printing*, 2 vol. in 1, *cuts*, 4to. 1677–83

Specimen of the several Sorts of printing Letter, given to the University of Oxford by Bp. Fell and Fr. Junius, 8vo. *Oxf.* 1695 — Cottrell's Specimen of printing Types, 4to. [4 copies]

Caslon's Specimen of printing Types, *with some other Specimens, and Papers relating to Typography*

Smith's *Printer's Grammar*, 8vo. 1755

Middleton's Dissertation on the Origin of Printing in England, 4to *Camb.* 1735

Ames's *Typographical Atiquities*, *cuts*, 4to. 1749, with *MS. Corrections by* Mr. Mores

Mr. Mores's *Account of English Typographical Founders and Founderies*, *8vo. never published (only* 80 *Copies were printed)*

Jackson on the Invention of Engraving and Printing in *Chiaroscuro* as practised by Alb. Durer, Hugo [*sic*] di Carpi, &c. *cuts in colours*, 4to. 1754

In the last day's sale were also *"three small note-books on early and rare Typography,* Foreign and English; *Oriental, Greek, and Saxon Characters,* &c. by Mr. Mores; — Specimens of singular Print-Letters — *Two Treatises of Penmanship and Arithmetic, with The Art of Making Ink,* in Spanish, by Juan De Yciar, with his portrait, quarto, *printed at* Zaragoca [*sic*], 1559 — *very curious, but the former imperf.*" This is the "maimed copy" that Mores alludes to as having been "mutilated by some fool who has had it before us."

From my copy of this Catalogue, partially priced, I should suppose that the books and papers were sold at low sums, even for that day. The best of the papers were purchased by Richard Gough. Those relating to Queen's College were the subject of a correspondence between him and its provost, Dr. Thomas Fothergill, in which the latter alleged that Mores had retained papers lent to him by the college to which he had no right, and which repeated demands had failed to make him return. Gough refused to give them up, alleging that the papers he bought were not those sought by Queen's. Whatever they were, Gough ultimately gave them, with other manuscripts, to the Bodleian, where they now are. And our sorry hero has one more black mark against his memory!

The remainder of Mores' papers seem to have been chiefly divided between Gough's intimate friend, John Nichols, and Thomas Astle, author of *The Origin and Progress of Writing.* A number of Mores' manuscripts are preserved in the British Museum.

Notes

PUBLISHED: Edward Mores Rowe, *A Dissertation upon English Typographical Founders and Founderies,* ed. D. B. Updike (New York: Grolier Club, 1924), pp. xix–xl.

The *Dissertation* by Edward Mores Rowe (1730–1778) is an important early history of English type-founding. Updike's edition was the first reprint of it; a second reprint, with more elaborate scholarly apparatus, was edited by Harry Carter and Christopher Ricks (Oxford: Oxford Bibliographical Society, 1961).

The are frequent references to Updike's "Notes" in his letters to Morison. For example:

"My own paper has grown, because I kept finding new things to put in; and I have tried to represent the gentleman just as he was: a sort of scampish, crotchety, whimsical individual, with a good deal of the 'cat' about his dispposition. And he wasn't very honest in his relations with other people. In short, he was a "poor lot," but he did some interesting things, and like many poor lots," had his uses. I hope that you won't think I have made him too wretched or too respectable" (28 January 1924).

"The Rowe Mores is coming along slowly. The Grolier Club have decided to put in Gough's rather long-winded notes which accompanied the memoir, so that it will increase the size of the book by some pages. Then, after various very unsatisfactory attempts to reproduce the title-page of the sale catalogues of Mores' library and types, from the very yellow copies that I have here, we have abandoned this, have set them up in type, and they have come extraordinarily near the originals" (21 March 1924).

1. This is not his daughter's initial. Her name was Sarah. [DBU]

2. Talbot Baines Reed, *A History of the Old English Letter Foundries*, ed. A. F. Johnson (London: Faber, 1952), pp. 148–49. The first edition—from which Updike quotes—was published in 1887.

3. Thomas James (d. 1736), son of the Rev. John James, vicar of Basingstoke, and father to the John James (d. 1772) from whom Mores bought his foundry, is remembered, not much to his credit, for his association with William Ged, whose invention of stereotyping (first put into execution in 1725) he was at as much pains to defeat in practice, as Mores was to explode it in theory. His brother, John James (dragged into the affair for his influential connections and ready cash), whom Mores curtly characterizes as "an architect at Greenwich," was a man of cultivation and clerk of the works at Greenwich Hospital,—a post in which he succeeded Nicholas Hawksmoor,—where he worked under Sir Christopher Wren and Vanbrugh, architect of Blenheim. James later became surveyor to St. Paul's Cathedral and the Abbey, and was the designer of St. George's, Hanover Square, and some other churches and country-houses. The Hancock papers show that he visited New England on a journey for health and pleasure, in the late seventeen-thirties; and the unusual plan and distinguished design of Shirley Place at Roxbury (Boston), the seat of Sir William Shirley, Colonial Governor of Massachusetts, have been attributed to him. This fine mansion, built in 1746 (the year of John James's death), known as the Shirley-Eustis House, is still standing, though the estate is altogether shorn of its lands and the house somewhat of it dignities. [DBU]

4. For Ged's pathetic story see *Biographical Memoirs of William Ged, including a particular Account of his Progress in the Art of Block-Printing*. London: Printed by and for J. Nichols, 1781. "The first part of this pamphlet," says Nichols, its editor, "was printed from a MS. dictated by Ged sometime before his death; the second part was written by his daughter, for whose benefit the profits of the publication were designed; the third was a copy of proposals, that had been published by Mr. Ged's son in 1751, for reviving his father's art; and to the whole was added Mr. Mores's narrative of block-printing." This last paper is an extract from

the *Dissertation* and to it John Nichols has added notes correcting Mores's misstatements: for his account of Ged is not merely prejudiced, but inaccurate. The *Biographical Memoirs* were reprinted in 1819 at Newcastle for T. Hodgson, whose *Essay on the Origin and Progress of Stereotype Printing* (Newcastle, 1820) may be consulted in this connection. [DBU]

5. Reed, pp. 215–16.

6. Son to the author of the *Dissertation*. [DBU]

7. The common term then used to denote gangrene. Nichols, in speaking of Paterson's demise in 1802, says, "The immediate cause of his death was a hurt in his leg, which happened from stumbling in the dark over a small dog-kennel most absurdly left by his landlady (as servant-maids too often leave *pails*) at the bottom of a stair-case. The wound turned to a mortification, which soon ended fatally." [DBU]

8. Reed, p. 223.

9. *Ibid.*

THE old and infirm have at least this privilege, that they can recall to their minds those scenes of joy in which they once delighted, and ruminate over their past pleasures, with a satisfaction almost equal to the first enjoyment; for those ideas, to which any agreeable sensation is annexed, are easily excited, as leaving behind them the most strong and permanent impressions. The amusements of our youth are the boast and comfort of our declining years. The ancients carried this notion even yet further, and supposed their heroes, in the Elysian fields, were fond of the very same

WHEN the exertions of an Individual to improve his profession are crowned with success, it is certainly the highest gratification his feelings can experience. The very distinguished approbation that attended the publication of the ornamented edition of Goldsmith's Traveller, Deserted Village, and Parnell's Hermit, which was last year offered to the Public as a Specimen of the improved State of Typography in this Country, demands my warmest acknowledgments; and is no less satisfactory to the different Artists who contributed their efforts towards the completion of the work.

13 Pica roman and italic designed by William Martin for William Bulmer.

Some Revivals of Printing
in the Nineteenth Century

THE President of the Massachusetts Library Association has paid me the compliment of asking me to say a few words to you today about printing—in particular about "Revivals in Modern Printing"—in connection with the typographical exhibition now held at this library, intended to illustrate the evolution of printing as an art. In this exhibition an endeavour has been made to trace the beginnings of the printed book in a brief way from the time of the invention of printing until now; and it has fallen to my lot to arrange, with the aid of Mr. Bruce Rogers, the Department of Modern Books.

For purposes of definition, modern printing must be generally conceded to begin with the introduction of the lighter and more modelled faces of type which came into fashion with the work of Didot in France, of Bodoni in Italy, and of some of the Scotch type-founders in Great Britain. This was the point of departure from which we may date the printing of the modern book. These types and these books were intended to be, and in many ways were, more readable than any which had preceded them; and although they had faults, which only of late years have been clearly seen, they were in some directions an advance over what had been done before. I have been much impressed while working over these volumes to see how constant has been the effort toward the improvement of the printed book. We have been accustomed of late to hear so much in regard to the modern revival of taste in typography that we are almost misled into believing that there have been, hitherto, no revivals at all. But the history of printing during the last hundred years has numbered several revivals.

[135]

I

There was, in the first place, the attempt to revive beautiful printing in England, which took place under the auspices of William Bulmer [*Fig.* 13], an interesting man, who, born in Newcastle and a friend of the Bewicks, the engravers, came to London to practise his craft. Through his intimacy with Nicol, the Librarian of George III, and of Boydell, whose patronage of art, as then understood, was very influential, Bulmer produced a series of very fine books, some of which are included in the exhibition of which I have spoken. The preface of one of his books—the Poems of Goldsmith and Parnell—shows that precisely the same thing was done one hundred years ago in book-making that is being done today, and Bulmer's interesting and characteristic "advertisement" to this work is quite worth quoting. Here it is: —

To raise the Art of Printing in this country from the neglected state in which it had long been suffered to continue, and to remove the opprobrium which had but too justly been attached to the late productions of the English press, much has been done within the last few years; and the warm emulation which has discovered itself amongst the Printers of the present day, as well in the remote parts of the kingdom as in the metropolis, has been highly patronized by the public in general. The present volume, in addition to the SHAKESPEARE, the MILTON, and many other valuable works of elegance, which have already been given to the world, through the medium of the Shakspeare Press, are particularly meant to combine the various beauties of PRINTING, TYPE-FOUNDING, ENGRAVING, and PAPER-MAKING; as well with a view to ascertain the near approach to perfection which those arts have attained in this country, as to invite a fair competition with the best Typographical Productions of other nations. How far the different Artists, who have contributed their exertions to this great object, have succeeded in the attempt, the public will now be fully able to judge. Much pains have been bestowed on the present publication, to render it a complete Specimen of the Arts of Type and Block-printing.

The whole of the Types, with which this work has been printed, are executed by Mr. William Martin, in the house of my friend Mr. George Nicol, whose unceasing endeavours to improve the Art of Printing, and its relative branches, are too well known to require any thing to be said on the present occasion; he has particularly patronized Mr. Martin, a very ingenious young Artist, who has resided with him seven years, and who is at this time forming a Foundry, by which he will shortly be enabled to offer to the world a Specimen of Types, that will in a very eminent degree unite utility, elegance, and beauty.

The ornaments are all engraved on blocks of wood, by two of my earliest acquaintances, Messrs. Bewicks, of Newcastle-upon-Tyne and London, after designs made from the most interesting passages of the Poems they embellish. They have been executed with great care, and I may venture to say, without being supposed to be influenced by ancient friendship, that they form the most extraordinary effort of the art of engraving upon wood, that ever was produced in any age, or any country. Indeed it seems almost impossible that such delicate effects could be obtained from blocks of wood.

Of the paper it is only necessary to say, that it comes from the manufactory of Mr. Whatman.

Here, you see, was made the same effort to produce beautiful types, the same effort to procure papers by special makers, the same effort for attractive illustrations, — the same effort, in short, to make a perfect book that we see today. Of course the view of what a perfect book consisted in was the view of 1806 rather than the view of 1906, but the effort was the same. This episode of Bulmer and The Shakespeare Press, which printed not alone a very fine edition of Shakespeare, but also the letterpress to Claude's *Liber Veritatis* and Dibdin's *Bibliographical Decameron* (with exquisite illustrations engraved on wood), shows, as I have said, that the printer of that date was not unmindful of what the perfect book should be, and that he strove to make it.

II

Another revival occurred about 1844 at The Chiswick Press through that agreeable combination of taste and skill which came about through the association of Pickering as a publisher and the Whittinghams as printers. A series of volumes, with which you are all familiar, was then issued, which has been—from my point of view—the soundest output of any English press during the last hundred years. These books revived the delightful eighteenth-century types of Caslon, which had fallen into disuse. In the octavo volumes of Jeremy Taylor, Herbert, Milton, and other classic English authors, as well as in the smaller volumes, in 16mo, of Vaughan, Herbert, and Selden, these Caslon types are used with a discretion and a taste which leaves nothing to be desired,—a discretion which never allows decoration to prevent the book from being readable, and a taste which always prevents its typographical appearance from being commonplace or dull. These books showed a revival of old forms in another sense, for it is an interesting by-path in the history of typography to see how deeply Pickering as a publisher was influenced by Aldus. His adoption of the Aldine anchor and dolphin and his motto, "An English disciple of Aldus," was very much more than a sentimental affair. Even the volumes, bound in calf, stamped in blind with little leaves and flowers, were an English version of a kind of binding practised by Aldus himself, not to speak of many of the effects in typography—in some cases the arrangement of the advertisements. I recall a little volume published by Basil Pickering in which the advertisements show a very close study of the Aldine manner.

III

But it is more particularly of the revival of printing today that I want to speak; because I believe that during the last ten years there *has* been a revival of printing which, while no more earnest than the revivals that have preceded it, has had an influence which is destined, I hope, to be lasting, and which is, I believe, in some respects a sounder influence than any which has arisen before it. When I say this, you may ask me the same question which was asked by an acquaintance of mine who had a taste for the French decoration of interiors, and had studied for many years the subject of styles of French architecture, furniture, and objects of art. Lately, when travelling in the West, where her reputation had preceded her, she was shown, by a number of hospitable ladies, houses which were furnished in a taste which might be called French, but which were sadly devoid of any resemblance to "the real thing." One day, after being conducted over a peculiarly ugly and pretentious house furnished in a so-called French style, the hostess threw open the door of one of the rooms and said to her, "This is my Louis XV boudoir." The visitor, thoroughly exasperated, turned to her hostess and exclaimed, "What makes you think so?"

Now perhaps you will ask, In what does the modern revival in printing differ from others, and what makes you think so? To this I wish to explain, first, though the modern revival of printing originated with William Morris, that Mr. Morris was not a great printer, but was a great decorator. He therefore saw in the printed book certain decorative qualities which, not being decorators, the printers had failed to perceive. While I believe that Mr. Morris has been overpraised as a printer, I do not think he can be overpraised for one point in his influence on printing. As you know, both from his books and from his art, he loved the Northern style of decoration and design. There was something a little Teutonic in his whole point of view He openly announced that he preferred Iceland to Italy, a liking which, counting out the climate, most of us scarcely share with him. He held, in common with Mr. Ruskin, a quaint view about the Renaissance, which he thought had done a vast deal of harm. About that matter, too, opinions may well differ. But, on the other hand, he grasped a principle and taught a principle in his books which had been, after the

[139]

first fifty years of printing, lost sight of, and which, to quote Mr. Charles Ricketts, is this: "*The novelty of a book made during the recent revival lies in the fact that it shows design in each portion of it, from type to paper, and from 'build' to decoration. Therein lies the difference between a book so understood and any other modern book printed before* 1891*; therein lies their affinity with the grand volumes of the Italian and German presses.*"

In other words, Mr. Morris's influence has made clear the unity of a book as a whole. Before he came upon the horizon, although there were many books that were good, it was often forgotten that merely beautiful paper, merely beautiful illustrations, and merely beautiful type did not make a beautiful book. A book is beautiful primarily—always granted that its treatment is appropriate to its subject—because the type, paper, imposition of the printed page upon the paper, presswork, and decorations are beautiful in themselves, *but above all beautiful in relation to each other.*

For instance, you all remember the edition of Rogers's Italy, in which the type is pretty and the engraved illustrations after Turner quite charming, but which is not a very beautiful or very charming book in itself. Why? Because one feels in it the lack of unity. On the other hand, if one looks at Mr. Morris's great books, the Chaucer and the trial pages of the Froissart, one is instantly struck with their harmony. It may be a harmony one does not like, the almost deafening harmony of a full orchestra; but, like all reformers, Morris made progress by overstating (typographically) his own case. And so his books do teach wonderful lessons by the proper accord of all their different parts into one delightful whole. Personally I do not care for Mr. Morris's books, because I am still of the opinion that books were meant to be read, and that no book is a good one that cannot be read, and read easily. I admire much more the remarkable volumes published by the Doves Press, in which the lessons which Mr. Morris taught have been applied in a lighter and more classical method of typographical treatment. Indeed, at the present moment it seems to me that the Doves Press Bible is among the most beautiful books of its kind which has ever been produced. But this sense of harmony and unity in the printed book has been brought about chiefly through the perception of Mr. Morris and others of the decorative quality that the properly printed page may have. The same conscious or unconscious sense of that quality was what made the earliest German and Italian books so beautiful. From that time to this the importance of this principle of unity and harmony has been generally lost sight of. The principle has now been happily revived. And this is the lesson of the modern revival of printing as an art. All classes of work, from the humblest to the highest, show the influence of this idea, so potent for good. It has taught, both to the expert and to "the man in the street," a different way of looking at books from any familiar to him heretofore. I may add that from the standpoint of the printer it is incomparably more difficult to arrive at success by this method than by the mere pitchforking of things pretty in themselves into a kind of typographical scrap-book.

On the other hand, there is coming to be, and must be, an end to those experiments in typography which gain a decorative and harmonious effect while disregarding clearness. It cannot be too much insisted upon that books were first, last, and all the time intended to be *read*, and that a public will soon be tired of books, however beautiful, which are not simple and unobtrusive mediums by which what is written shall be presented to the reader. And it is furthermore to be remembered that no printers have ever yet been able to revive old styles of book-making without unconsciously introducing a certain quality of the period in which they worked—just as the Renaissance sculptor and decorator believed himself reverting to the purest models of antiquity, while we of another age are so readily able to see the difference between Renaissance and antique work. We of today must not expect to be able to

[141]

eliminate the artistic feeling of 1906 from our reproductions of earlier work, however painfully studied. If we can lay hold of the lessons of earlier printing and apply it to the work of to-day, that is legitimate. Unfortunately, to apply these principles for today's need is no easy task. But I believe it can be and must be done.

In conclusion, I have always felt that the printer had something in common with the librarian and the cataloguer. Our tasks, perhaps, are not very gloriously rewarded, either in the estimation of the public or in satisfaction to ourselves; and as I conceive your own work from what I know of my own, it is made up of endless detail. To fail in one of these details means the failure of the whole work in any satisfaction it can give to us. To succeed in perfecting every detail is not perhaps very important to any one save ourselves. But we do know that we are trying to build up in the world and to make more perfect one department of work; and it is this patient, quiet performance that America so much needs, not alone in our ranges of effort, but in almost every department of her work, her thought, and her life. I fear that there come to us all moments when the effort for perfection does not seem much worth while. Then again there are other and happier moments when, taking a truer view of the relations of things, we know that our work has its value and its place. It is well that we should remember now and then those fine, strong words of Michelangelo in speaking of art, which run somewhat like this: "All art is noble and religious to the mind, if the mind producing it be so. For art is but the strife for perfection, and God is perfection; and he who strives after it is striving for something Divine."

Notes

PUBLISHED: *Printing Art* 7 (March 1906): 13–17.

A paper read before the Massachusetts Library Association at the Boston Public Library, 11 January 1906.

[142]

❧ Contemporary

ing, Take, eat, (c) this is my Body, which is given for you; Do this in remembrance of me. Likewise, after supper, (d) he took the Cup; and when he had given thanks, he gave it to them, saying, Drink ye all of this; for (e) this is my Blood of the New Testament, which is shed for you, and for many, for the remission of sins; Do this, as oft as ye shall drink it, in remembrance of me.

(c) And here to lay his hand upon all the Bread.

(d) Here he is to take the Cup into his hands.

(e) And here he is to lay his hand upon every vessel in which there is any Wine to be consecrated.

WHEREFORE, O Lord and heavenly Father, according to the institution of thy dearly beloved Son our Saviour Jesus Christ, we, thy humble servants, do celebrate and make here before thy Divine Majesty, with these thy holy gifts, which we now offer unto thee, the memorial thy Son hath commanded us to make; having in remembrance his blessed pas-

The Oblation

14 *The Form of Consecration of St. George's Chapel* (printed by the Merrymount Press for St. George's School, Middletown, R.I., 1928).

Ecclesiastical Printing

ECCLESIASTICAL printing, as practised at the present
day, falls under two heads,—liturgical printing and parochial printing. Under the head of liturgical printing may be
grouped, besides the authorised service-books of the Church,
portions of the Holy Bible, collections of prayers, collections of
hymns, books of devotion, and orders of service [*Fig.* 14]. Under printing for parochial purposes may be grouped calendars,
parish year-books, service lists, baptism and confirmation
cards, marriage certificates, parish notices, *et caetera*. I propose
to devote the present article to the first of these two divisions,
namely, liturgical printing; the second paper being devoted to
printing for parochial or diocesan purposes.[1]

In writing of liturgical printing I am confining myself more
particularly to liturgical printing as practised in England and
the United States. As is well known, the first liturgical books
were printed in black-letter, generally in two sizes of type
throughout, in double column. Why liturgical books should
have been printed in double column is not altogether clear, but
this form was no doubt chosen for its better artistic effect. It is
easy to see that a book made up of short sentences looks better in a rather narrow, than a very wide, "measure"; for most
liturgical books are made up of prayers, psalms, hymns, and
responses, many of these being extremely short. If a large type-
page is selected for the book and the prayers are printed across
its entire width, it leaves a very ragged-looking right-hand side
to the page, owing to the many short lines which do not fill
the " measure." Again, initial letters must often be introduced
into the body of the text, with type enough to surround them;
but a short prayer printed on a wide page would perhaps fill

only three lines of type and so leave a place only for a small initial letter. The same prayer printed in a narrow measure (in double column, for instance) would give room for a four or five-line initial, and a line or two of type would still be left to go beneath it, in which case the initial would be surrounded by type, as it ought to be. Then again for decorative purposes, double columns are better, because the initials, instead of all falling to the left-hand side of the page (as on a page printed in single column) fall some on the left and some in the centre; or, in other words, are more evenly distributed on the field of type. This series of considerations probably determined the form of the written or printed liturgical book.

The directions for the performance of Divine Service were often set in type of the same size as the prayers, but were distinguished by printing them in red, from which fact the word "rubric" is derived. These rubrics added incidentally a very charming feature to the early liturgical books, often making the pages very brilliant in effect. But their use, of course, was to distinguish the directions for the performance of Divine Service from what was actually to be said by the priest.

The black-letter books were, at the time they were first printed, perfectly readable, as there was practically no other character in common use except the gothic types. They were, in fact, nothing more than rough reproductions of manuscripts. When, however, the roman letters came more into fashion, the Church retained the black-letter as being the traditional and, in a sense, more suitable form for service-books; and to this idea is traceable the printing of theological books in black-letter, at a period when volumes of a more secular character were printed in roman type. After a time the black-letter began to be discarded, even in liturgical and theological volumes. The legibility of the book was becoming more and more the important feature in printing, and the greater number of books were being printed in roman type, so that the latter became more familiar to the eye than the black-letter. This substitution of roman for black-letter type was after a while general. Its survival in prayer-books and what is improperly called "church printing," for headlines, title, etc., is nothing more than the remains of what was once the type of the entire liturgical book. The names of the sizes of the black-letter types used today, i.e. Brevier, Little Canon, and Great Canon, allude respectively to the types used in the breviary and missal. This brief and very general account of the use of black-letter type is given solely to show why we find it still used for ornamental purposes in liturgical printing. It is an interesting example of the persistence of a certain traditional form, kept active by persons often quite ignorant of the historical tradition which they are unconsciously following. I must add that the printing of modern literature in black-letter may be accepted only in so far as one is aiming at reproductions of old work. Fine examples of work of this sort are found in the series of Pickering's Folio Prayer Books, issued about 1840. These are perhaps the best modern examples of reproductions of black-letter books; though the charming little Book of Hours which was printed by Curmer, in Paris, from a French gothic type, about 1860, if I am not mistaken, should not be forgotten. The Kelmscott Press revival of gothic types is too recent to require mention here [*Fig.* 15].

A liturgy is the means by which the celebration of Divine Service is performed. Anything, therefore, which sets forth the words to be said or the acts to be done must be above all legible: so that the words may be read without hesitation and the directions followed without mistake. Prayer-books and all works of a liturgical kind should be printed in roman type, as large in size as is consistent with the proper margins of a moderate-sized book: for the book must not be too large to be easily used, or too heavy to be carried by a child. The size of page having been selected, the sober "old style" Caslon type is perhaps best suited in form for the purpose, or else some type suitably designed on *readable* lines. It should be set in double column. The decorations should be, I think, confined to simple capital letters in red, which should occupy two or three lines. These should be introduced, one at the beginning of the office and perhaps at the beginning of each prayer. The important portions of the service, however, should carry initials slightly larger than the less important parts. The rubrics should be printed in roman type of exactly the same size as the prayers, the only difference, of course, being the application of red to the directions, which will give them the look of being printed in slightly smaller type than the same font of type printed in black ink.

In some cases, however, it is allowable to put the rubrics in smaller type for the sake of economy in space: and also because of late years there has arisen a great necessity for cheap prayer-books. In these prayer-books red cannot be used on account of expense. The rubrics in these cases are sometimes printed in a very small size of roman type, or else in italic to differentiate them from the larger text of the prayers. I regret to say that in some quite important books the rubrics have been set in italic *and printed in red.* When italic is used, and then printed in red, it is only because the printer is ignorant, or the publisher too thrifty to set the rubrics in roman type for a "red printing." It is the publisher who is generally to blame: for he it is who economically uses the same type, to make plates both for books to be printed in red and black, and for books to be printed in black only.

The above remarks apply chiefly to prayer-books used in the Anglican churches. Very fine specimens have been of late years turned out by the University Press, Oxford, for the Church of England, and by Mame, of Tours, for the Roman Catholic Church. One of the most successful books issued for the use of that Communion is the Ambrosian Missal, lately issued in Milan,—a very fine volume which is worthy of study by all students of liturgical printing. This was first brought to my attention by that very learned man, the late Monsignor

Ceriani, of Milan, who, if I am not mistaken, had a hand in its making. The strictly Protestant bodies, in so far as they use liturgies at all, generally follow *The Book of Common Prayer* as to typographical arrangement—in the main a good model. When they depart from it they very often land themselves in typographical absurdities—from the liturgical point of view.

Besides the books for the services of the Church there are, of course, many collections of prayers, anthems, portions of the Bible, lessons and books of devotion. What is applicable to other service-books is applicable to these. Collections of prayers should be arranged like a prayer-book, but the type must be small, the paper flexible, and the book must be easily adapted to the pocket. This is also applicable to collections of hymns, to selections from the Bible, and to all books of private devotion, such as preparations for Holy Communion, the devotions of Holy Week, etc. In passing, I wish to say that the binding of such books cannot be too plain and unobtrusive. If sacred emblems are used on the binding they should not be stamped in gold. These are books for the "closet," and restraint should mark them in every way.

In the printing of prayers and hymns there is one point which should be mentioned, i.e. the necessity of avoiding over-capitalization. Sacred things are not made more holy by the use of capital letters, and the very sober usage of the English Prayer Book is recommended. My own opinion is that capitals should be used for names of the Deity, for the persons of the Holy Trinity, and sometimes for pronouns referring to these persons. But the capitalization of words like altar, and adjectives referring to the Blessed Sacrament should be discouraged. There are a few particularly silly modern hymns, which are generally printed in a manner as silly as they are; and one of these, a perfect inventory of Church furnishings, capitalizes not only altar (which is occasionally permissible) but also lights, frontal, etc.!

Order of service proper for special occasions are, of course, to be printed exactly as an office in the Prayer Book should be—any interpolations, such as hymns, etc., being printed in brackets.

There remains one class of modern work which is becoming very common, namely, the service lists which show what music is to be sung in church and by whom it is composed, the words of hymns, anthems, etc. These are generally in the form of a leaflet, one Sunday being devoted to each page of the leaflet. These should be printed in simple roman type, not too small. All fancifulness should be avoided. If possible, the words of the anthems or hymns should never come partly on one page and partly on another. Nothing is more distressing than the crackle of the turning music-lists in the middle of an anthem. The Germans have got over this difficulty very cleverly by using unsized paper, which may be turned noiselessly. Its texture, however, is woolly and unpleasant, and it prints none too well. But the service-list belongs more to my second article than the first; though it is, however, partly liturgical in character.

When I have said that fancifulness should be avoided, I mean by this, that the trivial sprinkling of crosses and devotional emblems on printing intended for use of the Church is in wretched taste and is the resort only of ignorant incompetence. When a clergyman wants something "churchy and artistic" he usually means this kind of printing. The first page of any devotional book might *very properly* have a cross upon it or some religious emblem—*but nothing else.* One colour of ink is generally enough; and it is much better that black ink should be used and good paper, than two colours of ink, and paper of poor quality. For the service of God it is desirable to use the best material and to avoid all display and needless expense.

The subject of printing for parochial purposes, under which may be grouped such work as is called for in the ordinary activities of the modern parish, will be considered in another paper.

And loveth him, the which that right for love
Upon a cros, our soules for to beye,
first starf, and roos, and sit in hevene above;
for he nil falsen no wight, dar I seye,
That wol his herte al hoolly on him leye.
And sin he best to love is, and most meke,
What nedeth feyned loves for to seke?

Lo here, of Payens corsed olde rytes,
Lo here, what alle hir goddes may availle;
Lo here, these wrecched worldes appetytes;
Lo here, the fyn and guerdon for travaille
Of Jove, Appollo, of Mars of swich rascaille!
Lo here, the forme of olde clerkes speche
In poetrye, if ye hir bokes seche.

O moral Gower, this book I directe

To thee, and to the philosophical Strode,
To vouchen sauf, ther nede is, to corecte,
Of your benignitees and zeles gode.
And to that sothfast Crist, that starf on
rode,
With al myn herte of mercy ever I preye;
And to the Lord right thus I speke and seye:

Thou oon, and two, and three, eterne on lyve,
That regnest ay in three and two and oon,
Uncircumscript, and al mayst circumscryve,
Us from visible and invisible foon
Defende; and to thy mercy, everichoon,
So make us, Jesus, for thy grace digne,
for love of mayde and moder thyn benigne!
Amen.
Explicit Liber Troili et Criseydis.

Kelmscott

15   *The Works of Geoffrey Chaucer* (Hammersmith: Kelmscott Press, 1896) [reduced], a book that profoundly influenced Updike's liturgical printing during the 1890s.

PUBLISHED: *Christian Art* (Boston) 3 (July 1908): 177–84.
1. *Christian Art* ceased publication before Updike's second installment could appear.

Georges Lepreux and the
'Gallia Typographica'

THERE are old books in every branch of learning that impress us because of the comprehensive and far-seeing point of view of their writers. We are apt to think that such works *de longue halcine* were characteristic of a more leisurely day than our own; and the modern composite works on literature and history lend colour to this idea. But the production of great books by a single author is, after all, less a matter of period than of temperament. Their appearance is really the result of persistent enthusiasm for a subject; and the leisure, or lack of it, is of slight importance. In fact, the phrase "a man of leisure"—though I admit it to be a brave individual, nowadays, who confesses himself one — has come to connote a person whose leisure enables him to bore those who have none, while accomplishing little himself!

In the literature of printing there have always been such books, because there always have been such enthusiasts. In France the works of La Caille and Chevillier are seventeenth-century instances of them. And in the eighteenth century there was Lottin, whose *Catalogue Chronologique des Libraires et des Libraires-Imprimeurs de Paris* took him thirty-six years to compile, and six more to correct and print — a matter of forty-two years in all! Lottin perceived that such a work was needed, or he hoped it was — at any rate, he set himself to produce it. It was a list, rather than a catalogue, of Parisian publishers and publisher-printers from the introduction of printing in 1470 up to the year 1789. To this he added lists of the same, arranged under their proper names; a second list arranged alphabetically under Christian names; a table of the thirty-six

[153]

printers allowed by law from 1686 (when the number was first legally fixed) down to his own day; and chronological notes on publishers and those "artists" (as he calls them) who had occupied themselves with the cutting and casting of printing types. It contains much more which I need not mention; it is enough for my purpose to cite it as an example of a book conceived on a comprehensive plan, though based on some earlier works conceived, too, for their day, on a comprehensive scale. But Lottin's plan was bigger than any that had preceded it; he had a larger point of view; he did not permit himself to be upset by outside events, though he finished his Catalogue in very troubled times—"*dans ces temps,*" as he says in a passage in his dedication, "*où l'Église se trouve ébranlée, comme la Monarchie, par la choc des opinions nouvelles.*"

I fancy, too, that Lottin was quite sincere in saying (what appears to be a prerequisite in producing volumes of this sort) that it was "a work in which a public service has been the sole end in view, and one which does not offer to the author's *amour-propre* any gratification other than the sense of having performed a service to his fellow citizens." "For this compilation," he adds, "no expenditure of intellect, no exhibition of talent or genius was requisite—only patience." But if, as has been said, genius is the art of taking pains, it took something very like intellectual genius to have patience to this extent! Lottin was not, however, merely patient; he had a point of view. He was not merely large-minded in his conception of his field of effort; he had a broader outlook still. This he showed by his hope that what he had done in relation to Paris and its printers, others who came after him would do for the whole land of France. He urges the need of carefully kept records, which would so much assist future historians of printing. "There remains but a single wish to be expressed," he writes, "that in each of the fifteen Provinces of France, some zealous publisher would do for his own town what I have tried to do for my own. ... If such an enterprise was undertaken, what light would be

[154]

shed on French bibliographical and typographical history!"

About one hundred and twenty years had passed before Lottin's wish came to fruition through the efforts of Monsieur Georges Lepreux, the subject of this paper. Becoming interested in the history of French printing, he conceived the idea of a monumental work upon it, the scope of which is shown by its title: *Gallia Typographica; ou Répertoire Biographique et Chronologique de Tous les Imprimeurs de France depuis les Origines de l'Imprimerie jusqu'à la Révolution.* The work of Lottin was, after all, only a very elaborate compilation of names and dates, amplified by some historical in formation, but confined to Paris. Lepreux took France as his field, and proposed to write full biographical, bibliographical, and typographical accounts of every printer in the country from the introduction of printing to the French Revolution. The conception was simple, but the task enormous! "When the plan of the 'Gallia' was first unfolded a dozen years ago," writes Beaulieux, "we were terrified!" Any publisher might well be so!

Lepreux's programme for the *Gallia* is outlined in his *Avertissement* to the first volume. He does not attempt to write a history of printing in France, like the monumental work by Claudin, but to give the chronology and biography of French printers based on official documents, and some account of the productions of their presses. Works general in scope, monographs on particular printers or localities, original researches in national archives and libraries, and books produced by the printers themselves—all these coördinated, he tells us, form the *Gallia Typographica*. Each printer who has exercised his art in France, from the beginning of the industry up to the Revolution, has his biography. These are grouped by Provinces, subdivided into Departments. Beginning with the northern Provinces, these are followed by those of the east, west, centre, and *midi* of France, and in the south the author ends what he calls "this long but interesting bio-typographical journey."

Each division devoted to a Department, after some prefatory matter and general survey, is divided into two chapters. The first is a chronological list of all French printers by localities, the second a biography of each printer in alphabetical order of name, with exact indication of the authorities on which information is based. Each volume, containing either one or several Provinces, is completed by an Appendix called "Galliae Typographicae Documenta," comprising in chronological order the different original sources, which will supply when finished an inventory of the decrees pertaining to the history of printing for the whole country. Finally, an alphabetical index of names of persons and places closes this series.

The preponderance of the Parisian press in the typographical history of France, its remarkable output from the end of the fifteenth century, and the ability, knowledge, and number of the Parisian printers, as well as the superiority of most of their productions, made Lepreux decide to devote to it a special Paris series of the *Gallia*. So parallel with the "Série Départementale," the still more interesting "Série Parisienne" was issued. The scheme of both is the same. After chronological lists, the biographies of Paris printers appear arranged in alphabetical order, followed by an analysis of original "sources" and reproductions of the most interesting documents about them. His first volume is devoted to the distinguished succession of men who figured as royal printers by appointment, under the title of *Livre d'Or des Imprimeurs du Roi*, and it supplies a delightful series of masterly and very "documented" sketches of some of the chief figures of French typography. This was to be followed by two more volumes covering all the other printers of Paris—a fourth volume consecrated to the *Communauté des Imprimeurs* and the *Chambre Syndicale* of Paris, which played such a large part in the annals of the Parisian press; the series closing with a volume on the printers of the different localities of Ile-de-France—which for Lepreux's purpose he considered as including only Seine-et-Marne, Seine-et-Oise, and, of course, the Department of the Seine itself. The historical introduction—a sort of summing up, which one would expect to find at the beginning of the first volume of one or the other of these series—Lepreux decided to reserve for the very last volume of the entire work,—an admirable plan in theory, though how far justified will be determined by whether he completed it or not! But to return—this volume cannot be dismissed without calling attention to his bibliography of the history of Parisian printing, and the learned disquisition on the post of *imprimeur du roi* which he prefixed to it. The second part of the volume, issued separately, is devoted to documents illustrative of the notices of the ninety-eight *imprimeurs du roi*, and is furnished with indexes of names of persons, devices and signs, and their Latin equivalents.

The ordinary student of French printing will undoubtedly first turn to the Paris series, for some of the men treated in it are among the most famous French printers, and from one's previous knowledge of them it is possible to appraise how successfully Lepreux's work is done. The notices of the seven members of the Estienne family who were *imprimeurs du roi*; of Tory; of Vitré; of Vascosan; of the Ballard family of music printers; of the Coignards, printers to the French Academy; of Lottin, author of the *Catalogue Chronologique*; of Franklin's friend Pierres—are a few of particular interest. I do not say that every inch of ground in this great field is wholly covered. For instance, in his notice of J. G. Clousier, *imprimeur du roi* between 1785 and 1790, no mention is made of his interesting post as director of les *Enfants Aveugles*, which ought to furnish some sidelights on the early history of printing for the blind, inaugurated by Valentin Haüy; and no doubt similar *lacunes* exist elsewhere. This Lepreux foresaw. "Alas," he says, " I feel my inadequacy, and I fear there are many imperfections. I ought surely to excuse myself for these last, in advance. I prefer, however, to have them pointed out to me, and I shall hasten to profit by them in order to make all the possible rectifications and additions to my work that I can. So, in view of their use-

fulness, I beg the reader to tell me of them." Here the true
student speaks! A departure from faĉt was, to him, far more
disgraceful than the dreaded "errata" slip! "*O si sic omnes!*"

By an accident as brutal as it was unforeseen [writes Charles
Beaulieux¹], on the fifteenth of January, 1918, Georges Lepreux
was snatched from the affeĉtion of his family and friends and from
erudition. Asphyxiated in his study, by the emanations of a defective heating apparatus, he passed without transition from sleep
into death while in fullness of health and achievement, without
ever having had the joy of seeing the deliverance of his daughters,
who had been in the invaded territory of his native city, Valen-
ciennes. Born the sixteenth of April, 1857, Lepreux, his studies
ended, entered upon his career in the insurance business, of which
he became an inspeĉtor. He very soon developed a taste for historic and bibliographic research. First he published two books
upon the history of his native Department: *Nos Journaux. Histoire
et Bibliographie de la Presse Périodique dans la Département du
Nord* (1746–1889), 2 vols., 8vo, 1896; *Nos Représentants pendant
la Révolution* (1789–1799), 8vo, 1898. The first forms the first
part of the *Encyclopédie Historique du Département du Nord*. The
latter forms a second series with this sub-title: *Histoire Éleĉtorale
et Parlementaire du Département du Nord et Biographie de tous les
Députés, Représentants, Pairs et Sénateurs de ce Département.*

To such a degree was Lepreux seized with a passion for the history of printing that he abandoned his lucrative business post that
he might devote himself entirely to his *Gallia Typographica*. From
that time forward he arranged for himself an extremely laborious and carefully regulated life. His month was separated into
two kinds of employment. The first and much the least part of
his time was given to work that assured the material needs of his
family. The second absorbed all the remaining days of the month.
And what days! Getting up before dawn, Lepreux passed several
hours in the study where he was prematurely to end his life, pen in
hand. Then there were researches at the *Bibliothèque Nationale* or
at the *Archives*; and in the evening, up to a late hour of the night,
he classified the notes he had colleĉted, and mapped out a chapter
of his book. Furthermore, taking a part of the time which he so
jealously reserved for his work, he laboured in the Archives of the

Ministry of War, in order to contribute, as far as he could, to the National Defense. When, a dozen years since, he showed us the plan of his *Gallia*, we were actually frightened; but when we considered this solid man of northern France, whose whole physiognomy breathed health, strength, and determined will, and when we saw the considerable quantity of material which such intensity of application and such regularity of effort had enabled him to get together, we were reassured as to the possibility of bringing the great work to successful completion.

And when the lamented Honoré Champion, who had become enthusiastic over the beauty of the subject, had assured the future of its publication, Lepreux redoubled his efforts to hasten the realization of his project. From 1909 to 1914 five volumes, in seven issues, of the *Gallia Typographica; ou Répertoire Biographique et Chronologique de Tous les Imprimeurs de France depuis les Origines de l'Imprimerie jusqu'à la Révolution* appeared, with perfect regularity, as supplements to the *Revue des Bibliothèques*. These are volumes I to IV of the Departmental Series, comprising: I, Flanders, Artois, Picardy; II, Champagne and Barrois; III, Province of Normandy; IV, Province of Brittany, and the first volume of the Parisian series—*Livre d'Or des Imprimeurs du Roi*. It was in vain that, in a friendly way, we urged him to publish first all the volumes of this last series which is so particularly interesting. Nothing would make him deviate from his plan. The *Gallia* had a great success. The *Académie des Inscriptions et Belles-Lettres* twice rewarded with the *Prix Brunet* the author who had already been crowned by the *Société des Sciences, de l'Agriculture, et des Arts*, of Lille. Between times Lepreux published articles on the history of printing in the *Revue des Bibliothèques* under the general title of "Contributions à l'Histoire de l'Imprimerie Parisienne," in the *Bulletin de l'Union syndicale des Maîtres Imprimeurs de France*, under the title "Fastes Séculaires de l'Imprimerie," in the *Bibliographe Moderne*, etc. The war stopped the publication of the *Gallia Typographica*, but Lepreux, having no more proof-sheets to correct, prepared even more energetically the volumes which were to follow. Furthermore, on the eve of the war, he showed us a large number of volumes, as yet unpublished, of which several were completed and others in part prepared—manuscripts written in his superb hand. Thus we may hope that the sudden death of a scholar as conscientious as he was modest, of a man of such absolute integrity as was Georges Lepreux, will not interrupt the publication of this great monument for which we may search vainly any equivalent across the Rhine.

"May this collection," wrote Lepreux in closing his preface to the first published volume of the *Gallia*, "receive from the public a favorable reception; above all, may it be of some use to all those who have at heart the love of books and the studies connected with them, and who understand the obligation which we owe to those modest and often illustrious pioneers, the Printers, thanks to whom the face of the earth is renewed by the universal spread of the productions of the human intellect. These are my most cherished wishes; and if they come to fruition, I shall regret neither my labors nor my pains."

His labors will not be in vain. The number of volumes completed and the forwardness of the remainder of the work lead us to await the continuance of the publication of the *Gallia*. That it can ever have those delicate "finishing touches" that no one but its author would see the necessity of giving, is not in the nature of things; but in the care of Monsieur Edouard Champion, son of the late Honoré Champion, just returned to civil life after distinguished service in the French army, the work is in responsible, sympathetic, and erudite hands. It deserves the support of everyone who admires Lepreux's work and regrets his loss. No man more than he ever lived up to the device of his ancestor—Poncet Le Preux, sixteenth-century Paris printer and publisher—*Quidquid agas, sapienter agas!* All students of French printing will be immeasurably in his debt for what he did, and for what we shall yet receive from his pen. What more he might have done and did not live to do—that belongs to "the tears of things," and will be the lasting regret of every admirer of this brave, patient, modest, indomitable, and learned man!

PUBLISHED: *Printing Art* 35 (March 1920): 25–31.

    1. In the *Revue des Bibliothèques* (Janvier–Juin, 1918) under the same title as this paper. It was as supplements to this review that the *Gallia* was issued, through the interest of its publisher, the late Honoré Champion. [DBU]

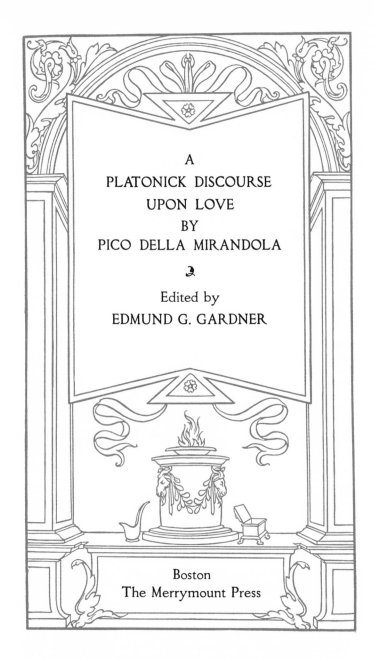

A

PLATONICK DISCOURSE
UPON LOVE
BY
PICO DELLA MIRANDOLA

Edited by
EDMUND G. GARDNER

Boston
The Merrymount Press

16   Title-page—designed by T. M. Cleland—of *A Platonick Discourse upon Love* by Pico della Mirandola (Merrymount Press, 1914).

Thomas Maitland Cleland

HERE is a beautiful book[1] which has taken more than five years of preparation and labour to produce. It is the most remarkable showing of an American designer's work yet published; and although Cleland's reputation was already established among those who were conversant with American decorative design, this book introduces him to a wider public than ever before. Even to those who have watched his work, the cumulative effect of this assemblage of drawings is surprisingly impressive, partly because it shows such mastery of every kind of technique, but even more because it displays a master's hand in so many different schools of design.

The first three decorations shown in this book were for title-pages of volumes which I myself published, and of these the earliest was drawn at a period when Cleland was particularly interested in Florentine woodcuts [*Fig.* 16]. Indeed in the year 1904 he had also produced for Mr. Edwin Gorham, of New York, a tiny portfolio which contained "Florentine Christmas Cards; Six Designs by T. M. Cleland," executed in Italian woodcut style. Although this drawing as shown in these cards is less assured than it afterwards became—the figures in particular showing certain lapses—nevertheless the same ability to seize salient points of design is exhibited, that he has continued to show throughout his later work. It would be easier to trace the various influences under which he worked if the designs in the present volume were arranged chronologically, thus showing his work in sequence, but for various reasons this has been impossible: though this defect might have been somewhat obviated by giving a second list of designs in order of date. But I hesitate to make even this suggestion to a man who

[163]

has made it possible for us to see this splendid showing: for we owe a great debt to Mr. Elmer Adler, of The Pynson Printers, for the care with which the designs have been assembled and the immense pains and expense he has been at, to represent Cleland's work as it was put forth by Cleland himself.

The designs in this book, which are chiefly made to accompany the text of luxurious advertisements, may be roughly grouped into periods, the first being when Cleland was more or less under the influence of the early Italian style; later under the influence of the French taste of about the same epoch; and later still under the influence of both Italian and French work of the eighteenth century. One becomes conscious too, if we examine these drawings according to the date of completion, of a much freer and more personal manner of employing the styles in which he worked. It is for that reason that such examples as the poster for the American Wing in the Metropolitan Museum of Art, the cover for the Westvaco brochure, the sketch for the proposed panel for Lord and Taylor, the water-colour illustration for the *Woman's Home Companion*, the extraordinarily effective pages advertising the Cadillac car [*Fig.* 17], and the Christmas cards in colour (done last year) are to me among the most interesting things in the book. Perhaps this change is best exhibited on the last page of the volume, in the difference exhibited between a design for a catalogue cover made in 1908 and an emblem for an architectural society made twenty years later. In the first Cleland was still somewhat imprisoned; in the second design he is free. But no one who looks at the folder advertising Strathmore papers done in 1921 could accuse him of lack of freedom. This charming representation of an eighteenth-century Italian piazza might have illustrated a comedy by Goldoni, though no comedy was ever so superbly mounted; and in this connection the selection of six out of twelve clever and "knowing" drawings in colour for the West Virginia Paper Company, made in 1927, present this same freer style.

[164]

17   Cadillac advertisement by T. M. Cleland.

Cleland's drawings are extremely sophisticated, but the most sophisticated of them have been done in most cases to advertise very sophisticated and expensive products; and one would scarcely consider a "return to nature" appropriate to the wine list of the Hotel Claridge, or, inversely, his drawings for the Locomobile or Cadillac cars suited to the advertisement of a Ford truck. These designs must be judged by what they are meant for, and the kind of product they were intended to advertise: granted that fact, a treatment less artificial or "opulent" would have been inappropriate. And then too he was often called upon to fulfil most difficult commissions—for instance, to make a series of advertisements illustrating statistical facts. Yet consider the charm of the series of advertisements made for the General Motors Company, which appear to me to be among the cleverest things in the entire book! Wentworth and Smith's *High School Mathematics* does not by its title particularly allure, but the illustrations which Cleland designed for it, in the manner of early French mathematical books, are perfectly delightful; while as a piece of book-making, as well as of harmonious illustrative design, nothing could be better than his *Grammar of Colour.* This ability to turn his hand successfully to the problem before him, selecting from the styles with which he is familiar the one best adapted to the work he has to do, places him head and shoulders above the "period" decorator, who in his zeal without knowledge protrudes the tip of a patent leather shoe through a lunette designed by Le Brun for the architectural decoration of Versailles.

Cleland began his career as a very untrained and unevenly educated lad with a remarkably acute and perceptive eye, and an immense enthusiasm for beautiful things. It would seem as if this lack of education must have been a handicap. But in Cleland's case it had great compensations. As the book before us shows, his education was perfected as he went along—an education not even yet completed. If he had experienced a more methodical training, either literary or artistic, or had followed a course in design, it might have taken off the "edge" of his enthusiasm for new forms of decorative expression as in turn he discovered them, and would very likely have ruined his talent. It was precisely because he began without such training, that historic styles of decoration often came upon him as something entirely new, and their impact, startling to him to a degree sometimes a little amusing to the onlooker, resulted in extraordinarily vivid reactions. When I first knew him he had just discovered (as I have before indicated) the Florentine Italian woodcut, but before he got through with it, or to put it more accurately, before it got through with him, he had squeezed out of it everything that it could teach him and was ready to proceed to other and equally thrilling discoveries. What each style, that for a time fascinated him, resulted in, we can very well see in cumulative fashion in this book, though by no means to such an extent as a really complete showing of his work would indicate. Indeed this volume might be called "The Education of Thomas Maitland Cleland," and perhaps the valuable point about the assemblage of designs is its showing of what a quick-witted, painstaking, and persistent man can do. The sources from which Cleland drew part of his inspiration are open to everyone, but it was not given to everyone to see the relation of these sources to the problem to be solved. It is because Cleland was so "curious"—in the eighteenth-century meaning of the term—about what had been done in design, because he saw the possibilities latent in different styles, and because he knew how to inject his personality into them, that he stands at the forefront of American designers, through sheer talent to do what appears, now that he has done it, simple for anyone to do.

The ingenuity and quick-wittedness which enabled him to perceive the possibilities latent in styles he also applied to decorative possibilities latent in things. Quick to seize any allusions potential in the content of the job he was undertaking, accordingly automobiles, machinery, etc., have been vehicles for delightful, whimsical, and ingenious decoration. These elements were all there, waiting to be discerned, and when discerned by him appear sufficiently obvious to all of us. But it remains a fact that no one with equal talent did study carefully the decorative possibilities of these somewhat discouraging subjects, did see how to utilize the qualities latent therein or did know how to cast them in the manner of the style in which he was working. This ability to see from both angles, and blend happily what he saw, is perhaps, apart from his admirable technique, Cleland's particular characteristic.

This technique has been slowly and laboriously perfected, by that enormous amount of disciplined effort that invariably lies behind what appears easy and graceful accomplishment. With the years his ability in this direction has become more and more assured, and in thinking of how it has been effected I am reminded of a passage that I lately read about a great journalist. "If it be asked," it ran, "how all this is done, not only without any dishevelment and discomposure of living, but with rather more than less attention to its airs and graces, the teaching which is contained in answer is easy to frame and hard to follow, since it requires no less than the whole of life. The rapid decision, the finished scheme composed against time, do not come of a position sometimes assumed and sometimes relaxed. The spring is easy because the pose is always maintained. The burden is carried because it is never laid down."

I commend this distinguished collection, therefore, to those who wish to see some of the best work that has yet been produced in the field of what is commonly called "commercial art"—a term I dislike, but use because I can think of none more agreeable or better—and which is meant to indicate, design applied to purposes commercial in their end. I also commend the volume to designers in the same field as (to use the word employed by another reviewer) "a swipe book," the meaning of which phrase needs, I fear, no explanation. But what I suggest "swiping" is the intelligence, knowledge, persistence and unconscious courage and idealism exhibited in Cleland's artistic career—all the more to be imitated if "the swiper" is at once blessed and cursed with a temperament, which by its very impressionability makes it difficult to steer an even course, when beset by unreasonable demands and ignorant flattery from without and by currents of feeling, waves of discouragement and gusts of temporary elation from within that seem to be part of the progress of the man who can both feel and see.

The work that I admire so much is open, however, to one criticism. It has been cleverly said that Cleland is first of all an actor, and his interest from boyhood in things theatrical has been shown in Mr. Hamill's admirable and discriminating notice which prefaces this book. Just as an actor sees the dramatic possibilities in the part he is to play, so Cleland sees the decorative possibilities in the particular school of decoration in which he is, like an actor, for the moment "cast." He seizes, therefore, the most outstanding characteristics of the style that he has chosen to work in, and to make them "carry across the footlights" he slightly exaggerates them. The result is usually charming. It amuses those who know, astonishes those who do not, and delights both the one and the other. Better yet, it accomplishes its end in a precise and definitive manner—or *an* end. But as we are puzzled as to the real character of the man behind the actor, so we are tempted to inquire what Cleland could do when, working in no particular "manner," he approaches things or Nature directly, and gives to these things or to natural forms that charming twist which he so well knows how to give in his more derived art. In the middle of the eighteenth century, the designers and silk manufacturers of Lyons petitioned for the establishment of a public school of design, and in that petition they emphasized the importance of a garden of growing flowers to be connected with the school, since, said they, it was only by perceiving the growing plant that they could take advantage of its subtle beauties. I am not saying that Cleland has never worked directly from Nature or showed us his personal view of inanimate objects, but I do feel that he has not done this enough. I perceive, through the various manners which the reproductions in this book display, a perpetual attempting and discarding, with more and more approach to a direct personal point of view. One looks forward to his complete emancipation, for Cleland is a man who will "die learning," and his potentialities as an artist are greater than anything he has yet accomplished.

What I have suggested in these last paragraphs is summed up in a fine passage in Emerson, very significantly—for my purpose—entitled: Quotation and Originality. "We cannot overstate," he wrote, "our debt to the past, but the moment has the supreme claim. The past is for us, but the sole terms on which it can become ours are its subordination to the present. Only an inventor knows how to borrow and every man is or should be an inventor. . . . This vast memory is only raw material. The divine gift is ever the instant life, which receives and uses and creates, and can well bury the old in the omnipotency with which Nature decomposes her harvest for recomposition."

Notes

PUBLISHED: *The Fleuron*, No. 7 (1930): 133–42.
On the relationship between Updike and Cleland, see W. S. Peterson, "The Correspondence of Daniel Berkeley Updike and Thomas Maitland Cleland," *Matrix* 20 (2000): 8–36; 21 (2001): 128–41, and Cleland's essay "A Tribute to Daniel Berkeley Updike" (Beilenson, pp. 81–85).

1. *The Decorative Work of T. M. Cleland:* a Record and Review with a Bibliographical and Critical Introduction by Alfred E. Hamill, and a Portrait Lithograph by Rockwell Kent. Large Quarto, xxvi + 100 pages. New York: The Pynson Printers, 1929. [DBU]

Rudolph Ruzicka: An Appreciation

IT is dangerous business for a man who knows nothing of the technique of engraving, nor has anything new or interesting to say about its relation to printing, to write a paper on an engraver's work. The profound remark of an architect—the late Mr. McKim—has not been lost on me. It may be remembered that he said—though if the reader does remember I shall be secretly disappointed—that he used to talk about music and painting, but that since he had been obliged to listen to what people said *to him* about architecture, he thought it wiser to hold his peace! So I shall spare Mr. Ruzicka the annoyance of an attempt to describe his work as an engraver would describe it, or as a printer might describe it, and prudently rely on what it suggests to me in relation to forms of artistic expression round about us today.

If we look back at a certain class of "big men" in the past, we find that an intimate relation to the life of their time was a very vital part of their "bigness." A Frenchman and an Englishman who had this quality—Callot and Hogarth—can scarcely be thought of nowadays, if we leave this characteristic out. Their alliance with their own period was so intimate that they made it belong to them as much as they belonged to it. They had a manner so personal in interpreting the life round about them that it is to them we look for a sort of epitome of it.

The unruly wills and affections of such original persons have always distressed the academic—the men who admired the Carracci in the seventeenth, Canova in the eighteenth, and Alma-Tadema in the last century; and the noble army of artistic standpatters whose legacies fill the cellars (elegantly called "reserves") of our museums—or should—are of course made uncomfortable by today's work if done in today's manner. They prefer men whose work can be accurately placed without thinking; for new thoughts produce in such minds an irritation analogous to "something in one's eye."

An amusing thing about going to Bernard Shaw's plays (often in parts of excruciating dullness) is the nervous attitude of the audiences. Being "Shaw" it must be clever and amusing, they think. So, in order to be on the very front seat of the dramatic "band-wagon," they titter anxiously, or exchange expressive glances over portions of drama not normally amusing to anybody. And there is a like class of artistic snobs "waiting for the hint." They are a dangerous class to "new men," much more dangerous than old gentlemen who like Henner's not very obviously repentant Magdalenes, or old ladies who buy Haghe's etchings of cathedrals (in sets) about Eastertide. These latter at least "know what they like"; but the "art snob" class never liked anything until someone they thought bigger than themselves liked it first!

To neither of these two classes—the standpatter or the artistic snob—will Ruzicka's engravings appeal. They are too extreme for the one and not sufficiently sensational for the other. But there is a class to whom they do appeal, a still larger class to whom they will appeal when they know them. My desire is to show why.

As I looked at the collection of Ruzicka's wood-engraving at the delightfully arranged exhibition at Newark, it did not occur to me to analyze the pleasure I felt. But as I have thought of it since, I perceive that much of my satisfaction was because the work so expressed the man who did it, was so little related to that of other engravers, and was so close to our time, as our time is understood by a truthful, thoughtful, and original man. A phrase in some chance reading occurred to me in this connection—that "to work simply one must think simply." These engravings result from thinking simply, seeing simply, working simply; and, too, seeing very individually, or in other words, for oneself. Such qualities of mind and eye and hand are much needed today, when we see so much and feel so little.

One of the qualities in Ruzicka's work is its actuality. He seizes the picturesque side of a "Gospel tent" at night, with its violent contrast of light and shade, or a gasometer, or a Ferris wheel, as some others have done; but actuality is not all, for he makes them pictorially his own, presents them always *more suo*. To be able to see picturesque qualities where other people see nothing is the power of the seer; to convey them to others is the power of the interpreter. It was, I think, Emerson who remarked that in what to the farmer was only "the back wood-lot," the poet saw all the glories of the autumn; and being a poet, naturally he conveyed what he saw in poetic terms.

Such prints as the night-view beneath the bridge at Pittsburgh—"Along the Monongahela"—with the white light of the furnaces glowing in the distance, making even the shadows luminous, and a figure on a tugboat silhouetted against the glare—is an example of what I mean. And another instance of it, though less attractive, is the view of the skeleton of a great building in course of erection, behind which a mass of steam rises against a background of towering construction. The men carrying lumber in the corner, the workers among the girders, the figures against the white vapour, waiting and considering, with that quality of repose which comes to all labourers momentarily at rest—all this is very true and very much of to-day. It is also very much Ruzicka. Such a print is the modern equivalent of the dreamlike "Carceri" of Piranesi, though it represents the Grand Central Station a-building !

Quite from another angle is an engraving of the sun-bathed façade of the New York Public Library, with passing pedestrians—a scene about which there is something so bright and American and yet Parisian!—for New York at rare moments recalls Paris. And in still another manner is the artist's sedate, workmanlike rendering of St. John's Chapel, Varick Street,

which a community pretending to a fashionable taste for eighteenth-century architecture has not spirit enough to save as a
church; though its oblations contribute to the building of an
exceedingly ugly cathedral in which some stodgy Victorian
"uses" flourish, which, it was hoped, were untransplantable
from the British Isles! The print of St. John's is as sober and
as ordered in its somewhat early method of presentation as is
the delightful building it portrays. And this design, so full of
the calm spirit of its subject, was the work of a Bohemian to
whom Anglicanism is a word, early New York a tradition, and
American architecture of the school of Wren as remote as the
Alhambra!

Ruzicka's work has not been confined to single engravings or
to wood-blocks for coloured illustrations in books. His agreeable black-and-white drawings of picturesque localities, of that
part of Rhode Island known as "the South County," illustrate
that whimsical book, Hazard's *Jonny-Cake Papers*. Sketches
of the buildings of Vassar College, four of which illustrate a
volume printed in connection with the fiftieth anniversary of
its foundation, which, with eight more, are issued by the College in portfolio form, further show the designer's abilities in
drawings in black-and-white with an added tint. In a third
book, Mrs. Charles McVeagh's *Fountains of Papal Rome*, the
illustrations, though still in black-and-white, are from wood-
blocks [*Fig.* 18]. These are among the most delightful things
Ruzicka has done. The differentiation of substances—the
dripping bronze figures on fountains, stucco buildings sleeping
in the hot sun, and shadowy granite basins full of water—are
very extraordinary in rendering, and very beautifully managed.
To be judged fairly these engravings should be seen in the
engraver's proofs, for the book did not have the advantage of
his supervision, and as far as illustrations are concerned, is but
a slovenly performance. Still it has indirect value, as have the
two volumes just mentioned, in bringing the artist's work to
the attention of a wider circle than is possible for single prints

18　The Fountain of the Tartarughe (a wood-engraving by Rudolph Ruzicka), from Mrs. Charles McVeagh's *Fountains of Papal Rome* (New York: Charles Scribner's Sons, 1915).

or special editions, both necessarily limited in number. For that reason, I hope that Ruzicka's activities in this direction will grow.

Of the series of prints furnished for the Christmas and New Year's cards of the Merrymount Press, chiefly devoted to "*les délices de Boston*," it is perhaps more fitting to quote an outside opinion. Mr. W. M. Ivins, Jr., curator of prints at the Metropolitan Museum, New York (whose excellent little paper about Ruzicka's work is, in artistic, technical, and historical knowledge, the best thing yet written about him), speaking of this series says that "in them he has given supple expression to a local psychology of a kind quite different from that with which he is more familiar. Such woodcuts as the Louisburg Square, Faneuil Hall, and Old State House are correct in every Bostonian sense of the word, a little dry, a little precise, quite restrained, and just a little backward looking to the older times of the shallow straight-backed chair which forbade lounging, in a word, charming records of a prim, provincial elegance which seems about to depart."

This brings me to Ruzicka's individual engravings for Christmas and the New Year, some of them little gems in their way; and among the best of the good things his hand has given us.

A clever circular design which he cut for himself in 1911 represents the Farragut Monument crowded with observers as a regiment passes down Fifth Avenue. Examples of Ruzicka's agreeable and penetrating treatment of work of this sort are the delightful view of an old pilastered brick house at Geneva, in its pleasant garden, for Mr. Beverly Chew (1916); the front door of 7 Washington Square, a Christmas card for Mr. De Forest (1914), and the view of Mr. De Forest's Sweet Hollow Farm, done earlier (1912); the Washington Arch seen against the red brick houses of Washington Square, with a passing 'bus just disappearing through it (for Mr. H. W. Kent, 1911); and a Newark church, Judge Raymond's card of 1912, this last among the most delicate and tasteful of these small designs. A charming example illustrates this paper, namely, the Christmas Greeting of Dr. and Mrs. Dennett—an open-air concert in Bryant Park on a hot summer night. Nor should the bookplates he has engraved be forgotten, notably a beautiful *fête champêtre* in the manner of the French eighteenth century for Mrs. Oliver Ames, and the horses *à l'antique* for Miss Florence Windom.

Several of the illustrations accompanying this notice are taken from a volume published by the Grolier Club in 1915, entitled *New York*. The first of these is a view of the Harlem River in winter. From a subject which seems unpromising, Ruzicka has made a distinguished picture, for he has perceived what very few people but himself would see. Both in colour and composition, I think it among his most charming prints. The second illustration is the impressive little view entitled "Down Town, a View from Union Square." The movement of which it is so full is partly due, perhaps, to figures in the foreground moving to the right, with smoke and mist above them driving to the left. Somehow this composition conveys the weary and restless quality of a life forever in flux—"a city consumed by its desire to live!" Next come three illustrations to *The Fountains of Papal Rome*, and on the opposite page Ruzicka's own Christmas cards for 1911 and 1912, and the Dennett card already spoken of. The views of Faneuil Hall, and of Louisburg Square, Boston, belong to the series executed for my own Press [*Fig.* 19]. The next illustration (engraved in 1909) is not a cañon in the Yosemite Valley, but a view of Liberty Street. Ruzicka has made other sketches of skyscrapers which seem to me preferable to this; for it is less original in suggestion than most of his work. The last illustration forms one of the tailpieces of the book on New York—an ordered view of a building that so well expresses plain living and high thinking—the Quaker Meeting House in Stuyvesant Square.

Through every piece of Ruzicka's engraving and design runs

[177]

MONTES ET COLLES
CANTABVNT

19   Louisburg Square, Boston (a wood-engraving by Rudolph Ruzicka), from a Merrymount Press Christmas card.

a secure and sufficient quality—the sane, self-respecting individuality of a man who has something to say and says it simply,
directly, calmly, and felicitously. In an hour of intellectual
mob-thought and artistic mob-fashion, of open advertisement
of self or tacitly permitted exploitation by others, he has the
poise to let his work speak and be himself silent. He reserves
his strength for his task and dilutes not his talents in criticism
of others' performance, or explanation of his own. This attitude to one's own effort is more foreign than American. We
can all learn from him not merely the technique of engraving,
but (incidentally) the technique of good manners, and admire
a man whose work shows that he possesses that rarest of all
possessions—himself!

Notes

PUBLISHED: *Printing Art* 30 (September 1917): 17–24.
    For the relationship between Updike and Ruzicka, see the
Lathems's edition of their correspondence, Ruzicka's essay "Frag-
ments of Memory" (Beilenson, pp. 118–29), and *Rudolph Ruzicka: Speaking Reminiscently.*

THE
PREFACE
TO
Johnson's
DICTIONARY
OF THE
English Language
1755

CLEVELAND
THE ROWFANT CLUB
1934

20   *The Preface to Johnson's Dictionary of the English Language* (Cleveland: Rowfant Club, 1934), printed at the Merrymount Press [reduced].

Some Tendencies in Modern Typography

NOT very long since I was asked by a printer to what extent he should accept or avoid modern trends in the design of types and books. I attempt here to answer that question.

I have a friend, connected with one of the great companies supplying machines for type composition. Not long since he spoke to me in unflattering terms of the examples of typography shown at an exhibition of the products of the Bauhaus School, originally of Weimar and later of Munich. He protested against a practice there manifested of discarding capital letters and depending solely on those in the lowercase. I consoled him by showing him a French book, printed entirely in this style. This volume, entitled *Typographie Economique*, was published in Paris in 1837 and so far as it had any influence on printing, then or later, is as dead as Queen Anne. The author, the Count de Lasteyrie, who promoted this scheme, was one of a race of French scientists, of some intellectual and social importance—one of the daughters of Lafayette married into that family. In the eighteenth century no less a person than the German writer Grimm tried a similar typographical plan. In the *Fairy Tales* containing "Snow White and the Seven Dwarfs," later compiled by Jacob and Wilhelm Grimm, the practice was not continued. This supports the contention that many new and disturbing experiments, under the patronage of distinguished names, are merely survivals or revivals of ancient failures. Thus in the light of experience, there is in Bauhaus typography nothing for my acquaintance—or anybody else—to be excited about.

Now Bauhaus typography is of the essence of modernism. That its position may be fairly stated I quote the following from a *Bauhaus Year Book*:—*verbatim* and (I may add) *literatim.*

why should we write and print with two alphabets? both a large and a small sign are not necessary to indicate one single sound.
A = a
we do not speak a capital A and a small a.
we need only a single alphabet. it gives us practically the same result as the mixture of upper- and lowercase letters, and at the same time is less of a burden on all who write—on school children, students, stenographers, professional and business men. it could be written much more quickly, especially on the typewriter, since the shift key would then become unnecessary. typewriting could therefore be more quickly mastered and typewriters would be cheaper because of simpler construction. printing would be cheaper, for fonts and type cases would be smaller, so that printing establishments would save space and their clients money. with these common sense economies in mind . . . the bauhaus made a thorough alphabetical housecleaning in all its printing, eliminating capitals from books, posters, catalogs, magazines, stationery and even calling cards.
dropping capitals would be a less radical reform in english. indeed the use of capital letters occurs so infrequently in english in comparison with german that it is difficult to understand why such a superfluous alphabet should still be considered necessary.

Now in German printing all nouns have capital letters. In the sentence "A Dog chases a Cat into a Barn," dog, cat, barn are all capitalized. No one can be blamed for wanting to be rid of so much capitalization. But when Germans purge anything, the innocent invariably suffer with the guilty. Thus all capitals must go. While it may have overcome a difficulty felt in Germany, this imported missionary zeal corrects no difficulty in the printing of English prose or poetry. In some instances such a custom brings about surprising results. Suppose, for example, a newspaper says "the white house favors black and prefers even green to a dyed-in-the-wool red." To make the sentence intelligible would need the addition of a number of words—which would not be *typographie économique!* We need labour this point no further but leave these experiments to the advertising of Coty and Elizabeth Arden. Such effects have what is called attention value—like Neon signs—but I am not considering that kind of typography. I have, however, here traced the source of a current fashion of printing signs and advertisements without capital letters.

I have been classed by my work as a conservative, but I am a liberal conservative or a conservative liberal—whichever you like or dislike. All I wish to conserve, either in traditionalism or modernism, is common sense. What little I have was gained by experience. I regard many typographic experiments with good will and many traditional viewpoints with tolerance. I agree wholeheartedly with neither. I remember—or try to do so—that every generation has in turn to be told that there was once a man named Caesar, who wrote a very dull book called the *Commentaries*, of which the first sentence is all that most people remember; that the makers of Baker's Chocolate did not invent the familiar picture of a chocolate girl, which was an eighteenth-century painting by Jean Etienne Liotard now in a Dresden picture gallery, and that William Blake did not write, but only illustrated, the Book of Job. We who have long known these things forget that people are born not knowing them. We should therefore look tenderly on many typographic experiments. To us elders they may seem akin to lighting a fire with kerosene or applying one's tongue to metal in zero temperatures, but it is by such unwise ventures that we outgrow them. And as I have spent a long life learning, and to most questions do not yet know the answers, I have no right to frown on more youthful and enterprising enquirers.

Obviously some of the eccentricities of present-day typography are a natural reflection of that rather tortured world in which we find ourselves. If art, the drama, literature, and music reflect current trends of life it is natural that printing should in a measure do so. If we throw overboard old standards of conduct, we may far more readily throw over old standards of taste. When one casts a convention away as useless and out-moded, we often learn for the first time why it was there! It is urged that fuller expression of individuality, unhampered by rules, is development. It seems to me more accurate to say that through the experience of trying these experiments develop-ment comes—though not always of a kind expected. Such development ought never to stop until in the exact sense of the word we are "accomplished"—finished—which few live to be.

The *problem* is to distinguish between a true development and a false one. In judging either modernistic or retrospective typography, that is what must be decided. Do these develop-ments, wise and otherwise, produce a well-made and readable book—in short a good book? "In the printing of books meant to be read," says an authority, "there is little room for 'bright' typography. Even dullness and monotony in the typesetting are far less vicious to a reader than typographical eccentricity or pleasantry. Cunning of this sort is desirable, even essential in the typography of propaganda, whether for commerce, pol-itics, or religion because in such printing only the freshest sur-vives inattention. But the typography of books, apart from the category of narrowly limited editions, requires an obedience to convention which is almost absolute—and with reason."[1]

It is the fashion, just now, to decry typographic conven-tions. Some conventions and traditions deserve to be decried and some have already been laughed out of existence. There are, however, good and bad conventions and traditions in printing, just as there are true and false developments, and the trick is to know which is which! Convention and particularly tradition are, generally, the crystallized result of past experi-ments, which experience has taught us are valuable. In some of the extreme modernistic typography a little more tradition might come in handy. The trouble with the modernist is that he seems afraid not to throw everything overboard and mis-takes eccentricity for emancipation. Thus some books of today seem to be the arrangement of a perverse and self-conscious eccentricity. Such printing is often the work of eager, ambitious, and inexperienced men, and because they are young and God is good, one can afford to be patient; sure that they will, in the long run, outgrow the teething, mumps, and measles of typography. Their convalescence will possibly be hastened by meditating on the saying of Lord Falkland that "when it is not necessary to change, it is necessary not to change."

No movement ever accomplishes all that its first promoters intended or hoped for; almost all movements make some lasting contributions to our common stock. Every new idea, every new invention brings along with its expected benefits unforeseen evils. Modernistic architecture is at present exciting because new and unusual; when more common it will become commonplace. When it becomes difficult to differentiate the exterior of a modernistic church from a warehouse, we may get very, very tired of it. Then a compensating reaction will set in and balance will be restored. The same thing is true of modernistic typography. At present, it shocks us into attention, but we get tired of being shocked, for we do not want printing to surprise but to soothe us. The modernist must remember, too, that "such a thing as an underivative work of art does not and cannot exist, and no great master in the arts has thought or asserted otherwise." We gladly admit that some modernistic formulas have had good results. In architecture, perhaps to some degree in typography, they have taught us to get rid of clutter and useless ornamentation. But neither the one nor the other leads anywhere—except to a dead end.

The conservative, however, need not think that all truth is on his side. However much he tries to practise retrospective or "period" typography, consciously or unconsciously his work will show the influence of his time. Just as there is a popular idiom in speech which varies in each decade, so there is a current idiom in printing. All these idioms, literary and typographic, have not come to stay, but some become accepted terms. Under Theodore Roosevelt we suffered from the word "strenuous." President Harding inflicted the word "normalcy" on American speech. We now have "reactions," and "contacts." Clergymen "challenge" things, have "spiritual adventures," talk of "strategic positions" for their parish houses and aid parochial charities by "clarion calls," though if confronted with a "clarion" (if this instrument exists outside of sermons) they would be quite unable to blow it. All these catch-words and stock phrases are in the air. We suffer much the same thing in typography, about which there is also a new jargon which replaces the old *clichés* of my youth about rhythm, balance, and colour. Neither in speech nor printing can one make a clean sweep of the past nor help being of the present, no matter how hard one tries. I deplore violent attempts to make current printing accord with the spirit of the age. It always has, always will, and does now.

Nor need the conservative sniff at typographic experimentation. To turn to another department of daily life, what would happen if no one had ever tried experiments with food? In the distant past there was the first human being who—as an experiment—ate an oyster, though perhaps first trying jelly-fish with less comfortable results. Others died of eating toadstools before people learned that they could survive on mushrooms. Almost all our vegetable food we owe to gastronomic adventurers. Thus the most hide-bound conservative owes his sustenance to the fruits—and vegetables—of experiment.

To speak more seriously, both modernist and conservative should lay to heart what Benedetto Croce says in his *Autobiography* about "the impossibility of resting on the results of past thought" and the necessity of modesty in stating one's present position. "I see," he writes, "a new crop of problems springing up in a field from which I have but now reaped a harvest of solutions; I find myself calling in question the conclusions to which I have previously come; and these facts . . . force me to recognize that truth will not let itself be tied fast. . . .

[186]

They teach me modesty towards my present thoughts, which tomorrow will appear deficient and in need of correction, and indulgence towards myself of yesterday or the past, whose thoughts, however inadequate in the eyes of my present self, yet contained some real element of truth: and this modesty and indulgence pass into a sense of piety towards thinkers of the past, whom now I am careful not to blame, as once I blamed them, for their inability to do what no man, however great, can do . . . to fix into eternity the fleeting moment."

There is, to the reasonable mind, no real quarrel between modernism and traditionalism in printing, *except in degree.* Modernism must and does influence the conservative in spite of himself—if by modernism we mean a healthy awareness of the needs of the time in which we are living. Tradition must and does influence the modernist, if by tradition we mean patient and respectful appraisal of what that accumulation of yesterdays, which we call the past, has to teach. It is only by experience that we can effect a wise blend of the two. Then we produce books which, while representing the best practice of our time, will outlast it. The appraisal of their ultimate values we must leave to the future.

"There is no past that we need long to return to," said Goethe, "there is only the eternally new which is formed out of enlarged elements of the past; and our real endeavor must always be towards new and better creation."

Notes

PUBLISHED: *Some Aspects of Printing*, pp. 41–49. Delivered as a lecture at Harvard University and Pasadena, Calif., 1940.

Updike, comparing it with "The Essentials of a Well-Made Book," said that about modern typography "there was more that was new to say, and perhaps I have arrived at some helpful conclusions on the subject" ("Foreword," *Some Aspects of Printing*, p. 2).

1. Updike is quoting from Stanley Morison's *First Principles of Typography*, published in 1929 and frequently reprinted.

American University Presses

WHETHER American University Presses so-called are always worthy of a university, and what their needs and aims are, from a typographical and scholarly point of view, I propose to consider briefly in these pages. There are more university presses in the United States than in any other country in the world or in all other countries combined. The last sixty or seventy years have seen their rise. For my purpose I define a university as any institution of learning that so describes itself and grants accredited degrees for scholarship. Not all these *soi-disant* university presses are what their names imply. I suspect that some of them are the result of that sort of emulation which forces minor colleges to inaugurate certain courses of study, not because they are needed but because other larger institutions offer them. While almost every important college or university has some sort of publication or printing agency—whatever may be its official title—like applicants for positions in a printing-house, these fall into sub-divisions.

In the first category are commercial printing presses not officially connected with the college they serve but which use a college or university press imprint on work for the institution. Another class has some official connection with the university and takes care of its printing. They might describe themselves more accurately—and modestly—as "Printers to the University." Such presses do not publish books at all, so no equipment for publication is needful. To adopt the nomenclature of the librarian of the University of Omaha, Mr. Robert Frederick Lane, the first of these presses would be an "imprint press," the second an "imprint and printing press." The third variety is an "imprint and publishing press," which uses the university

[189]

imprint and publishes books under it but does not print them. We now come to what we usually think of in using the term "University Press." That is a press which prints, publishes, and sells books under the university imprint and supplies the printing needed by the university. This is the kind of press of which I wish to speak. Of the two hundred self-styled university presses set up in this country, some sixty or more both print and publish under the imprint of the institutions they represent. This class of press is less common, however, than the others.

If we count out the press established in Cambridge under the auspices of Harvard College in 1639, and continuing in existence until 1692, Cornell (a press no longer existing, though such an imprint is employed) appears to be the earliest to use the term "University Press"—in 1869. Notre Dame is the oldest institution to use the term continuously. The largest output of publication in 1940 seems to have come from Columbia, Harvard, Yale, and the University of Chicago, Teachers College and Princeton coming next in order. The relative standing of the presses varies, however, from year to year.

The aim of a university press should be, and is supposed to be, the publication of scholarly work produced in a scholarly way. One of the presses I have mentioned announced its primary aim as follows. It was "to issue books that had an essentially educational value. It was understood that in many cases, these books, whose intrinsic value made their publication desirable, would never yield a profit. A committee was formed whose duty it was to examine works offered for publication. If they were found to be of little educational and scientific value they were refused. If, on the other hand, they were distinctly worthy they were recommended to the Trustees for publication. And in such cases the fact that they might not pay the expenses of publishing did not shut them out from favorable consideration. It is not to be understood that the books published by this University Press were never financially profitable . . . but they were not always paying ventures and were not always expected to be. They were books worth printing and were a part of the educational service of the University to the world." This quotation outlines very well the aim of a "learned" or university press, though I am not in a position to know how well this programme has been sustained by the press whose statement of aims it is. In fact, the claims made for the various university presses in their prospectuses contain a good deal of wishful thinking.

From the typographical point of view the product of the rank and file of these university presses is extremely uneven. Few of them compare favourably with the output of such English presses as those of Oxford and Cambridge. In the annual exhibition of the Fifty Best Books of the Year from 1923 to 1938 only eleven university presses had any representation at all. Of the eight hundred books shown during sixteen years the university press proportion was about one-eighth. Yale, Harvard, Chicago, and Princeton led the list in this order. It is significant that each of these universities had printing plants of their own—in other words, they belonged to the fourth class of press which I have been discussing. It appears that typographical excellence must depend on the enthusiasm of individuals about printing and the types which make printing scholarly and good. Save in cases where this has been in some degree true, uniformity in style has not played much part in the products of a given press. Chicago, Yale, Princeton, and Texas have, among others, tried for consistent styles of work and have issued "style books" to this end. The collection of types shown in the loose-leaf specimen book of Yale issued in 1937 is good, of Chicago University Press, as shown in its *Manual of Style* of 1937, mediocre, and of Princeton, which has issued no recent specimen but whose list of current types I have lately seen, is entirely creditable.[1] Nor is the proof-reading of all university presses by any means impeccable. Not long ago a university press of high reputation printed a book which

was meant to be its author's *magnum opus.* When the book arrived the writer retired to his closet—for some reason writers
and parsons, in trouble, always have closets to retire to—and
when he got there turned his face to the wall and wept over the
misprints he had detected. The list of errors shown me made
tears pardonable. Another establishment of still higher claims
to scholarly distinction, in quoting the famous passage in
Gibbon, where he describes how the thought came to him of
writing *The Decline and Fall,* "Amid the ruins of the Capitol,"
spelled the last syllable of that august word with an *a—Capital.* The displaced *o* flying homeless about (like Noah's dove,
or perhaps more like a cuckoo) finally nested in a collection of
ancient ballads, with the surprising result of *The Not Brown
Maid!* The pirate *u,* no doubt ready to swoop, lurks in the off-
ing. These negligences and ignorances are amusing, but they
are also disheartening. They signify hurried work, careless
proof-reading, slovenly typography. Such things may occur in
commercial printing, but they appear inexcusable in a press
operating under the auspices of an institution of learning.

It has been a tendency of late for a number of the larger
university presses to go into a somewhat ambitious range of
publications. They do not confine themselves to the work of
scholarly teachers or graduates of the colleges or universities
they represent or to works of scholarship of either a profitable or non-profitable kind. Some of them have cast sheep's
eyes at successful publishing firms. To emulate their success,
they allow on their lists of publications books of more popular appeal than a learned and scholarly press has much call
to put out. To compete with publishers such a press is forced
to conform to the methods of publishers, and to tolerate the
kind of output with which a publisher, for purely economic
reasons, has to be content. In the long run this may debase the
kind of product one has a right to expect from a learned press,
eventually deflecting its course from the ideals it should hold
to. There is no valid reason why a university press might not

publish text-books for collegiate and high-school clienteles, and make money by doing so, nor need pamphlets or periodicals be excluded from its output. The Cambridge University Press (England) has been very successful with publications of this class.

One may say that there is no adequate reason why a university press should confine itself to works of scholarship which have very little chance of paying for themselves; and that, for instance, the Oxford University Press publishes miscellaneous books. But not all books bearing the Oxford University Press imprint are of necessity scholarly books. Responsibility for scholarship, format, etc., is indicated by the special imprint, "Oxford: At the Clarendon Press." This has a special meaning, which is that books like Thompson's *Greek and Latin Paleography*, McKerrow's *Introduction to Bibliography*, or Murray's *Aeschylus, The Creator of Tragedy* are published by the authority of the University, and the contents as well as form are certified by the University through the delegates of the Press. In other words, the imprint "Oxford: At the Clarendon Press" is the hall-mark of scholarly work. The imprint "Oxford University Press" does not imply that the books bearing it have necessarily a relation to the University delegates. It is the imprint of a publishing house of very high repute whose English publications are printed at the University Press, Oxford. At the Cambridge University Press there is not the same division of responsibility as at Oxford. Every book published by the Cambridge Press has the approval of the syndics as to its contents. One can also assume the approval of the syndics of the format of the books in its catalogue.

Tendencies towards undue popularization of output of university presses may in time, however, be remedied. In the words of Cowper's hymn,

God moves in a mysterious way
His wonders to perform

[193]

So the fulfilment of what seems startling and fantastic prophecy may come to pass through very commonplace and natural causes. Thus the lion and the lamb may ultimately lie down together, not from change in disposition, but because land is so dear that economically there is nowhere else for them to lie! For analogous reasons American university presses may ultimately be obliged to confine their activities to scholarly non-profitable work intimately connected with the university they serve. For it is a question how long an untaxed university press will be allowed to compete with presses subject to taxation.

If no really outstanding press conceived on the lines I have suggested and connected with a university has been developed in the United States, the chief reasons are a lack of large vision, a practical conception of how to achieve it, a belief in the wisdom of that programme, and an endowment adequate to make this course possible. Of these desiderata the first is in the long run the most important. If one has the vision it will lead him to get the money. Such a press should do the work, ephemeral or otherwise, of the college of which it is a department, but it primarily should exist to publish books that the ordinary publisher cannot afford to produce and could not sell—to issue books independently of commercial consideration which, as contributions to scholarship, ought to be printed. This requires adequate mechanical equipment. It requires a collection of all the best types—and only the most approved types—used in the printing of English. It requires a collection embodying the best Greek and Hebrew types, and so-called exotic types. These may be used very seldom, but they should none the less be available to a learned press. It requires the best library of books of reference available and a working library on the history of printing independent of the library of the university and available at a moment's notice. It requires scholarly proof-readers—a few competent to read and correct Latin, Greek, and at any rate the chief modern languages. That such a press should pay in dollars and cents is very unlikely and this, I may add, is not only a secondary matter but a wrong conception of that for which such an institution should stand. This may sound visionary and idealistic, but there is no serious danger that vision and idealism will become epidemic. I wish I thought so. If, too, we are not to look to universities for idealism in practice as well as precept, to whom shall we look?

The English presses I have named have had a great advantage over American university presses, for they possessed until comparatively recent times a back-log in their monopoly of printing the Bible and the *Book of Common Prayer.* This lack must now be supplied by large endowments or a number of smaller annual gifts. In this country the "back-log" must be something in the nature of an endowment. It may be said with reason that in these uneasy days, endowment of such a press on a large scale is unlikely. An endowment has been defined by President Hutchins of the University of Chicago as a "capital sum, provided from the superfluities of the very rich, the interest on which pays all or part of the cost of an educational activity." And he adds, "Where is the very rich man who feels that he has any superfluous possessions, or even that he is very rich? How can the return on invested capital, at present rates, pay all or part of the cost of anything? . . . People who give away capital are people who have capital to give away. Few endowments have been created out of the annual salaries of the donors." His conclusion is that "for their ordinary needs in less critical times, the universities must look to broad popular support expressed in a large number of comparatively small annual gifts to operating expenses."

This was said in reference to the general maintenance of a university, but it is germane to our subject. Apparently even a great endowment for a learned press cannot be depended on to produce a stated income. If so, is not the simpler and more practical method to aid the development of a university press by smaller gifts and more of them? The sum required annually need not be large. Here again is a task for the educated man who is enthusiastic in his support of scholarly publishing and scholarly printing. Such ventures need enthusiasm and a certain disdain for the politic solution of questions.

In some quarters it has been suggested that the workrooms of a university press could be a kind of classroom for teaching how books should be made and a laboratory for typographic experiment. There it is claimed future master printers might profitably take part. To me this seems a fanciful idea with an impractical application. A going concern cannot stop to teach and experiment for the precise reason that it is "going." There may be, however, a need somewhere for a school that would correct (in the words of a correspondent) "the unfamiliarity of allegedly academic printing houses with the traditions and history of type faces; it would show that the proper use of type faces can only come to one who studies them; and indicate that scholarship is very seriously needed in the printing world and in few places more than in university presses." A university might supply the *rudiments* of such a school but not more than the rudiments. It might provide some very simple apparatus for the teaching of printing processes. Further than that I do not think it could safely go. To carry out, with any completeness or effectiveness, the making of a book involves far more equipment, machinery, and speed in execution than anything in the nature of an experimental laboratory could supply. It is of course open to anyone to make private experiments along these lines, but a thorough knowledge of printing and presswork can probably be most successfully accomplished for beginners by courses in good trade schools.

Furthermore, if even the best of the university presses in this country has not reached its highest ideal in scholarly production and typographic excellence, it is, besides the reasons already stated, through a lack of patrons alive to its needs. We know what great patrons the Oxford Press had in Bishop Fell, Archbishop Laud, Archbishop Sheldon, and Junius. Harvard College had a very early patron in Thomas Hollis, who in

1726 gave founts of Hebrew and Greek characters, and in our day a patron in the late James Loeb.

The Oxford University Press owns over five hundred and fifty founts of type, in some one hundred and fifty different characters, for Sanskrit, Greek, Hebrew, Arabic, Syriac, Ethiopic, Amharic, Coptic, Armenian, Chinese, Tibetan, Burmese, Sinhalese, Tamil, Russian, Gothic, Cyrillic, and Bengali types. The English Cambridge Press also has a fine assemblage of Oriental founts. The University of Chicago Press appears to possess Greek, Hebrew, Syriac, Arabic, Coptic, Ethiopic, Russian, German, Egyptian Hieroglyphic, and Chinese. The Yale University Press owns Armenian, Sanskrit, Arabic, Samaritan, and Nestorian Syriac types. These, however, were bought in Germany by a private individual in 1852 and have but lately come into its possession. This seems again to show that for the acquisition of this kind of material enthusiastic patrons often have to be depended upon.

The kind of education nowadays most valued by the printing industry seems to be technical rather than literary or historical, but none the less in the guidance of a learned press the humanities have a part to play. It is because of this that to the serious and practical man with university training, who wishes to pursue the trade of printing as a vocation, splendid opportunities are offered by working in a great press, wherever it may be, adequately supported by a university and the friends and patrons of that university. "The best use of our colleges," said William James, "is to give young men a wider openness of mind and a more flexible way of thinking than special technical training can generate . . . the habit of always seeing an alternative, of not taking the usual for granted, of making conventionalities fluid again, in a word the possession of mental perspective." This means an educated approach to the problems such work daily presents for solution. I can imagine no employment that will call for more all-round intelligence, flexibility, and cultivation than a place where the highest ide-

als of a learned press are from year to year increasingly fulfilled.

Notes

PUBLISHED: *Some Aspects of Printing*, pp. 60–71.

Delivered as a lecture at Harvard University and Pasadena,
Calif., 1940. Updike believed that it "has been long over-due—or
has long been needed—and is to my mind the most important in
the book" ("Foreword," *Some Aspects of Printing*, p. 2).

1. The Library of Congress copy of *Some Aspects of Printing*
contains an earlier, variant passage that Updike evidently decided
to suppress. The comment about Princeton University Press's
types reads: ". . . of Princeton very poor indeed. A man of educated taste in typography could have discarded three-quarters of
these latter types and done a better job with the remainder."

❧ The Merrymount Press

IN THE DAY'S WORK
By
Daniel Berkeley Updike
.·.
Limited Edition

Cambridge
Harvard University Press
1924

21 Title-page of the special issue of Updike's *In the Day's Work* (printed by the Merrymount Press for Harvard University Press, 1924).

A Description of the Merrymount Press

THE Merrymount Press was begun by Mr. D. B. Updike in the year 1893. It was then a Press in name only, as its actual mechanical work was done by other printers, the style of its work alone being arranged by Mr. Updike. About a year after this experiment was tried, type was acquired in small quantities, and a single fount was cut for the Altar Book [*Fig.* 2] issued by Mr. Updike and the late Harold Brown of Rhode Island. The type of this volume was setup in a small dingy workroom, rented for the purpose, at the back of some warehouses opposite the South Station,—to be exact, at the corner of Estes Place and Aldine Street. The office of the Press was then at 6 Beacon Street, in the building, since torn down, which stood at the corner of Tremont Place. Later the Press was moved to the first floor of a pleasant old house in Tremont Place, formerly occupied by the Winthrop family; and from there, needing larger quarters, to the house at 104 Chestnut Street [*Fig.* 22], where the two lower floors were used as work-rooms and office, and the upper floor was occupied by Mr. Updike himself. Although the next house was later added thereto, these quarters finally were outgrown; and as the introduction of very heavy presses, necessary to increasing work, was impossible in an old building, the present situation at 232 Summer Street was chosen, and has been occupied since 1903

The name Merrymount is derived from the ancient estate of a certain Thomas Morton, an Englishman, who with a company of friends emigrated to New England in 1628 and settled at Wollaston, near Quincy, calling his place Ma-re Mount, or Merrymount, a name still attaching to that neighbourhood. There he set up a Maypole, which is the emblem of the Press

[201]

Mʀ. *D. B. Updike desires to announce that the work of The Merrymount Press requiring larger quarters, he has removed from 7 Tremont Place, to the house number 104 Chestnut Street, a few doors from Charles Street. The present telephone number, 389 Haymarket, remains unchanged. All communications should be addressed The Merrymount Press, 104 Chestnut Street, Boston.*

New fonts of type, some interesting papers, including a supply of old Italian hand-made printing paper, marbled papers of the last century, etc., and other materials for the work of the Press, have been bought during a recent journey abroad. The new types alluded to are supplied, in many cases, specially from old matrices; and fonts of all of them sufficiently large for the printing of books have been obtained.

104 Chestnut Street, 1898.

22   Notice of removal of the Merrymount Press to 104 Chestnut Street, 1898.

[*Fig.* 1], and is intended to signify that one may work and yet have a good time. One of Hawthorne's *Twice-Told Tales* has "The May-Pole of Merrymount" as its theme.

THE ANTE-ROOM

This room, which opens directly from the hallway, is used as the general office of the Press. From it two arched glass doors communicate with the Counting-Room and the Reception Room. These doors, which are of *Directoire* style, were originally in the old Boston Museum Theatre on Tremont Street, and were then windows which opened into balconies overlooking that thoroughfare. On the right of the left-hand door is a framed specimen of *Caractères d'Écriture*, from the Parisian foundry of Léger, nephew and successor of Didot. This rare sheet formerly belonged to the French author and bibliophile, Antoine Auguste Renouard (1765–1853), whose *Annales de l'Imprimerie des Aldes* is still a standard book on the Aldine Press.

On the left of this door hangs a specimen sheet by Baskerville (also from the Renouard collection), issued about 1762, entitled "A Specimen by John Baskerville of Birmingham, Letter-founder and Printer." It contains eight sizes of types. The only other copy of it known is in the Birmingham Free Libraries, Birmingham. Beneath it is the specimen of William Caslon, of 1734.

Between the windows is an announcement, in French, of the sale of the Baskerville types, printed in red and black from Baskerville's characters. This, which was also the property of Renouard, is supposed to be unique. By the phrase "*vis-à-vis les ruines de la Bastille,*" it was evidently issued in Paris *after* July 1789. Mr. Ralph Straus, in his memoir *John Baskerville* (London, 1907), has reprinted this *affiche* in connection with the later history of the Baskerville types. He believes that the sale to which it relates took place about 1800. Beneath is a framed "Specimen of Type used at the Ashendene Press," the gift of its owner, Mr. St. John Hornby.

On the right wall, on either side of the door into the Reception Room, are two Specimens from the Renouard Collection—that on the left, with an extremely effective border, from the foundry of Gillé, *fils*, of Paris; and the other—a particularly fine one—from the foundry of Delalain and Boucher. Beneath the Gillé sheet is the rare "Specimen by Isaac Moore and Co., Letter-founders, in Bristol, 1766." This particular copy is alluded to by Reed in his *History of the Old English Letter-Foundries*, who says: "Renouard mentions a Specimen by Isaac Moore, Bristol, in 1768, of which he possessed a copy mounted on linen and which he describes as displaying '*charactères assez bien gravés, et imitant ceux de Baskerville.*'" Beneath the Delalain broadside hangs a specimen sheet of "Joseph Fry and Sons, Letter-founders, Worship-Street, Moorfields, London, 1785," printed on both sides and therefore framed between sheets of glass.

Over the small service door is a mezzotint of William Strahan (1715–1785), the English printer and publisher, a friend of Benjamin Franklin and of Dr. Johnson, and the publisher of his Dictionary; a member of Parliament and King's Printer. This print is after the portrait by Strahan's friend, Sir Joshua Reynolds, and was executed in 1792 by John Jones.

On the right of the service door into the Library is a specimen sheet of the letter-foundry of Dr. Alexander Wilson & Sons, Glasgow, 1783. Beneath it hangs a specimen of the "learned types" of William Caslon, the younger, issued in 1748. A facsimile of the first known printer's specimen sheet of type—that of Erhard Ratdolt, issued at Venice (though dated Augsburg), in 1486—hangs on right of the entrance, and on the left of the door are facsimiles of the second type specimen sheet known—that of Johan Petri of Basle, issued in 1525—and of the Boston printers, Mein and Fleeming (*c.* 1766).

Over the other service door is a rare mezzotint of Jacob
Tonson (*c.* 1656–1736), the famous London publisher for Dry-
den, Pope, Prior, Addison, and Steele. He was secretary of the
Kit-Cat Club, and this print, by Faber, was after one of the
Kit-Cat portraits painted by Kneller.

THE RECEPTION ROOM

On either side of the entrance door of this room [*Fig.* 23] are
two prints after pictures by Poussin, engraved by Baudet, from
a series of plates now owned by the Chalcographie du Louvre.
These, however, are original impressions. Beneath that on the
left is a copy of Drevet's print of Bossuet—well known in the
history of engraving.

On the left wall is a print of Le Tellier, prefect of the *Bibliothèque Royale* under Louis XIV, after the picture by Largillière.
Below is a portrait of d'Hémery (1722–1806), inspector of the
French publishing trade. In the centre of the left wall is a glass
case which contains various specimens of printing done by the
Merrymount Press. Beyond it is a framed autograph letter of
the celebrated Italian printer, Bodoni of Parma, written to
the artist Rosaspina; and framed with it is Rosaspina's print
of Bodoni, inscribed *Amicus Amico*. Near it is a document ap-
pointing Pierre-Robert-Christophe Ballard as private printer
to the Comte d'Artois, afterward Charles X, on his marriage
with the Princess Maria Theresa of Savoy. It was signed at
Versailles by Louis XV, in September 1773. This document
is countersigned by Phelypeaux, Comte de Saint Florentin, a
print of whom, from a painting by Tocqué, finished in 1740,
and engraved by the German, George Wille, resident of Paris,
in 1761, hangs near by. Phelypeaux was secretary of state to
Louis XV, and to him Louis Luce dedicated the frontispiece of
his celebrated *Essai d'une Nouvelle Typographie,*—a specimen
book of some types and ornaments bought by the *Imprimerie
Royale* at the instance of Louis XV.

On the south wall of the room, on the left, above the *brevet*

23   The Reception Room of the Merrymount Press.

to Ballard, is a large engraving of Robert Ballard II (d. 1673), a distinguished member of this family, who were music-printers to the Crown, and whose catalogue of publications furnishes almost a bibliography of French printed music from 1552 to the middle of the eighteenth century. Beneath is an Italian manuscript indulgence of 1688.

On the right of the window is a photograph of the portrait of Baskerville now in the National Portrait Gallery, the gift of Mr. Emery Walker, associate of the Kelmscott and Doves Presses. In the same frame is an autograph of Baskerville, and a letter from his wife, Sarah, dated Birmingham, 18 March 1779, in which she alludes to sending a copy of Baskerville's Sallust to a purchaser. Below is a copy of Baskerville's "Proposal" for the publication of his first book—the Virgil of 1757—showing a specimen of its types. Beneath this is an engraving by C. N. Cochin, *fils*, of the *Imprimerie du Louvre.*

On the fourth wall of the room, the centre of which is occupied by another of the doors formerly in the Boston Museum, is a portrait of Frederic Leonard of Brussels, engraved by Edelinck after Rigaud, and one of the finest engravings in the iconography of printing. Beneath this is a print after Lawrence's sketch of Horace Walpole (1717–1797),—"Elzevir Horace, as Mr. Conway calls me,"—whose private press at Strawberry Hill connects him with the art of printing. The antique chest of drawers on this side of the room is filled with a collection of decorative engravings of considerable scope and importance, as well as many signed prints presented to the Press by their engravers from time to time. Upon it stand two engravings—one of Walpole's printer, Thomas Kirgate, and the other a decorative medallion of Louis XV. Beside these is an autograph letter from Walpole to Thomas Astle, the author of *The Origin and Progress of Writing,* written from Strawberry Hill on 15 August 1785. A copy of the little book Louis XV printed under the direction of the Parisian printer Collombat, entitled *Cours des Principaux Fleuves et Rivières de l'Europe*—*composé & imprimé par Louis XV, Roy de France & de Navarre, en* 1718, lies beside two framed examples of Henri Didot's microscopic types. On the right of the door is an impression of a large diploma of the Royal Academy, designed by Cipriani and engraved by Bartolozzi. This diploma was granted to a water-colour artist named Edmund Garvey, and bears the autograph of Reynolds as President of the Royal Academy. It is engraved in two pieces, the joining of the plates being concealed by an ingenious *trompe-l'œil*. Beneath, in a frame, are ten tickets of admission to lectures at the Royal Academy, signed by West, President; Richard Cosway, miniature-painter; J. Nollekens, sculptor; Chantrey, sculptor; Stothard, illustrator and painter; James Fittles, illustrator; Northcote, painter; Flaxman, sculptor; Fuseli, painter; and Edward Ward, historical painter.

The seventeenth-century high-boy on the right of the entrance door contains a collection of French, Italian, Swiss, English, and American wood-blocks, both old and new, used in the work of the Merrymount Press. The chief feature of its contents is a series of nearly one hundred blocks, many of them cut by William and Thomas Bewick of Newcastle, about 1780, for the illustrations of *Select Fables*.

THE LIBRARY

This is Mr. Updike's private work-room [*Fig.* 24]. On two sides are open bookshelves. The books printed at the Press occupy three compartments of the bookcases at the end of the room. The other compartment is devoted to volumes which for various reasons are of special interest in the history of printing,—including examples of the work of Aldus, Tory, Ratdolt, the Estiennes, Bodoni, Baskerville, Didot, Ibarra, Pickering, Morris, the Doves Press, the Ashendene Press, the Vale Press, &c. In the two glazed cases on the left side of the Library and the three bays of open bookshelves on the right is a collection of books on the history and technique

24   The Library of the Merrymount Press.

of printing, of considerable importance. This collection has been chosen with a view to the value of the book as part of a working library, and though small, it comprises some hundreds of the best works on the subject, and some rarities. Many valuable books were purchased from a bequest from the late J. Montgomery Sears, Jr. (whose father was also a friend to the Press from its earliest days), and from the late Harold Brown. The specimen books and broadsides include those of Plantin, Bodoni, Didot, Unger, Fournier, Baskerville, Caslon, Wilson, Fry, Luce, Gando, Pierres, the *Imprimerie Nationale* of Paris, the *Imprenta Real* of Madrid, the Oxford University Press, the *Typographia Medicea* and the *Propaganda Fide*, Rome. Many of these books have autograph letters inserted in them or autograph inscriptions; for example, the *Manuale Tipografico* of Bodoni contains a letter from his widow announcing its completion; the Didot specimen, autograph verses by Didot addressed to the Debures; in a copy of Bernard's *Life of Tory* six letters of Bernard are inserted, &c. Among other curiosities is the copy of the Lord's Prayer in 165 languages, printed by Bodoni, and given to Firmin Didot by Eugene Beauharnais, Viceroy of Italy.

The inscription on the weatherbeaten wooden panel at the back of the room above the bookcases was the sign formerly on the outside of the Press in Chestnut Street, and was designed by Mr. Bertram G. Goodhue, the architect. In front of it is a bust of Sir Robert Liston, English Minister to the United States, the gift of the late Charles Eliot Norton, one of the warmest friends of Merrymount. On the central support of the bookcase is an inscription in memory of two friends of the Press, the late John Nicholas and Harold Brown; the latter enabled Mr. Updike to undertake the issue of an Altar Book, which first brought the establishment into notice. Beneath this are four medals, (1) in honour of William Blades, the authority on Caxton; (2) of Senefelder, the inventor of lithography; (3) of Franklin, by Dupré, with the familiar inscription attributed to Turgot; and (4) of the Italian printer, Bodoni of Parma; and some medals awarded to the Press for its work. Over the two service doors are decorative architectural prints designed by Bibiena. Beside one door hang engraved portraits of Beaumarchais, printer of the monumental Kehl edition of Voltaire, engraved by St. Aubin after Cochin; of John Boydell, the famous London publisher, after the portrait by Stuart, and of Francis Junius (1589–1677), benefactor of the University Press, Oxford, to which he gave punches of Anglo-Saxon, Gothic, Runic, and "Icelandic" types. Beside the corresponding door are prints of Richelieu, founder of the *Imprimerie Royale*; Francis I, patron of Garamond; and Archbishop Laud, whose intended benefactions of learned types for a learned press were (with his own head) cut off untimely! On the right side of the room, over the bookcase, are prints of the vestibule of Stᵃ· Maria Maggiore and the Cortile di Belvedere (showing the *Biblioteca Vaticana*, where the first *Stamperia Vaticana* established by Sixtus V in 1587 was placed), after G. P. Pannini; and a portrait of Carlos III of Spain, patron of Ibarra and Bodoni. The inlaid Spanish cross which hangs on a pillar near by was formerly in the sacristy of Burgos Cathedral. On the left side of the room hang two more prints after Pannini, of the interior of Stᵃ· Maria Maggiore, and of the Sistine Chapel (the latter the gift of Miss Amy Lowell). On the side of the glazed bookcase is an eighteenth-century terra-cotta medallion of Franklin, by G. B. Nini. Beneath are other "Frankliniana." On the wall toward the street hangs a remarkable print of Denise Camusat (d. 1675), daughter of Jean Camusat and wife of Pierre Le Petit, both printers to the French Academy; beneath is a frame containing photographs of Georges Lepreux, the lamented author of *Gallia Typographica*; of his publisher, the late M. Honoré Champion, and his son, M. Edouard Champion; a note from Lepreux, and some of his exquisite manuscript. Gaucher's delightful print of Fournier *le jeune* hangs on the neighbouring bookcase; and above, framed, is a bill for printing in the handwriting of Samuel Richardson, the novelist, rendered to A. Millar, the publisher; an item upon it being Richardson's own novel, *Sir Charles Grandison.* In the same frame is an aquatint of Richardson reading *Grandison* (to what Walpole called his "petti-coterie") in his uncomfortable-looking "grotto." Lower down is an autograph of Valentin Haüy, teacher of the blind, whose disciple, Braille, is well known. On the edge of the bookcase above is another of the books mentioned in the account, *The Art of Torment-ing* (the gift of the late Mrs. S. Van Rensselaer Thayer). On the corresponding wall on the opposite side of the room are framed manuscripts, &c., of personal interest to Mr. Updike. Among these are a certificate of membership in the American Antiquarian Society, signed by Isaiah Thomas, and an eighteenth-century document admitting a French printer to the University of Paris in 1762.

The eighteenth-century furniture in this room is American.

PROOF-READERS' ROOM

This room is devoted to the use of the Correctors of the Press—to use the quaint term anciently employed. On the left wall is an eighteenth-century map of Naples. In the corner, on the wall toward the street, are the well-known circular print of Plantin (a gift from the curator of the Plantin Museum, Mr. Max Rooses); a photograph of the room devoted to the Correctors of the Press in the Plantin establishment at Antwerp; and a small print of Justus Lipsius, Corrector of the Press. Near by is a print of Baltasar Moretus of the Plantin-Moretus family. Over the door hangs *Le Bonheur de ce Monde*, printed at the Plantin Press from ancient types (the gift of Mrs. Max Farrand), which completes this group of "Plantiniana."

Between the windows is a portrait of Charles I, engraved by Sir Robert Strange in London in 1770, after the picture by Van Dyck. It is the gift of Mrs. Wharton, the novelist, a valued and effective friend of the Press, whose earlier books were printed here. Next is a map of Rhode Island, published in 1795 by Carter & Wilkinson of Providence, who were printers there in the eighteenth century—John Carter being an ancestor of the founder of the John Carter Brown Library in Providence. This copy was found by the late Daniel Goodwin, among the papers of his ancestor, Mr. Wilkinson. It is the gift of Dr. Goodwin. In the corner is a signed portrait of Charles Eliot Norton, engraved by Kruell (the gift of Miss Sara Norton). Below hangs a copy of a French table for correcting proofs, published at Paris in 1817; and portraits of the late John C. Gray and Mrs. John Lowell Gardner (her gift), who were valued friends, are placed near by.

On the glass screen separating the proof-room from the composing-room are prints of some famous dictionary makers, namely, Worcester; Florio, Latin reader to Queen Anne and compiler of the first English dictionary; Baretti, the compiler of eighteenth-century Spanish-English and Italian-English dictionaries; and Noah Webster, with his autograph. Further on are prints of Samuel Johnson and the Greek scholar, Richard Porson, together with a letter written by him from Eton, on 17 September 1789, to Dr. Beloe, in which a Greek word occurs. The Greek type commonly called "Porson" was named in honour of this eccentric man. Above these hangs a caricature from *Punch*, referring to Mr. Roosevelt's attempt to change English spelling (the gift of the late T. Shaw Safe).

THE COMPOSING-ROOM

This long and narrow room is filled with compositors' cases, a proving-press, imposing-stones, &c., and contains a valuable collection of types and ornaments. The Caslon types are cast from the original Caslon matrices, and many of the ornaments were refitted especially for the Press. In fact, almost all the founts employed are from their original founders and not the reformations, deformations, or transformations too easily obtained elsewhere. The few interesting founts special to the Press are all named after it, viz.: Montallegro, Mountjoye, Merrymount, &c.

Over the green baize door leading into the proof-room is a plaster relief of the Blessed Virgin and Holy Child, after Luca della Robbia. On each side are two old Flemish sconces of engraved brass, which (according to a custom of thirty years' standing) are lighted on the eves of Christmas and a few "gaudy days."

The right wall of the room is hung chiefly with engraved portraits: the first space on the right contains prints of men connected with the history of the four great Polyglot Bibles—the Complutensian (1520), represented by its promoter, Cardinal Ximenez; the Antwerp or Plantin Polyglot (1572), represented by its patron, editor, and printer—Philip II, Arius Montanus, and Christopher Plantin; the Paris Polyglot (1656) by its printer, Antoine Vitré; and the London Polyglot (1657) by its editor, Bryan Walton. This learned but time-serving prelate was helped to complete his work by Cromwell, but on Cromwell's death and Charles II's accession he rewrote part of his preface in honour of the King, styled Cromwell "that dragon," and was made Bishop of Chester for so doing !

Beyond the door, the screen separating the composing-room and press-room is divided into four glazed partitions, and on the supports of these partitions are hung a series of engravings illustrating the history of printing. On the first bay are prints of Antoine Vitré, type-cutter and printer, after the celebrated portrait by Philip de Champagne; of Jean-François Rosart, the inventor of modern music types; of William Caslon, two views of the Caslon foundry, and a rare print of Mrs. Caslon, who for some years successfully conducted the business of this famous house. In the picture of the interior of the old Caslon foundry, the figures at the window are those of Jackson and Cottrell, both of whom afterwards established foundries of their own. The children at the table in the middle are breaking off "jets" from the newly cast type. Nearby is a print of Johannes Enschedé (b. 1708), of the celebrated firm of Haarlem letter-founders, another of the type-cutter, J. M. Fleischman, so much employed by Enschedé, and an eighteenth-century view of the interior of the Enschedé foundry. Prints of Bodoni and Baskerville, who both designed their own types, and of Joseph Jackson and the Caslon foundry as it is today, finish the group.

The second bay of the screen contains more engraved portraits, namely, Sébastien Mabre-Cramoisy (1642–1687), director of the Royal Printing House of France; Aldus Manutius, engraved by St. Aubin; a remarkable engraved portrait of Albizzi, the Venetian publisher, by Piazzetta, who illustrated some of Albrizzi's most important books; Paul Manutius, a companion print to that of Aldus and by the same engraver; Pierre Guillaume Simon, printer to the Parliament of Paris, 1722–1741, engraved by St. Aubin; and Robert Estienne.

The third bay contains the following prints and autographs: Ambroise Firmin Didot; an etching by Webster of the Rue St. Jacques, a street devoted to industries connected with the book since printing was first practised in Paris; Béranger, the printer-poet; Jules Claye, the enlightened Parisian printer, with a letter in his handwriting; a print and an autograph letter of Firmin Didot, written as director of the *Imprimerie Impériale*; Le Mercier, the lithographer, after Devéria; Christopher Oberkampf, printer of decorated linens, or *toiles de Jouy*, whose charming products were made fashionable by royal favour in the reign of Louis XVI, with a letter signed by him; and a print of Balzac, who (though it is generally forgotten) was for a time a printer.

The last bay contains seven more engraved portraits, mostly English. The first is that of William Blades, the learned biographer of Caxton; the next that of William Bowyer, "the learned printer," who is described on this engraving as *Architectus verborum*; and a portrait of William Bulmer (1757–

1830) of the Shakespeare Press, and of James and John Ballantyne, printers of Scott's novels. In the centre hangs an interesting picture of the Court of the Louvre, during the exposition of products of French industry held in the complementary days of the year IX, for which an inscription commemorating stereotyping, by Herhan (mentioned later), was printed. Further along is a portrait of Isaiah Thomas; a print of Benjamin Franklin, designed by Cochin and engraved by St. Aubin; and at the end of the row an autograph letter from Sarah Goddard, one of the first women in the American Colonies to publish a newspaper under her own name. A print of her son, William Goddard, ancestor of the Rhode Island family of that name, hangs near by. Mrs. Goddard, an amusing person of considerable attainments and energy, was the daughter of Lodowick Updike (1646–1736) of Rhode Island. Further on are prints of Thiboust, the Coster Statue at Haarlem, &c. On a case on the opposite side of the aisle is placed a Latin inscription in honour of stereotyping, produced by L. S. Herban in Paris in 1801. Herhan was associated with the Didots in early experiments in stereotyping. The "lay-out" for this inscription, probably in the handwriting of Herhan, is framed with it. Beneath Herhan's inscription is Mr. F. W. Goudy's interesting type specimen.

Opposite the door leading into the press-room are prints of William Goddard, J. I. Breitkopf, John Murray, the publisher, Henry O. Houghton and the late George H. Mifflin of the Riverside Press. In the middle is the framed "specimen" of the titling letters of Léger, the type-founder, nephew and successor of Didot, printed some time after 1806.

Between the windows on the other side of the room are framed specimen sheets of Andre Gallé, *ainé*, of Paris; the Pelican Press, London; the Marchbanks Press, New York, &c., &c. Between the next two windows is a cast of the lion of St. Mark, holding a book, followed by the charming broadside of Mr. Carl P. Rollins's Montague Press. Next comes a page from the Kelmscott edition of Chaucer, a gift to the Press from Mr. Douglas Cockerell; a portrait of William Morris, the printer-poet, the gift of his associate, Mr. Emery Walker; a portrait of Mr. Walker himself; an illustration from Morris's Life of John Ball, Kelmscott edition (given by Mr. E. E. Chandler), and a print of Joseph Moxon. On the same wall is a portrait of Mr. De Vinne and near it a reproduction of Loggan's engraving of Lely's portrait of Bishop Fell. Further on is the rare English specimen of the Phoenix Foundry of Myles Swinney of Birmingham, printed about 1802. Below is a reproduction of an old view of the interior of a sixteenth-century composing-room, engraved by Galle, who worked for Plantin. At the extreme end of the room hangs a framed leaf from William Caxton's *Dictes and Sayings of the Philosophers* (first edition), printed in what is known as Caxton's type 2, in 1477—the earliest English book bearing a date and place of printing—the gift of Mr. E. P. Warren. Above this is the old specimen of Delalain and Boucher of Paris.

The glass screen between the composing-room and proof-readers' room is hung with five very rare examples of Spanish printing. In the centre, on a piece of yellow silk, is a memorial of a mission preached at Saragossa in 1757. The text is printed from type, the border from wood-blocks, and the portrait of St. Peter Nolasco from a copper-plate. The other four are eighteenth-century Valencian typographical essays executed by the famous houses of Monfort and De Orga. These are broadsides in honour of the festival of St. John before the Latin Gate,—traditionally the patronal festival of printers,—and consist of verses in honour of the day. The elaborate decorations made of typographical units represent a printing-press, a tower, a tabernacle, and a pyramid, and were executed, respectively, by Monfort (1771), De Orga (1767), Monfort (1761), and De Orga (1770).

THE PRESS-ROOM

This room, which occupies the remaining width of the building, contains five printing-presses, with stocks of printing-paper, plates, &c. A window to the north commands a varied view of Boston harbour. Between the windows on the east wall are hung views of famous Presses. Beginning at the lower end of the room are cuts of the Harvard University Press, Cambridge, Massachusetts, and the De Vinne Press, New York. The next print is of the University Printing House, Oxford, 1832, engraved by Le Keux, and a view of its quadrangle. Next comes a view of the Pitt Press (University Press), Cambridge, England, while above is a view of the courtyard of the Plantin printing house at Antwerp; beneath it is a view of Hammersmith, which shows the Doves Press (indicated by a cross), the venture of T. J. Cobden-Sanderson and Emery Walker. Next come two eighteenth-century prints of the Clarendon Building (University Press), Oxford, which took its name from Lord Clarendon, the copyrights of whose *History of the Rebellion* accrued for its erection. Between these is a view of Stonor Park, near Henley-on-Thames (the gift of Lord Camoys), where a clandestine Press was established in the seventeenth century by the English Jesuits, Campion and Parsons. Beyond these is a view of College House, Chiswick, where the old Chiswick Press (presided over by the Whittinghams) remained until 1852; and a rare aquatint of the "Farm Yard and Printing House" at Strawberry Hill,—the "Officina Arbuteana," as Walpole jokingly called it (the gift of Mr. Lewis Hatch). On the next space between the windows is still another view of the Clarendon Printing House, Oxford; beyond it are prints of the Lee Priory Press, at Ickham, near Canterbury, established in 1813 by Sir Egerton Brydges. In the centre of the end wall is Loggan's fine seventeenth-century engraving of the Sheldonian Theatre, the basement of which was used as a printing house before the erection of the Clarendon Press—hence the imprint "Oxford: At the Theatre." Beneath it is a view of the

Mission Press connected with the Mission of St. Mary the Virgin, Sagada, P.I., worked by Igorots (the gift of its director, Fr. Stanton), Basire's view of the Sheldonian Theatre, Clarendon Building, etc., and a view of the same buildings in reversed order. The group is completed by a view of the Shakespeare Head Press, the gift of Mr. Newdigate, its director, and a view of the old Ballantyne Press, Edinburgh, and of the hand-press on which Scott's novels were printed.

THE COUNTING-ROOM

This room is occupied by the junior partner, Mr. John Bianchi. It is hung with five prints of Roman buildings, &c., by Piranesi, the one of Stᵃ⁺ Maria Maggiore being from the original edition of Piranesi's etchings—the gift of Mr. George Dorr. On the north wall is a facsimile of the sale sheet of the Elzevir types, many of which were cut by Christoffel van Dyck. The original was issued in 1681. On the west wall hang three very imposing folio engravings of printers to the *Académie Française*—J. B. Coignard I, after Pesne; J. B. Coignard II, after Voirieau; and P. A. Le Mercier, after Van Loo. Beneath this is a print of Sébastian Cramoisy of Paris, appointed by Richelieu as first director of the *Imprimerie Royale* (d. 1669), and a document signed by him. The engraved sheet advertising Piranesi's plates, with additions in manuscript (probably in his own hand), hangs opposite—possibly one of the finest broadside advertisements ever produced. Leaving this room by an arched glass door, we reach the Ante-Room, and the circuit of the Press comes to an end.

PUBLISHED: pamphlet (Boston: Merrymount Press, 1928).

Unsigned. Colophon: "Five hundred and twenty-five copies of this Description of the Merrymount Press, Boston, have been printed for the Members of The American Institute of Graphic Arts, by D. B. Updike, in April, 1928." Other versions of this pamphlet were published in 1913, 1917, 1926, and 1932.

Notes on the Merrymount Press and Its Work

PRINTING became the occupation of my life by pure accident. Books, as literature, have been familiar to me as long as I can remember, for my mother, a woman of very remarkable intellectual powers who knew thoroughly both English and French literature, trained my taste in reading; but I knew nothing about how books were printed or put together. However, an experience that occurred after my father's death in 1878 familiarized me with the outside and inside of many volumes I should never have known about otherwise. This was a winter passed as an assistant at the Providence Athenaeum, when the librarian, being invalided, asked me to relieve him by taking some hours of duty there each day. I had access also to the interesting but then crowded library of Brown University; and when in Newport I spent many hours among the books at the Redwood Library. All this was done without any particular aim. How the books were made never interested me; least of all did it occur to me that I should ever make books myself. But this substratum of familiarity with books of all sorts, their appearance, titles, contents, stood me later in good stead. My mother, who was a thorough student, was impatient at my miscellaneous and ineffective browsings. "You are not a scholar," she used to say. "You do not love to learn as I do." Nor did I love to learn. I was unhappy at school, and as I look back upon it I had reason to be. The only thing I ever got there was a deepened religious sense, for the master, an Episcopal clergyman of real "Evangelical" piety, in the short daily morning talks before lessons began, made an impression that I have never forgotten. Eagerness for knowledge about things I wanted to know was not lacking, but most of the knowledge imparted did not concern the things I wanted to know about. One scar inflicted on me has never been effaced—nor forgiven. On the last Friday of each month a torturing hour was devoted to an exercise called "declamation." I was paralyzed by the necessity of speaking in public, not so much because I feared to speak as because I could put nothing into the dreary selected "pieces" I was set to declaim. Such was my dread of these occasions that by the time the fateful Friday arrived I was ill with apprehension. I trace to these oratorical forced marches a lifelong inability to address with ease any assemblage large enough to be considered an audience. By inheritance I ought to have had some capacity in this direction, for my father and my grandfather were both effective speakers. The latter constantly spoke on public questions and was for many years a factor to be reckoned with in the General Assembly, and my father was presiding officer of the Rhode Island House of Representatives during the first two years of the Civil War.

The temporary employment at the Providence Athenaeum of which I have spoken became more regular on the death of the librarian, and I held for a few months the place of assistant to the librarian *pro tempore* until the election of a new librarian-in-chief. Then came the question: what next was I to do? Some members of my family proposed a position in a bank, being ignorant or forgetful of the fact that I could not then (or now) readily add a simple column of figures. Having made this "gesture," and having met with a refusal—which may be numbered among the few wise decisions of a long life—they washed their hands of the matter and me. College was impossible in the state of our affairs and although I ostensibly regretted this, my previous experience of education was so little alluring that I privately counted necessity a virtue.

But in the spring of 1880 this lull was broken by a telegram from a cousin[1] in Boston: "A place is open for you with Houghton, Mifflin & Company." I replied that I would take the position, and the next day I left Providence for the city where I have lived ever since. The place I was given was that of errand boy—I was told that everyone began there in that way, and I certainly did. The firm had been driven by a fire from its quarters in Park Street and occupied some dreary temporary offices in Franklin Street, near Hawley. The installation was provisional, and as uncomfortable and inconvenient as provisional installations generally are. The *personnel* of the office was unattractive, the hours were long, the duties new and wearisome. Later a return was made to Park Street. But by summer I was so tired that at the end of a two-weeks' holiday, after much searching of heart, I gave up the place. Four days later a letter arrived. The firm was so pleased with my efforts and saw in me (God knows why!) so much promise that I could return on shorter time. That was enough to arouse an already uneasy conscience.

The Park Street offices to which I returned were in a pleasant old house formerly belonging to the Quincy family, fronting the Common, with back windows giving on the Granary Burying-ground. Park Street was still residential, and this situation was an improvement over the Franklin Street quarters. At first my work was much the same. After a time, however, my occupations became a bit more congenial. I began to help the advertising manager in small ways, and was deputed to look through the endless newspapers that came to the firm for notices of its books. It does not seem as if this occupation could have any bearing on my future work as a printer, but it did; for my eye became so trained to the kinds of types employed in the press of the country that I was able to tell at sight from what paper an extract had been cut. My next step was to prepare "copy" for advertisements, and, after a while, to direct how it was to be set up; and this led to making up material for catalogues and revising those already made, and trying to put into them some uniformity of arrangement and harmony of style. The havoc that I created for the compositors and the expense I caused the firm did not occur to me, for since I had never seen type and did not know how it was set (no one thinking it worth while to instruct me), I treated it as if it were made of india-rubber. What those extra corrections must have cost the establishment I have never cared to contemplate.

My expensive performances in this direction arose chiefly from a love of order. The only event I recall that had any effect upon my typographic efforts was an exhibition of early books and manuscripts held by Quaritch of London at the old Tremont House. I visited this exhibition several times and in my work for the firm tried to imitate in a modern way some of the early printing displayed, and, as I look back upon it, anticipated by some years the essays of people who had a definite objective and really knew what they were about. In those days knowledge now commonplace enough was not available, nor were axioms current on unity of style and "rhythm, balance, and colour"—terms which I yet but dimly understand, but evidences of which (I am told by those who know) are often artlessly exhibited in my own work.

I was in the employ of Houghton, Mifflin & Company for twelve years, broken by one short and one long and delightful stay abroad. My interest in typography was even then so slight that I troubled myself little to see fine books when in great centres, or to visit places where good books could be seen. My aim seems to have been *not* to know about printing, but to forget a work that had been so full of drudgery. On my return from my second journey, which lasted a year, and the most interesting parts of which my mother and I passed in Morocco, Spain, and Italy, I began to be treated as a person who had taste in typographical arrangement—a fact which never would have been discovered if after my departure the work I had been accustomed to do had not shown a sudden slump. Instead, however, of making better terms before returning, I went back to Park Street at my inadequate salary and received compliments instead of the dollars I so much needed. But the return was depressing.

And yet the experience of those years—too long drawn
out though they were—was not fruitless. I made in Park
Street some lasting friends: Mr. Francis Garrison, with whose
opinions I wholly disagreed and whose character I as wholeheartedly admired; Miss Susan Francis, assistant editor of *The
Atlantic Monthly*, upon whose efforts a succession of often indolent editors depended for the impeccable scholarship of the
magazine; Dr. Abner Post, of the *Medical and Surgical Journal*, which was published there; and many other interesting
people—Mr. Howells, Miss Sarah Orne Jewett, Mrs. Fields,
Mrs. Bell, Mrs. Whitman, and Mr. Aldrich. In my position
I naturally met Dr. Holmes, Mr. Lowell, Mr. Longfellow,
Mrs. Stowe; and I remember Miss Ellen Emerson conducting
her father to a desk whereon lay a visitor's book in which the
old man tremulously signed his name. Aldrich, then editor of
The Atlantic Monthly, had an office next to mine. His talk was a
constant firework of witticisms. I remember how he confused
the man on the Common who, for a consideration, permitted
one to peep through his telescope, by asking him seriously: "Is
Venus naked to the visible eye?"

Mr. Houghton and Mr. Mifflin both had a sincere desire
for excellence in book-making. Mr. Houghton, the senior
partner, was a Vermont man, and his character had in it much
of "the strength of the hills," though I did not perceive it then.
His taste typographically was of the sixties, and it was a sound
taste of its kind. He had travelled abroad and had met printers
like-minded with himself—I remember a line in one of his
letters: "The people of Holland are industrious and happy,"
which was received by the stay-at-homes with derisive smiles.
To me his manner appeared somewhat hectoring, and perhaps
I had, unconsciously, the power of irritating him. But a gruff
and sometimes rasping speech concealed a tender heart for
those in trouble, especially if they were old associates or former
workpeople. I have seen tears in his eyes as he parted from some
old friend less fortunate in life than himself, who had come to

ask aid, and who was never sent empty away. Mr. Mifflin, of a different outlook on the world, was equally earnest in his wish that the firm publish good and well-made books. To both men a new publication was an event, and they could talk of nothing else until the next publication day with its new books arrived. In particular I remember Mr. Houghton's pride in a new issue of Webster's Dictionary. Everyone who came to Park Street was told of the Dictionary, shown the Dictionary, and—if possible—made to praise the Dictionary. One day Mr. Edwin Whipple arrived. Mr. Houghton showed him the volume, and gently leading the conversation in the direction of further commendation, asked: "Mr. Whipple, when you don't know the meaning of a word, what do you do?" "Well," said Mr. Whipple meditatively, "I generally use another word."

It was a tradition of the establishment that no one—unless for grave cause—was ever dismissed. Accordingly, when persons were not agreeable to those in authority, the tactic of Louis XIV was adopted whereby it was signified to uncongenial courtiers or those who would not "court" that retirement to a distance from Versailles would be appreciated. There in retirement they languished. Something like that happened to me, though for a quite different reason. The work I was beginning to do with efficiency I could do better under Mr. Mifflin's eye at the Riverside Press than in Boston, and so it was thought best that I should be sent to Cambridge. I was sent there, and I, personally, languished to such an extent that after two years of it I decided it was not worth while to languish more. Meanwhile I had, in an inadequate and half-hearted fashion, learned to set type or, more accurately, learned how it was set. And I then also learned how much time and money I had wasted by not knowing this earlier.

In the summer of 1892, while still at the Riverside Press, I was asked by the rector of Grace Church, New York, the Rev. William Huntington, to help him and some colleagues out of a difficulty. The 1892 revision of the *Book of Common Prayer* had just been completed, and a "standard copy" on vellum and an edition on paper had been handsomely printed by Theodore De Vinne in his chilly but workmanlike style. The idea unfortunately occurred to Dr. Huntington, Dr. Doane, Bishop of Albany, and some others that a reissue might be made of this Prayer Book from the existing plates, with margins adorned with symbolic decorative borders. With more haste than discretion they launched the scheme before completing the arrangements for it; and a relative of a member of the committee was chosen to make designs "because he could draw," without much consideration as to whether he could draw what was wanted. When I saw the designs submitted, I also saw the committee's dilemma. The offer of a very decent sum was made if I would plan some general scheme of decoration and select a competent designer. I declined. The offer was doubled. I reluctantly accepted it, and chose Bertram Goodhue to make a series of borders based on the *Benedicite omnia opera*, for which I picked out appropriate texts. In these decorations Goodhue's line was very far from DeVinne's typography, and I fancy it was a painful task for the latter to reprint his uninspired but dignified book with the *appliqués* so continuously, unremittingly (and sometimes unwillingly), supplied by Goodhue and myself. I remember that we begged those in authority to be allowed to omit borders on the Gospel for Good Friday; but this could not be. The borders were to go on *every* page—so the committee had promised—and on every page they accordingly went. The best things about the book were the cover and charming end-papers which Goodhue designed for it. Sad to relate, the edition had an immediate and astounding success! We were congratulated, and we blushed. Our shame was taken for modesty and we were congratulated more! While the book is indeed a strange one, it is by no means so strange as the designs originally made for it. These I preserved until lately as *pièces justificatives* for a performance about which Goodhue and I often exchanged "the augur's wink."

The time spent at the Riverside Press had convinced me that I must do something on my own lines, and through a commission to print an Altar Book [*Fig.* 2], which my old friend the late Harold Brown of Rhode Island stood ready to finance, the opportunity was offered.[2] Had I not had this definite work to do I should not have had the courage to leave my position there. Although I did not then know it, I was starting at a fortunate moment. The repercussion of Mr. Morris' work at the Kelmscott Press was greatly felt in New England. The printing of forty years ago is, to quote a friend's words, "just old enough to awaken reminiscences." "What days those were," he adds, "when we first began to realize that beauty could become, even in New England, an integral part of life. What names rush to our minds: Bertram Goodhue, Will Bradley, Carl Heintzemann, Copeland & Day, and dozens of other brave companions from the time when to be young was very heaven, and we all were young!"[3] With all these men I was acquainted, but Goodhue was the only one I knew well. The best and most consistent printing of that time was done at the instance of Mr. F. H. Day and his partner Herbert Copeland. What they printed was little to my taste, for there was about their performances a certain conscious pose of the kind that made Lord Minto say at the soulful house-party: "I hate clever people—they're so damned silly." But their books were the best of that period.

When I left the Riverside Press in 1893, Mr. Mifflin, who liked my work and had come to trust my judgment, was considerably disappointed, and did not conceal his impatience with my projects; but later our happy relations were resumed, and I always saw him once or twice a year as long as he lived. On these occasions he always said the same words, meant as a compliment. "You know," he would exclaim, "I can only say that I think your success *Perfectly Remarkable!*" He was probably right. As I look back upon it, the venture must have seemed to my elders and betters a desperately silly enterprise,

and they were quite correct in estimating my valour as ignorance. I required capital and had little; comprehension of my
own trade, of which I had less; and business experience, of
which I had none at all. I had no equipment whatever when I
began work on my own account. My innocence was such that
I thought I could obtain orders and have other printers undertake the composition and press-work at my direction; and to
differentiate myself from wiser colleagues, I announced—for
a short time—that I undertook "decorative printing." The result was that though other printers did my work they charged
the prices ordinarily charged to a customer and I had to make
what profit I could over and above that. Thus my prices were
higher than those of other printers, and higher than was warranted by any betterment I could give the work; and when my
results appeared an improvement on current typography, the
printers whom I employed copied the feeble thing they called
my "style" with varying degrees of success. So I was forced to
invest, most unwillingly, in a small amount of type and ornaments, and by this tortuous path I arrived where most printers
begin! Perhaps the reason that I survived, in spite of mistakes,
was that a simple idea had got hold of me—to make work better for its purpose than was commonly thought worth while,
and by having one's own establishment, to be free to do so.

The first quarters occupied by the Press consisted of two
connecting rooms on the upper floor of a building at the corner of Beacon Street and Tremont Place. These rooms, which
were lofty of stud, had been formerly occupied by an architect,
who had installed a tasteful wooden mantel-piece and a hearth
on which it was possible to light a fire. The narrow windows,
lofty ceilings, and hardwood floor made a good background for
some pieces of old furniture, which presented a much better
effect than the office equipment of that day. The back room,
looking out on an angle of the Boston Athenaeum, was occupied by Mr. J. E. Hill, who did much of the designing of ornament which I required, as well as work on his own account.

The first book printed under my supervision was a volume of selections for each day in the year, compiled by Lucy Bradlee Stone, under the title *Vexilla Regis Quotidie.* The Riverside Press was responsible for the composition and press-work, but the arrangement of the little volume was mine. Originally privately printed, it became by the printing of a second edition in 1895 the first book bearing my name as publisher. It was set in a "modernized old style" type.

Several other books were printed while the Altar Book was being planned and produced, and before any varied stock of type was acquired. Perhaps the best one was *The Hazard Family of Rhode Island*, 1635–1894, a genealogical book by Caroline Robinson, the expense of production of which was borne by her sister, Sarah Rodman Woodward. This book, issued in 1895, was very carefully schemed and was set up by that conscientious and thorough craftsman, the late Carl Heintzemann of Boston. Its decorations were redrawn from the fine series used by the eighteenth-century London printer Bowyer—ornaments among the best of their kind, and splendidly used in some of his folios. These embellishments, with strips of Caslon "flowers," were combined in a quarto book set in various sizes of Caslon type.

After a stock of type was acquired, the first volume set up by us was *The Governor's Garden,* by George R. R. Rivers, a romance based on the life of Governor Hutchinson and his house at Milton. I was familiar with this place, which belonged to the author's aunt, Miss Rose Russell, and the garden with its arbours and pleached alleys remained much as the Governor had left it. It occurred to me to illustrate the book with a series of fictitious silhouettes representing the characters of the story. The headpieces, each one different but all made up of combinations of but two Caslon "units," were the clever arrangement of Mr. John Bianchi, then foreman of our composing-room. What I remember chiefly, however, is the small amount of type I had with which to print, and the patience of the author under the consequent delay. The "period business" is perhaps a bit overdone for the reader's comfort, but its format attracted considerable attention when the book came out in 1896.

The same year saw the second of my few publishing ventures, in Hans Andersen's *The Nightingale*, cleverly illustrated by Mary Newill of the then popular Birmingham Guild of Handicraft, for whose short-lived magazine *The Quest* we also were agents. My old friend the late Edward Hort New of Oxford contributed some charming illustrations to that periodical, as did Gere, Gaskin, Miss Newill, and others. And in the same year the Altar Book [*Fig. 2*] appeared.

It was largely the dissatisfaction felt with the "decorated" Prayer Book that suggested the publication of this volume, and Mr. Brown, who was of my way of thinking in such matters, stood ready to back the undertaking. His stipulations were that the book should be as fine a piece of work as I could make it, and that while strictly conforming to the text of those parts of the *Book of Common Prayer* containing the altar services, it should yet fall in line with missals of an older period. When musical notation is introduced, the canon law of the Episcopal Church allows a departure from the uniformity required for all service books without music. Accordingly a few notes of plain-song were placed before the collect for the First Sunday in Advent, with which the book opened. Thus the book was strictly canonical, and having received the authorization of the Rev. Samuel Hart, the registrar of the *Book of Common Prayer,* we were able to place "By Authority" on the title-page. Dr. Huntington, when he saw the volume (which he did not much like), exclaimed: "'By Authority'! We must look into that!" But as when he looked he found nothing to see, we heard no more about it.

To enumerate the difficulties met with at that period in obtaining what is now easily available would take longer to tell than is here desirable. It is enough to say that after various essays a type was designed for the book by Bertram Goodhue, who also drew the borders and initials—no two of the latter exactly alike—the illustrations being by Anning Bell. The amount of work the undertaking involved was increased by the difficulty in obtaining hand-made paper, in cutting the type, and by various troublesome details. And when the type was designed and cast a separate workshop had to be found where it and a hand-press could be installed and a proof-reader could work. For this purpose an office at the corner of Aldine Street and Estes Place, near the South Station, was rented, and there, through a hot summer, the work was carried on. The press-work was placed with De Vinne, who turned out a magnificent piece of work, although he was frankly out of sympathy with the style of the volume. Begun in 1893, the book was finished at Easter, 1896.

Whatever satisfaction I might have taken in its completion was destroyed by my mother's sudden illness and death, which seemed to deprive me of any incentive to continue along the path on which I had set out. Probably I should not have gone on if I had not already had the nucleus of a tiny organization. When at the Riverside Press I had made the acquaintance of Mr. Anselmo Bianchi, and when I started for myself I asked him to join me. This he could not do, since he was bound by an indenture for a certain period of service there, but he suggested his brother as a man suitable for the place. It thus came to pass that John Bianchi came to the Press. He was later joined by his brother Anselmo, who remained with us for several years, finally returning to the Riverside Press in a position which he has developed into an important one. Miss Ellen Powers, also a former employee of Houghton, Mifflin & Company, was acting as proof-reader and accountant at that time. To the loyalty, patience, and confidence of these three, and to friends who supplied work to do, the Press owes its existence in those early and difficult years. In looking back one realizes the truth of Emerson's phrase: "Every man's task is his life preserver."

The following summer I passed abroad. In London I visited Kelmscott House, where I was kindly received by Mr. Cockerell. This was shortly after Mr. Morris' death, and the London Society of Arts and Crafts was at the moment holding an exhibition where the Kelmscott books were magnificently displayed. I remember making some rather ineffective researches at the British Museum, and there meeting Mr. Alfred Pollard; our first contact with the Caslon house was also made at this time. Between this date and 1914 I made several other foreign journeys, but as I travelled chiefly in Spain and places somewhat remote from printing interests these have little to do with this narrative. I did, however, go to Parma on one of these journeys and saw the splendid collection of Bodoni's books preserved in the library there, and I also went to Mainz and Leipzig. And on my last foreign journey I visited the Plantin Museum at Antwerp, partly because I was so tired of saying "No" when anyone asked if I had seen it. I doubt if visits to homes of great and good printing amount to much except from the sentimental point of view. To my mind, a printer can learn more from a few visits to such an exhibition of printed books as is shown in the King's Library of the British Museum than by desultory wanderings to less well arranged and more distant collections.

Owing to the demolition of the Beacon Street building in 1896, the Press, so called, had to go elsewhere, and rooms were secured in a building round the corner, at 7 Tremont Place, in a house formerly, I believe, occupied by the Winthrop family. The ground floor was used by our landlords, Messrs. Ginn & Company, as a shop or shops, and we occupied the next floor, or "noble storey," consisting of two drawing-rooms connected by folding doors and a small side room occupied as a private office. The front room on Tremont Place covered the width of the house, and here a composing-room was installed; the back room, which commanded pleasant glimpses of the Granary Burying-ground, was the general office.

It was while occupying these quarters that I first met Mr.

[233]

Bruce Rogers. I was already familiar with a book in which he had had a hand—*Notes on the Walters Collection*—so he needed no introduction. The splendid results of his eighteen years' work at the Riverside Press are known of all men. At that early period we saw much of each other, both in town and in country, for in summer I had a country house at Harvard, Massachusetts, where he, Cleland, and others were often visitors.

The further story of the Press, from this time on, is chiefly the history of such outstanding books as it has printed year by year, save for those years—and they were not uncommon—when nothing interesting is to be chronicled. A connection with the house of T. Y. Crowell & Co. of New York that lasted for a long period was inaugurated in 1897 by the appearance of a book, set in Clarendon type, called *What is Worth While?*, which in my absence abroad was planned by Mr. John Bianchi. This book showed the influence of Mr. Morris' ideas upon commercial work, and the long series of similar 16mo volumes printed for this house followed the general style of the first one, though with varying degrees of success. The covers—rather tasteless affairs—were usually supplied by the publishers, though this first book and *Ships and Havens* had the advantage of a binding designed by Bertram Goodhue. Our first use of Scotch-face type was made in the same year for Messrs. Crowell & Co. in a little book by Richard Le Gallienne entitled *If I were God*.

We remained at 7 Tremont Place only two years, for in 1898 another move became necessary when the whole row of old houses had to make way for an office building. The next situation for the Press was 104 Chestnut Street—commonly called (since those were the days of stables in that neighbourhood) "Horse Chestnut Street" [*Fig.* 22]. This house was three storeys high, and had two large and two small rooms to a floor. The composing-room was placed on the first floor, the main office on the second at the back, my own office on the same floor at the front, and a proof-readers' room in a hall bed-room. Two views in this book show the library in this modest Victorian dwelling-house. The third storey I at first occupied as an apartment. Later on, in 1903, we utilized the third storey as a proof-readers' room and added No. 102 Chestnut Street to No. 104, connecting the lower floors of both houses and using them as a composing-room. The two upper floors of No. 102 I moved into, this apartment being completely sepa-rated from the Press.

In 1899 appeared under my imprint a book that had a family interest, namely, a diary kept by my great-great-uncle, James MacSparran, D.D., between the years 1743 and 1751. MacSparran was an Anglican missionary sent to Rhode Island from London by the Venerable Society for the Propagation of the Gospel in Foreign Parts. There he became rector of St. Paul's Church, Narragansett. His diary is a quaint affair recording the daily life of an American Parson Woodforde. In printing it I conformed to his manuscript—superior let-ters, odd spelling, and all. This volume was edited by the Rev. Daniel Goodwin, a former rector of the same church.

The Press has been fortunate in its friends, but never more so than in the friendship of Mrs. Wharton. I had known her before she wrote *The Greater Inclination*, her first book of short stories, and when the volume came to be published, in 1899, she stipulated with the Scribners, who issued it, that I should be employed to print it. In this and in all her later books that we printed, we employed a Scotch-face type that, common enough in England then and in America now, had not be-fore been used for fiction in this country. To Mrs. Wharton's thoughtful act the Press owed not merely the prestige of print-ing her books, but also the printing of many other volumes for Scribner's—indeed we were constantly employed by the firm until it set up a press of its own. Nothing could have helped the Press more, just then, than the Scribner connection, for it showed we were not amateurs but could hold our own with larger printing houses; and this was all due to the friend who used her influence as generously, intelligently, and effectively then, as many times before and since, for persons or causes that she thought deserved a "lift." Besides the volume mentioned the following books written by Mrs. Wharton were printed here: *The Touchstone* (1900); *Crucial Instances* (1901); *The Valley of Decision* (1902); *Sanctuary* (1903); *Madame de Treymes* (1907).

The most ambitious book of 1900 was printed for Mrs. J. V. L. Pruyn—a description of a pastoral staff given by her to the Diocese of Albany. The pictures of the staff were reproduced in photogravure, which made an odd alliance with a text set throughout in black-letter type. Goodhue designed the elaborate frameworks of the opening pages and, in fact, all the decorations and the binding. The book is an exhibition of his cleverness as a draughtsman rather than of any skill of mine.

In the same year a little book that had a great success was printed for Scribner's, set in Scotch-face type. This was Stevenson's *Christmas Sermon*, bound in boards, with a green cloth back and paper sides of that gloomy shade of blue known to my childhood in Seidlitz powders. This was reprinted several times, and was followed by a number of short essays in the same format. A genealogical book of importance typographically, set throughout in Caslon, was *Mumford Memoirs*, by my old friend the late Dr. James Gregory Mumford. Another genealogy was printed for the late Josiah Henry Benton, the first of a series of books brought out by him. The best of these volumes were the catalogue, set in Mountjoye and Oxford types, of his splendid collection of English and American Prayer Books now in the Boston Public Library; and a memoir of Baskerville, read by Mr. Benton before the Society of Printers and printed later in amplified form—a book now rare and much sought after. For the latter we used a Caslon type of the period when Caslon's founts showed the influence of Baskerville, and its title-page is a good bit of "period" printing. Between Mr. Benton's wife and my mother's family there was an ancient friendship, though I became aware of this only after our first meeting. Mr. Benton, under a brusque manner, concealed great sensitiveness and a warm heart; but these were not always apparent. On my first visit to him at his office in the Ames Building accompanied by Mr. Bianchi, Benton, expecting to see one person and seeing two, exclaimed: "Who's that?—plumber's helper?"

Possibly the most ambitious "period" book in the so-called colonial style that we ever attempted was an edition in quarto of Irving's *Knickerbocker's History of New York*, printed for R. H. Russell in 1900. The arrangement of its complicated and voluminous preliminary matter I am proud of, and the book "hangs together" in spite of Maxfield Parrish's eight illustrations (then the vogue), which are only pseudo-"colonial." This volume was set up at the Press, though it was printed outside it. A catalogue of Doubleday, Page & Co.'s books also deserves attention for its use of Clarendon type—one of the few times I have used it to my own satisfaction.

Mr. Charles Goodspeed first became a customer in 1901 by commissioning me to print Sanborn's *Personality of Thoreau*. For this slim volume, printed in a limited edition, Scotch-face type, much leaded, was used, printed on a highly calendered paper, with some copies on Japan paper. The result was a somewhat attenuated elegance, but it found favour and was followed by more books in the same style. A more sympathetic piece of work was a little volume printed for Miss Sarah Cooper Hewitt called *Some Old Letters & Bits of History*, a paper written by her aunt, Margaret Adelia Cooper. Its cover of Empire paper, with white label, yellow edges, and end-papers printed from wood-blocks in green and pink, and the Bewickian decorations accord with its leisurely well-bred text. The book-marker in blue and pink was much consulted about, and Miss Hewitt—very much *la maîtresse-femme*—adjured me that under no possible pretence should like end-papers and ribbons adorn the books of any other living being! Only two hundred copies were printed, to be used as gifts.

Two French *bâtarde* types that I acquired in Paris were first used in a tiny rubricated volume printed for Edwin S. Gorham of New York, *The Form of Solemnization of Matrimony*, issued in 1901. We later used the same type in a circular, *Merrymount: Being a few Words on the Derivation of the Name of The Merrymount Press*, brought out after our removal to Summer Street. Of these two interesting founts, the larger is a true *bâtarde*, the smaller a *lettre de somme*. The same year brought to the Press the service for the consecration of a lifelong friend, the late Charles Brent, as Bishop of the Philippines; several of Brent's books we afterwards printed. This service was one of a long series of similar services for consecrations of bishops and of churches, the institution of rectors, and the like, that have been printed here. As these ceremonies usually included a celebration of the Eucharist, we began the composition by first printing the two pages containing the prayer of consecration facing each other and worked back from that point, so there should be no noise of turning leaves at the most solemn moment of the service. All "turnovers" were planned as far as possible to occur at liturgical points when they would not disturb the congregation: for three thousand people turning a leaf at once gives the effect of the sudden flight of a flock of pigeons.

The year 1902 was marked by my publication of *Four Addresses*, by Henry Lee Higginson. Its cover, as were those of several other books printed at the Press, was designed by Mrs. Henry Whitman, a figure in the artistic circles of Boston, who for many years designed the best of the covers for Houghton, Mifflin & Company's books. She was a woman of taste and charm, though the personal impression she produced was perhaps greater than any definite accomplishment. Somewhat fantastic in phrase and manner, she dealt with us, to use her own words, "very handsomely." I remember at the first exhibition of the Society of Arts and Crafts, in 1897, on seeing a folio leaf of our Latin Tacitus set in Goodhue's Merrymount type, she cried: "Phoebus, what a page!" This year saw also the beginning of a set of octavo books finished in 1903—*The Life and Works of Charles Lamb*—printed in Scotch-face type and issued in twelve volumes for the Pafraets Book Company of Troy, New York.

The Poet Gray as a Naturalist, edited by Charles Eliot Norton, is an essay based on a copy of a book in Mr. Norton's library—the *Systema Naturae* of Linnaeus—interleaved for annotation and illustration by Thomas Gray. From the text pages and those interleaved a few of the most interesting drawings were chosen for reproduction, and selections from Gray's manuscript notes were also printed. These facsimiles are extraordinary pieces of reproduction. The book was published by Goodspeed in an edition of five hundred copies in November 1903—or so the colophon says—though as I recall it, it was early in December and much too late for the Christmas trade. As I look back I am impressed with the casual manner in which I then regarded practical affairs.

Mr. Norton was from the beginning of our work most sympathetic and helpful. We were brought together more particularly because of some projects for an endowed University Press at Cambridge. He gave my own Press one or two books to print, presented it with proofs of interesting types and ornaments, and placed at our disposal any books in his library at Shady Hill. He was a great aid in these early years, before other people had found me out or—what was more important—I had "found" myself. But about the business end of the Press he was always a bit nervous, fearing that it might be diverted from the Service of Beauty to the Worship of Mammon; and he grieved at my "defection," as he considered it, when we abandoned the amateur atmosphere of Chestnut Street for the commercial air of Summer. In vain I pointed out that the presses would go through the floor if we had to install them in Chestnut Street. I had, he thought, gone over to the "enemy," though what particular enemy he was loath to specify. For as work increased it was obvious that however much we enlarged the Chestnut Street quarters we could not go on without printing-presses, since without our own machines our press-work was uneven and expensive. The construction of the Chestnut Street houses would not bear much weight, and if a press-room were built out over the small back-yard, this would consume capital and obstruct light. Wandering about in the neighbourhood of the South Station one Sunday afternoon, I found a building just completed on Summer Street, and the top floor, although only a well-built loft, seemed to have possibilities. After much cogitation this floor was taken. Some old glass Directoire doors[+] I had found in East Cambridge, which formerly figured in the Tremont Street façade of the old Boston Museum, were fitted into "compo board" partitions, arranged as nearly as possible on an axis in a building in which nothing was symmetrical. To the old furniture we had, more pieces were added—notably some fine chairs, the gift of two well-disposed friends; and a collection of framed engravings pertinent to printing was begun. All this gave the rooms a certain effect. Three presses were installed and a decent composing-room was arranged. The offices consisted of an ante-room, a reception room, a counting-room, and a library. It was from this locale that we issued the first of a series of illustrated pamphlets describing the Press. All our work was done here for twenty-eight years. It is amusing to remember with how much perturbation of spirit we made each move, only to regret that it was not made long before.

No particularly interesting book was produced in 1903 except the two-volume set of the poems of Dante Gabriel Rossetti—the Cheyne Walk edition—edited by Herbert Copeland, of Copeland & Day, and with a decorative design on the title-page by T. M. Cleland, who also designed the cover. Set in Caslon throughout, the book somewhat reflects the aesthetic movement of which Rossetti was patron saint.

Cleland had been living in Boston a little before this time and occupied a small studio, or office, in Cornhill, which was then more of an old-world locality than now, the picturesque effect of its low brick buildings on the curve of the street being then unspoilt by modern erections. Besides designing, Cleland produced several little books at what he called the Cornhill Press, which, like my own, was a press only because we chose to call it so. Our friendship—and I may add my admiration of his talents and his work—dates from those remote days. He was an idealist—quite impractical—often in difficulties; but he produced delightful things then, as in maturity he has continued to do. Perhaps none of us at that period were very sensible or businesslike, and if we had been would never have been heard of more.

Of the long series of music-books turned out for Messrs. Oliver Ditson Company under the title *The Musicians Library*, the major part consisted of lithographic music, all we contributed being the title-pages and introductory matter. For this reason these are not included in the list of work. In this connection sheet-music covers should be mentioned. These were executed chiefly for Schirmer of Boston and New York, the larger number being printed for the New York house. For these titles little money was available, and most of them had to be produced in a hurry. How to vary them attractively without expense was the problem. Some could be printed solely from type and type-ornaments, but for those requiring decoration we reproduced designs from the engraved ornamentation of the seventeenth and eighteenth centuries. A collection of such engraved work belonged to the Press, and we drew from these plates and procured others for the purpose. Many of the most successful designs were reproduced from the elaborate and often beautiful *cartouches* on old maps. Others were taken from the *Chinoiseries* of Pillement, designs by the Du Cerceau and other *maîtres ornementistes*, Pompeian wall-paintings, German silhouettes—everything conceivable was pressed into service.

We continued to turn out this work until 1914.

Music programs also were brought to the Press to be printed. Among the earliest friends of my undertaking was the late Montgomery Sears, whose house during his lifetime and since has been known for the *musicales* at which famous artists have assisted. The programmes for these concerts Mr. Sears always brought personally to the Press to be printed, and these leaflets brought that class of our work into notice, leading to more commissions from other quarters. As I look back on the small beginnings of my establishment, I am grateful for the sympathetic interest in its work that my friends have all along shown. I like to record here in addition to those mentioned in connection with the books I am describing the names of others—and these are by no means all—who in ways great and small have been as friendly as Mr. Sears was in those early days: Bishop Brent; Mrs. John Carter Brown; Mrs. Harold Brown; Mr. and Mrs. John Nicholas Brown, Sr.; Mr. John Nicholas Brown, Jr.; Mrs. William Gammell; Mr. John Chipman Gray; Miss Eleanor Burges Green; Miss Belle da Costa Greene; Mr. Rowland Hazard; Miss Caroline Hazard; Mrs. Cadwalader Jones; Mrs. William Vail Kellen; Mr. Henry W. Kent; Miss Amy Lowell; Mr. John Pierpont Morgan, Sr.; Mr. John Pierpont Morgan, Jr.; Dr. Charles L. Nichols; Miss Elizabeth Norton; Mrs. J. M. Sears; Mr. Edward Perry Warren; Professor Barrett Wendell; Mrs. Henry Whitman.

The year 1904 was to us notable for the launching of a type designed for the press by Herbert Horne of London, whose essays in typography in *The Hobby Horse* had already attracted attention. The type was a roman letter of fourteen-point size modelled on early Florentine founts, named Montallegro as an Italian equivalent of "Merrymount." Horne stipulated that the first volume printed in it should be designed by him, and for the text he employed his own translation of Ascanio Condivi's life of Michael Angelo, or, as Horne preferred to call him,

Michelagnolo Buonarroti. He chose as a format for the book a small square quarto resembling early Florentine woodcut books, with type closely and solidly set; and he also designed the title-page and initials. This type was afterwards employed in volumes of *The Humanists' Library*, where it had a more open and, I think, more agreeable treatment. Horne afterwards designed for other firms two similar types, the Florence and the Riccardi, all three being cut by E. P. Prince, who executed the types used by Morris and Cobden-Sanderson. I have never considered Montallegro a complete success—there is about it a rigidity which makes one conscious of the type instead of the text. The same year Bertram Goodhue's Merrymount type, hitherto used only in the Altar Book, was utilized for a large folio edition of the *Opera Minora* of Tacitus, a text suggested by Mr. Norton and edited by the late Professor Morris Morgan of Harvard University. Only one hundred copies were printed of this volume, which was designed to display the Merrymount type—a fount solely adapted to an enormous page. I sent specimen pages of the book abroad, and our choice of this text suggested its use to the Doves Press, whose first book, the *Agricola* appeared in 1901.

Another book which attracted attention for its type was Thackeray's *Letters to an American Family*, printed for the Century Company, New York. Here we employed a Mountjoye (or, as it would now be called, "Bell") fount, and although this was not its first use by us, it was our first use of it in a book of popular appeal. This Mountjoye type was much the same, if not the same, as some founts existing at the Riverside Press known in my time as "copper-face," but afterwards called "Brimmer" because they were first used in an address by Martin Brimmer, delivered at Wellesley College at the opening of the Farnsworth Art School. This address was published in October, 1891, and its format and typography were designed by Mrs. Henry Whitman, who was a great friend of Mr. Brimmer's. Mrs. Whitman also arranged the more ambitious volume by Mr. Brimmer, entitled *Egypt*, which was printed in the same type and published at the Riverside Press in December, 1891.

For the Mountjoye type I traced the history of the fount until I found what British type-foundry owned the matrices and then obtained strikes of them for our own casting. As I write, this fount (discovered by Mr. Stanley Morison to be the production of John Bell of London, 1745–1831)[5] has just been placed on the market—twenty-nine years after its first use by the Press in a little volume of sketches by Frances Dabney entitled *Saudades*, privately printed in 1903 for Miss Amy Lowell. This same type was also used in 1904 for the text of a fourteen-volume set of the Bible printed in several editions on various papers for the R. H. Hinkley Company of Boston. With the commonplace illustrations we had nothing to do—except to deplore their use; and of the various bindings only those in cloth were ours.

One more book must be mentioned under 1904: *The Letters of Three Dutiful & Affectionate Rhode Island Children to their Honoured Parents*—the children being Master Nicholas, Miss Hope, and Miss Joanna Brown, whose letters were written between 1779 and 1781. This and two succeeding volumes, *The Course of True Love in Colonial Times*, issued in the next year, and *James Browne—His Writings in Prose and Verse*, printed in 1917, seem to me as good "colonial" typography as the Press has ever put out [*Fig. 25*]. But few persons have ever seen these books, for the limited numbers printed were chiefly for family distribution.

A volume devoted to the dedication of the John Carter Brown Library in 1903, issued in 1905, was the beginning of a long connection that still continues with this library, of which I am a member of the board of management. In the following year use was made of the Mountjoye type in *The Life of Benvenuto Cellini*, for Brentano's, New York. The title-page of this edition was designed by Cleland. The edition was a great

JAMES BROWNE
HIS WRITINGS
In Profe and Verfe

Concerning the *Firſt Settling* of the Town of *Providence* and a Memorandum of his Efforts to prevent a Separation in the *Baptiſt* Congregation there in *Oƈtober*, 1731: Together with Some *Metrical Obſervations*

Therefore I pray You be ſo kind
In theſe Few Lines proceed
And ſomething in them You ſhall find
That's worth Your While to read

Printed by *D. B. Updike* at *The Merrymount Preſs* in *Boſton*, Maſſachuſetts, 1917

25   Title-page of *James Browne: His Writings in Prose and Verse* (Merrymount Press, 1917).

success, but the early issues are the only ones in which the presswork was executed here. Later editions showed an unfortunate declension in this feature.

In the next year the first volume in *The Humanists' Library* was published. This series was under the general editorship of Lewis Einstein, and Maurice Baring translated for its initial issue Leonardo da Vinci's *Thoughts on Art and Life*. These books employed, as I have said, Horne's Montallegro type, and for them Horne designed the initials and title-pages of the first series, which consisted of four volumes in editions of 303 copies. The other three volumes of the first series were *Erasmus Against War*, edited by J. W. Mackail, brought out in 1907; *Petrarch and the Ancient World*, by Pierre de Nolhac, issued in 1907; and Sidney's *Defence of Poesie*, edited by George Edward Woodberry, issued in 1908.

In January 1906, we printed a handbook of an exhibition, *The Development of Printing as an Art*, arranged in honour of the bicentenary of Benjamin Franklin by the Society of Printers of Boston. This modest organization—of which I was at one time president—still exists, largely because, having no definite programme, it has done such necessary work as occasion has presented. Their show was held at the Boston Public Library, and I had a hand in the preparation of the text of its catalogue as well as charge of its typography. Many of the specimens exhibited came from our library. A somewhat elaborate volume was also issued in 1906 for the Club of Odd Volumes, Harold Murdock's *Historie of the Life and Death of Sir William Kirkaldy of Grange, Knight* [*Fig.* 26]. The decorations and initials for this edition of 114 copies were cut on wood, and although great pains were taken with the entire production, I have never thought the book as successful as it should have been. It was printed from a late Caslon fount.

I must mention Mrs. John Lowell Gardner as another good friend to the Press. The pamphlet guide for visitors to her house, Fenway Court, we printed for many years. On

HISTORIE OF THE LIFE AND DEATH OF
Sir William Kirkaldy
of Grange, Knight

WHEREIN *is declared his many Wise Designs and Valiant Actions, with a True Relation of his Heroic Conduct in the Castle of Edinburgh which he had the Honour to defend for the Queen of Scots. Now set forth from Authentic Sources by* HAROLD MURDOCK.

PRINTED *for* The Club of Odd Volumes *at* BOSTON *in* NEW ENGLAND *in the Year of Our Lord*, MDCCCCVI

26   Title-page of *Historie of the Life and Death of Sir William Kirkaldy* (printed by the Merrymount Press for the Club of Odd Volumes, 1906).

each revision I spent a morning there, and Mrs. Gardner and I, acting as "visitors," made a tour of the house, guidebook in hand. In this way we were able to test the convenience of arrangement in each succeeding issue. These mornings were always enlivened by Mrs. Gardner's talk about her acquisitions and the way in which she came to possess them. One of our dealings was, however, less fortunate. Mrs. Gardner had endeavoured to have prepared for her a catalogue of her books, and, failing to find the desired co-operation in several quarters, she decided to compile it herself, entitling it *A Choice of Books from the Library of Isabella Stewart Gardner, Fenway Court.* Now the compilation of catalogues, like the keeping of hotels, appears within the powers of most Yankees until they try it; and Mrs. Gardner's cataloguing was no better nor worse than the work of most amateurs. When the manuscript was in type I detected so many errors that I was sure there were more, and so I told her. But she was positive that all was right, and in spite of my begging that some competent person might revise the work, she held to her opinion. We accordingly printed the catalogue as it stood, but omitted the imprint of the Press. When the volume was distributed—it was privately printed in 1906—numberless errors were found, and the omission of the imprint was (I hoped) thereby accounted for. No one was very happy about the matter, least of all Mrs. Gardner, who corrected in pencil such errors as she caught and sent the book out, its blunders naturally being attributed to our carelessness. Some of my friends (who perhaps did not know Mrs. Gardner) said I should not have "permitted" her to make such mistakes. Mr. Norton in particular was severely critical and declared one evening at Shady Hill, in the presence of a number of people, that I should have insisted that some competent person look over the final proofs. "But I did suggest a very competent person," said I, "and it was not well received." "Whom did you suggest?" asked Mr. Norton. "You, sir," I replied. Everybody laughed, and the point was not laboured—nor I belaboured further. For some time after this my friendship with Mrs. Gardner, as Horace Walpole said of his with Lady Lucan, "rather waned than improved." But before long the difficulty was forgotten—indeed, we printed in 1922 a companion volume, *A Choice of Manuscripts and Bookbindings from the Library of Isabella Stewart Gardner, Fenway Court*. Mrs. Gardner was then ill and the consultations about the book were held in her motor, in which, rain or shine, she punctually kept any appointment she had made. "You must hurry, hurry," she said one day with a humorous expression. "I am dying, and if we don't make haste I shall die first." She had an indomitable spirit—never more finely shown than in those last years.

The chief work of 1907 was the issue, in three volumes, of a second edition of Wilkins Updike's *History of the Episcopal Church in Narragansett, Rhode Island*. This book, by my grandfather, first published in 1847 in a very casual manner, I had long intended to reissue, and had collected a mass of material to that end. But when I had assembled it I had neither the time nor the ability to arrange it, and the project lay dormant. As luck would have it, a later rector of this ancient cure, the Rev. Daniel Goodwin (editor of the *MacSparran Diary* already mentioned), was greatly interested in the church's history and was free to edit the work, using the material gathered by me; and no man was better fitted for the work or could have done it better. The book is much more than a history of a country parish. It is the history of the whole countryside, and gives especially a picture of social life and manners in eighteenth-century southern Rhode Island that has been the basis of everything written on the subject from that day to this. Fortunately, too, a distant kinsman of mine, Mr. Moses Goddard of Providence, also much attached to Rhode Island traditions, stood ready to help me out, his only stipulation being that the editor should annotate the work to his heart's content. When the manuscript was complete the amount of text had been enormously increased—fourteen hundred printed pages as against four hundred in the first edition! Encouraged by Dr. McVickar, then Bishop of Rhode Island, I cast about for means of publishing the manuscript, which was effected by the aid of several Rhode Island friends: Mr. George Gordon King; Mr. William H. Potter; Mr. George Peabody Wetmore; Mr. William Watts Sherman; and Mr. Goddard, who took the largest share in the production of a book which, alas, he did not live to see completed. A feature of the work is its fifty illustrations, chiefly from portraits hitherto unpublished.

On the publication of the original work in 1847 its author received an honorary degree from Brown University, and the completion of the second edition was signalized by degrees given by Brown University to Dr. Goodwin and to me. The German ambassador Bernstorff received a degree on the same day, and I was deputed by our host at a luncheon afterwards to look after him, since he was not familiar with the intricacies of Providence streets. As we walked along he said to me: "You know, I have to give an address before the alumni of the University this afternoon. I have given twenty such addresses in thirty days. None of them amounted to anything. If I say anything worth hearing I am called to account by Berlin. So my speeches give no pleasure to me nor to anyone else."

The connection of this Press with Brown University began in 1905. The printing of its catalogues set a style somewhat new in college publications—a style widely copied all over this country. Ever since, a large part of the University's "academic" printing has been done here, and also books such as Bronson's *History of Brown University* and ephemera for special occasions, such as the Sesquicentennial of the college, requiring programs, tickets, orders of service, and the like.

I am often asked if it is not uninteresting to undertake the printing of catalogues and similar material. As a matter of fact, such work is often both interesting and difficult, for in no class of printing is it so necessary to preserve clearness and simplicity. Refractory tabulation has to be so managed as to conceal its refractoriness; type arrangements that will be suitable to all the varying classes of instruction have to be schemed; and that a college catalogue is a book of reference has to be kept clearly in view. To the printer such work appears interesting, to the layman dull. For at the risk of digression I may add that the attitudes of mind of a professional and of an amateur about printing—as in most forms of creative endeavour—are quite different. The onlooker supposes the printer to enjoy doing what he enjoys seeing and to be bored by what bores him; and he also believes that the feeling of a man who does a piece of work successfully is "joy," when it is mostly relief. The *problem* is what interests all but beginners in typography. Its solution may be, and often is, moderately exciting; although if the problem is successfully solved no one perceives it has existed. Because all persons who work realize this, it is easier for one worker to talk to another, however dissimilar their occupations may be, than it is to talk with (or to be talked to by) an admirer of one's own class of work—whose likes or dislikes are often based on quite the wrong reasons.

A great mass of work for schools, colleges, and institutions followed in the wake of the academic work for Brown University. Even more important than the printing for Brown has been a long connection with the Carnegie Foundation for the Advancement of Teaching. This printing requires ingenuity in its arrangement and in the co-ordination of material, and accuracy as absolute as can be attained. The Foundation has shown the Press much consideration; the Press in turn has given the best it has. Begun in 1909, the work continues today, and will, it is hoped, *ad multos annos.*

A volume of Oakes Ames' *Orchidaceae*—one of a series the Press has since turned out—which showed what could be done typographically with a learned botanical work, and the *Catalogue of a Memorial Exhibition of the Works of Augustus Saint-Gaudens,* printed for the Metropolitan Museum of New York, were the two pieces of work most notable in 1908. The inscriptions in the Saint-Gaudens catalogue presented a problem that was interesting to solve.

An important work printed in six volumes in 1911, at the expense of the late Mr. J. Pierpont Morgan, was the *Archives of the General Convention*, devoted to the correspondence of John Henry Hobart. It was intended to issue more volumes, but the Hobart correspondence was so interminably strung out by the editor and the prospect of arriving at the end of the series became so remote that the project was given up. These severely plain volumes were set in Mountjoye type combined with those Oxford founts which accord well with it. Another book set in Mountjoye type that was thought successful is the "period" volume, *Letters of Bulwer-Lytton to Macready*, printed for the Carteret Book Club of Newark.

The second series of *The Humanists' Library*, set like the first series in Horne's Montallegro type, was begun in 1912. These volumes we thought great improvements over those of Series I in two respects: (1) by the adoption of a more ample paper-page, and (2) by a reduction of price. The first idea was a good one, the second was not; for collectors, a skittish race unaccustomed to good books at low prices, were thereby scared off, fighting shy of the very feature intended to attract them! And the general public was not interested in such books at all. Both series of *The Humanists' Library* have, however, long been out of print, and so the project justified itself financially. The four volumes in the second series were: *The Correspondence of Philip Sidney and Hubert Languet*, Albrecht Dürer's *Records of Journeys to Venice and the Low Countries*, Pico Della Mirandola's *Platonick Discourse upon Love* [Fig. 16], and Della Casa's *Galateo of Manners & Behaviours*, edited, respectively, by W. A. Bradley, Roger Fry, Edmund G. Gardner, and J. E. Spingarn. Of the title-pages, two were by Cleland and two by W. A. Dwiggins, and plain initials were substituted for the decorated series by Horne used in the first four volumes.

As will be seen, the number of types used by the Press

shows little variety. For most books, Caslon, Scotch-face, or the Mountjoye–Oxford combination of founts is the best, and a departure is desirable only when a new type performs the task to be done better than these types can. But new material—borders, initial-letters, and type-ornaments with which to vary the effect of the types used—was all along acquired, some of it during my several journeys abroad. And here, in parenthesis, I may say that one's attitude towards new movements in typography, and to new types produced under their influence, may be summed up in a comment on literary criticism,[6] which I adapt to printing: "The new should be welcome, the old not forgotten. What one misses in most contemporary work is a sense of proportion. Men do not remember what has been produced in the past, and do not distinguish between the briefly novel and the permanently valid"—between which one cannot too carefully differentiate. When one sees some ancient type-horror revived as new, one remembers the words of Marie Antoinette's milliner: "There is nothing new except what is forgotten."

The Club of Odd Volumes began to commission the Press to do work as early as 1904. Good examples of the printing for this organization are *A Catalogue of an Exhibition of Waltoniana* (May 1912) and the more important volume by the late Dr. Charles Lemuel Nichols of Worcester, *Isaiah Thomas, Printer, Writer & Collector.* Both pieces of work were set in Oxford type, and *Isaiah Thomas* is as satisfactory a book in that fount as we have ever printed. The most important books of 1913 were the *Ordinary and Canon of the Mass*, printed in Goodhue's Merrymount type, set in double column and rubricated; and Mr. F. B. Crowninshield's *Story of George Crowninshield's Yacht, Cleopatra's Barge*, in quarto, set in Scotch-face type, somewhat in the style of the period. The amusing "ship" end-papers were designed by Mr. Dwiggins.

In 1915 Mr. John Bianchi was made a partner as some recognition of effective work in carrying out the aims of the

Press and his steadiness and patience in tiding over times of my indifferent health and discouragement at the slow pace of advance. Addressing himself to the problem from a different angle than mine, and bringing to the undertaking thorough knowledge of the processes of production and sound financial judgment, he has always been at one with me in objective. Furthermore, his taste in typography and an instinctive Italian sense of order and proportion have made his collaboration, when planning work or producing it, invaluable.

The *Jonny-Cake Papers of "Shepherd Tom"* ("Shepherd Tom" being Thomas Robinson Hazard) was, like the edition of the *Narragansett Church*, a reprint of a Rhode Island book. It is chiefly notable for its illustrations from pen-and-ink sketches by my old friend Rudolph Ruzicka. It was issued in 1915 and was followed in the next year by another book illustrated by Ruzicka commemorating the fiftieth anniversary of the opening of Vassar College—views of the college buildings enhanced by the introduction of colour. But Ruzicka's best-known work for the Press is the series of Annual Keepsakes he has designed and engraved since 1912. These are listed on a later page.

The *Catalogue of the Collection of Prints from the Liber Studiorum of Joseph Mallord William Turner, formed by the late Francis Bullard . . . and bequeathed by him to the Museum of Fine Arts* was printed as a memorial to Mr. Bullard for Mr. Grenville Winthrop, in an edition of three hundred copies for private distribution. It was brought out in 1916. The reproduction of the prints was attended with difficulty, for the originals could not be taken from the Museum, and so trial proofs of each of our plates had to be brought there, compared, and corrected. I have spoken of problems in printing which, if surmounted, should be invisible. There was such a problem in this book. Many of the pictures were not uniform in depth, so that if they were to occupy the same relative position from the top margin of the book throughout, the distance between them and the first line of type, which also had to be invariable in position, differed. We overcame this difficulty by never allowing two pictures to face each other, so that in turning the page the eye did not catch the discrepancy.

The War brought a number of books to the Press in the shape of memorials to single individuals or to groups of men. The most ambitious of these publications is *The Book of the Homeless*, edited by Edith Wharton. Besides the articles in prose and verse contributed by "eminent hands," the illustrations were to be reproductions from a number of original paintings and drawings. To unify all this material was a considerable undertaking, and, when unified, to select the various *media* which would do justice to the originals was a further task. Accordingly, while the title-page and half-titles were printed from blocks engraved by Ruzicka, the illustrations were reproduced by photogravure and in coloured half-tone. The latter were printed here. Besides the regular edition, a special issue of 175 copies was printed in a large format with some extra features. The book was sold for the benefit of the American hostels for refugees, and other war charities.

Apropos of Ruzicka's work, in 1917 we printed for the Carteret Book Club of Newark a book illustrated entirely by him. The volume, which was entitled *Newark*, was by Mr. Walter Pritchard Eaton, and the text illustrations were printed at the Press, but the five delightful full-page coloured plates Ruzicka printed himself. Another volume brought out in the same year was Percival Merritt's monograph *The Parochial Library of the Eighteenth Century in Christ Church, Boston*, printed to accord with the subject, which made a pretty little "eighteenth-century" volume. Also in 1917 we printed for Brentano's the two-volume edition of Madame Campan's *Memoirs* (in a sense a companion set to the *Cellini* made for the same house), a handsome book set in Mountjoye type. The title-page is a reproduction of an old French engraved title-page; and the cover reproduces a binding said to have been executed by Derôme for Marie Antoinette, called *De Présent,* its design covering uninterruptedly the whole back, the old-fashioned "ribs" being done away with. The bindings of many books printed at the Press have been arranged here. Some of them are simple affairs with cloth backs and marbled cloth or paper sides; others adaptations of old designs which, while not always remarkable, have the advantage of being "on good terms" with the printing inside the cover—which is saying a good deal.

In 1919 we finished the *List of Books Privately Printed by William K. Bixby and those Privately Printed by Book Clubs from Manuscripts in his Collection.* This recalls Mr. Bixby's various brochures printed at this Press, such as *Two Letters of Charles Lamb* and *Martha Washington's Letter,* issued in 1922, which both include facsimiles of the letters themselves. The cover of the Washington letter is an adaptation by Ruzicka of the design of a *toile de Jouy*—an Indian introducing Liberty to the French Monarchy; and this same design was used, though with a different combination of colours, on a reproduction of letters from Wayne and Washington (1922). The most interesting of these books, of which there were a good many, is *Benjamin Franklin on Balloons.* I had chosen for the title-page a reproduction of an old engraving of Franklin's house at Passy, with a Montgolfier balloon riding the sky, and as luck would have it I received at just the right moment a visit from the representative of the French paper-makers Canson and Montgolfier. Finding that the Montgolfier of this firm was a descendant of the famous aeronaut, I procured from him the paper for the booklet, water-marked with a balloon—for the Montgolfier balloon was made of paper from this same mill. For the cover paper an amusing "balloon" design used by Oberkampf for a printed chintz was chosen, being redrawn for our purpose by Mr. Dwiggins. A quotation on the title-page from Franklin's prophetic letter about the future of air warfare is not the least interesting feature of the book.

In the same year (1919) we printed Part I of the first volume of the Catalogue of the John Carter Brown Library's magnificent collection of Americana—a series still in process [*Fig. 27*]. The typographic requirements of this work in diacritical marks, symbols, superior letters, and the like, and the careful proof-reading needful for entries in Latin, Italian, German, Dutch, and other languages make the production one requiring constant care. Three volumes have so far been published, the first two in two parts each, and the third in one.

A Grolier Club edition of Washington Irving's *Notes and Journal of Travel in Europe*, 1804–1805, is specially to be remarked for Ruzicka's three illustrations and title-pages, executed in aquatint with details heightened in water-colour. This was issued in three volumes in 1921.

The Wedding Journey of Charles and Martha Babcock Amory was a journal kept by Mrs. Amory during her travels in France, Italy, Switzerland, Holland, and Germany in 1833 and 1834 and afterwards copied by her into a finely bound blank-book, the tooling of which was reproduced on the binding of the printed volumes. To set up this book seemed an easy task, but as Mrs. Amory's "fine Italian hand" looked legible and wasn't, and as the journey was taken by carriage, the proper names of the less known towns and villages through which the carriage passed—or sometimes broke down—had to be verified by road-maps of the period. The titles of pictures, statues, and the like, had to be verified from guide-books of that period, for modern guide-books described galleries wholly rearranged since 1830. The preparation of the manuscript, therefore, proved an almost endless piece of work, and was a triumph of patience and ingenuity. The *résumé* of the contents of chapters, as well as the preface, I wrote myself. The book was issued in two small quarto volumes, and but one hundred copies were printed.

Mrs. Gordon Dexter, for whom the book was printed—great-granddaughter of Copley, grand-niece of Lord

Bibliotheca Americana

CATALOGUE OF THE

John Carter Brown Library

IN BROWN UNIVERSITY

Providence, Rhode Island

VOLUME I

PROVIDENCE

Published by the Library

1919

27   Title-page of *Catalogue of the John Carter Brown Library* (printed by the Merrymount Press for the Library, 1919).

Lyndhurst, and daughter of the diarist—was one of the most remarkable figures of the society of her period, and had the most original and distinguished personality I have ever known. Whimsical, unreasoning, autocratic, she belonged to the eighteenth century, and might in appearance have stepped out of one of the many Copley portraits that hung on the walls of her splendid house. Underneath an extremely sophisticated exterior she had the simplicity of a child, and went straight to the heart of matters much as a child does, and sometimes with the same devastating results. She retained her charm to the day of her death. Through all the vicissitudes of life, one trait never varied—Mrs. Dexter's devotion to her mother. These volumes were one of many testimonies to that devotion.

The production, in 1922, of my own book, *Printing Types*, which was printed here though published by the Harvard University Press, came about through an invitation to give some lectures (or, as I preferred to call them, "talks") on printing in the School of Business Administration at Harvard University. As I have said, I have always been tongue-tied when obliged to address an audience, and it was with something akin to panic that I found myself in Cambridge, one late autumn afternoon, to open the course. The subject assigned me was "type and composition," and to veil my inability to speak fluently *ex tempore* I wrote out what I had to expound in as colloquial a style as I could manage, so that I might run for shelter to the manuscript when too confused to remember what I wanted to say next. To my surprise, my efforts appeared to those in authority a success; the lectures were extended to some sixteen sessions, and continued up to the entrance of this country into the War. It was then proposed that these discourses should be made into a book, but since a successful spoken style is by no means satisfactory as a written style, my elaborate informalities had to be transmuted into a more chastened text before they could be printed. This was a terrible job, and would never have been completed except for the help of one of our own force, William Smallfield.[7] He it was who hunted up references, verified dates, corrected my grammar, and did the thousand and one odd jobs inherent in the preparation of a work full of names, dates, titles, and like matter requiring accurate transcription. In those last days the "sunny solidity of the *pax Victoriana*" was coming to an end. The lengthening shadows of war darkened too many lives to make the shape of a letter or the characteristics of a fount of type seem of importance, and indeed much of the task was in such "hours of gloom fulfilled" that I doubted whether there need be any book at all.

When the text was in final shape, Mr. Bianchi suggested that it would be far more interesting if illustrated. I had not much faith that what I had written would interest anyone, so I saw the value of his suggestion with dismay; for this new plan involved more delay and difficulty. Some of the illustrations I could easily lay my hand on in the library of the Press, but there were many gaps to be filled from books outside it. The Harvard College Library, largely through the kindness and influence of the late Archibald Coolidge, let me take rare books from the Library and photograph the required pages; and the Boston Athenaeum and the Pierpont Morgan Library in New York also gave me valuable special privileges. But the Boston Public Library was bound by law to keep certain books in its possession. To meet this requirement a small Irish boy was deputed to represent the Library. Wherever I went he had to go. Thus we passed interminable hours that summer in the hot, stifling lofts of photo-engravers, the boy dangling his legs from a bench while I examined negatives of the illustrations. Day after day, I and my unwilling twin left the Library in the morning with books, and wearily returned with them at night. Finally, after infinite labour, the illustrations, the little boy, and I were all "done" together, and the book was printed. By that time I was so convinced that no one would ever read it that I left for a month in the country without seeing the finished volumes. The book has, by those who know, been called a monumental work, and came, so far as I was concerned, fatally near being so. For it I received the medal of the American Institute of Graphic Arts.[8] The issue of three successive editions was no doubt instrumental in bringing me in later years a master's degree from Harvard University and membership in the Massachusetts Historical Society, as well as in the Harvard chapter of the Phi Beta Kappa Society; of this society I am also an honorary member at Brown University. Later on, a paper which originally had been a part of the course of lectures but which was not included in *Printing Types* was combined with two others and issued under the title *In the Day's Work* by the Harvard University Press [*Fig. 21*].

The year 1922 also saw the production of *The Felicities of Sixty*, by I. K. Lionberger, printed for the Club of Odd Volumes in an edition of one hundred copies. For this book we used a fount of Dutch type somewhat on the lines of the Fell type, cut by Janson in the seventeenth century,[9] which has long been in our possession. This type we have employed in many of our subsequent books.

Another journal written by a member of the Amory family was produced in the next year, in printing which, as in the former book, expense was not spared. This was *The Journal of Mrs. John Amory*, 1775–1777, issued in an edition of one hundred copies. It was illustrated with some delightful portraits and other material, and was susceptible of interesting treatment typographically. The arrangement of the first page of text is satisfactory, but the title-page would have been improved by making the panel of ornament smaller—reversing the arrangement shown on page one. The cover reproduces a very fine English binding. That same year Mrs. Meyer's *Chinese Painting as Reflected in the Thought and Art of Li Lung-Mien*, 1070–1106, appeared. This volume gave the establishment a reputation for scholarly printing not wholly deserved, for the insertion of lines of Chinese characters had an impressive effect—if one did not know each one was supplied in written form for reproduction by photography and had to be carefully marked "This side up" before we dared place it in the text!

That eccentric English amateur of printing, Edward Rowe Mores, wrote a paper entitled "Of English Founders and Founderies." This was published after his death in 1777, in a very small edition, by John Nichols, who gave it the title by which it has since been commonly known: *A Dissertation upon English Typographical Founders and Founderies.* The book is very queer—its author was even queerer—but it contains a mass of curious information on the subject. I had always been interested in this work, and, after some correspondence, induced the Grolier Club of New York to publish it. The issue of the volume depended, however, on finding someone to write a short introduction. This I offered to do, as our library contained some material for it. The result was that the short introduction became a long one, and the most careful literary performance I have ever attempted, though I have never met more than one or two persons who have taken the trouble to read it. The format of the book was determined by that of Mores' original essay. The decorations, made up from varying combinations of two or three typographical flowers, are worth looking at.

Two books issued in 1925—more interesting to print or to look at than to read—fell into the category of printing problems. The first was *The Record of Those who Gave to an Endowment Fund collected by The National Society of Colonial Dames of America for the Maintenance of Sulgrave Manor, the Home of the Ancestors of George Washington*—a title which sufficiently describes what the book is about, and also suggests that it is scarcely more exciting to the reader than a telephone directory. Our problem was to make "something" out of it, and the result was a great folio volume of considerable typographical splendor enhanced by a beautiful heraldic design by Ruzicka. Forty-eight copies were all that were needed to supply one copy for Sulgrave Manor and copies for branches of the Society of

Colonial Dames throughout the country, which subscribed at ten dollars each; and even then there were a few to spare. A college library purchased the last example of this unreadable and unread volume for a sum that would supply a very decent representation of the "world's best books."

The second volume, printed for the Boston Latin School Association also in 1925 and entitled *The Public Latin School of Boston in the World War*, 1914–1918. *A Roll of Honor*, shows the part played in the war by masters and students of this ancient school. The book at first sight seems easy to print, but the proviso that it was to be kept in a glass case and a page turned every day involved the presentation of entries which must be complete on each two facing pages. The pages dedicated to men who died in war were rubricated and each inscription had a page to itself; but for men still living the inscription had—in printer's language—to be "run in." Further stipulations were (1) that the names should be arranged in strictly alphabetical order, and (2) that there could be no omissions in each record. To see how these difficulties were overcome and the rules complied with, one must see the book. It was set entirely in Poliphilus and Blado types. The pages were surrounded by emblematic borders, in which the arms of the United States, eagles bearing olive branches, and heads of Liberty figure in white on black backgrounds—one of the earliest "native" American type ornaments, produced just after the War of 1812. I have had quite enough of books "with borders on every page," but bordered pages were adopted here since no more than two pages were to be shown at once.

The Lutetia type designed by J. Van Krimpen we first used in 1927, in a little book entitled *The Higher Citizenship*, by Alfred L. Baker, and we also employed it for some specimen pages for a folio *Book of Common Prayer* that were discarded in favor of pages set in Janson type. We also prepared for the Enschedé Foundry of Haarlem, which brought out the Lutetia series, some Latin pages that displayed some of the sizes of this type. In the same year appeared the only book printed at this Press ever placed under a ban: Adam H. Dickey's *Memoirs of Mary Baker Eddy*, set in Mountjoye. The Christian Science authorities suppressed this volume, and as many copies were recalled as possible. To those outside the fold it appears innocuous—and a "collector's item."

The completion of thirty-five years of the work of the Press was signified by an exhibition of Merrymount books in New York under the auspices of the American Institute of Graphic Arts, one book being selected from the output of each year from 1894 to 1928. I was not present at the opening, on the principle that one would rather have it asked why one was not, than why one was, there. But I sent this letter to the president of the Institute, Mr. Frederic Melcher:

When you kindly suggested an exhibition of the work of the Merrymount Press to inaugurate the use of your new room at the Art Centre, I was only too glad to fall in with the plan; though when it was pointed out that 1928 rounded out thirty-five years in the life of the Press, it caused some searchings of heart. Furthermore, the proposal that the exhibition should be a chronological display of its books presented some very disconcerting possibilities, and reminded me of the proverb that "Old sins have long shadows." In looking back over what (I now realize) is more than a third of a century, instead of having a sense of orderly progression in one's work, these years appear to have been nothing more than (as the late Barrett Wendell said of life) "a confused getting ready to begin." So perhaps my feelings about this thirty-fifth birthday are best expressed by a phrase often used by a great-grandfather of mine, an unworldly man, who kept silk worms that produced no silk, and wrote a poem called "The Sabbath" that none but his family ever read. When children came to see him on their birthdays, he had, when told their age, an invariable saying which serves me very well now. And this saying was: "What! So old and no better?"

Three books of typographical interest: *Notes By Lady Louisa Stuart on "George Selwyn and His Contemporaries," by John*

Heneage Jesse, an edition of Walton's *Angler*, and *The Form of Consecration of St. George's Chapel* [*Fig.* 14] appeared in 1928. In the Stuart book, printed for the Oxford University Press, New York, a complicated problem was presented, for the original passages in Jesse's Selwyn had first to be given, then Lady Louisa's notes upon them, and finally the editor's notes on her annotations. Only a printer can realize the difficulties of getting all these notes on one page—successfully—and yet making a readable volume. The *Angler*, in a small 16mo format, is chiefly remarkable for the delightful *en-têtes* by Mr. Dwiggins, printed in colour, and for its cover, also designed by him. The typography was kept simple that it might be subordinate to the illustrative decoration. The St. George's Chapel service is a piece of liturgical printing set in one of Janson's seventeenth-century founts. Except for rubrication (which is always decorative), it has no ornamentation at all. The cover we designed. Apart from its use, the book had a great success as a piece of typography, and copies have since sold at an absurdly high price.

For the Harvard University Press we printed in 1930 a selection of David Garrick's letters, somewhat whimsically entitled *Pineapples of Finest Flavour*. This also was set in Janson type, and preserves with fidelity the spelling, abbreviations, and peculiarities of the original. It also contains some successful facsimiles of letters. The same year produced an edition of La Fontaine's *Fables*, illustrated with designs engraved on copper by Ruzicka, whose delicate line required a cool and restrained employ of the Janson founts used. Another book of this period was Caspar Whitney's life of his father-in-law, Charles Adelbert Canfield, in quarto, the first book printed at this Press in Bodoni type—perhaps rather too elegant a letter for Mr. Canfield's rugged personality, but chosen by Mr. Whitney.

The chief accomplishment of 1930 was the completion of an edition of the revised *Book of Common Prayer* for which I and three other printers were asked to prepare specimen pages, and for which our pages seemed to the Commission on Revision the most practical.[10] It was an enormous task, and one which taxed our resources in many different directions, but in which what knowledge I had of the history of a Church to which my family have been for nearly three hundred years adherents and of the liturgical requirements and practical use of the Prayer Book stood me in good stead. The proofs were read not only by our own proof-readers and by those members of the Commission in charge of the work, but also by the readers of the Harvard University Press and of the Riverside Press, Cambridge. The planning of the book was complicated by the fact that from the beginning of Morning Prayer to the end of the Psalter this edition set the pace for all Prayer Books in small format, which by canon law must conform in pagination thereto. Then again, some new features were introduced for which previous books supplied no liturgical precedent, and finally, some solecisms in the typography of the Standard Book of 1892 had to be corrected. The various tables preceding Morning Prayer were the most difficult portion of the book to arrange. In the edition of 1892 these were "boxed" in rules. These rules we did away with, spacing and leading being depended on to separate the figures in the tables from one another. We also induced the Committee to permit the rubrics to be set in roman type printed in red, these directions previously having been set in italic and then rubricated—an unfortunate piece of typographic redundancy. Besides the copies printed on paper, five examples were printed on vellum, and one of these became the "Standard" *Book of Common Prayer*, which was presented with considerable ceremony to the Convention of the Episcopal Church, sitting at Denver in the autumn of 1931. The expense of the whole undertaking was borne by Mr. J. Pierpont Morgan, who thus repeated his father's generous gift to the Church of the Standard Prayer Book of 1892. Copies were given to the members of the Commission on Revision, to all dioceses and missionary jurisdictions and their cathedral churches, and to dignitaries of Churches in communion with the American Church throughout the world. The book was begun in 1928 and was finished in the autumn of 1930.

Mr. Lawrence C. Wroth, librarian of the John Carter Brown Library, is the author of a scholarly book entitled *The Colonial Printer*, published by the Grolier Club, New York, and printed by us in 1931. This very straightforward piece of work was executed in Mountjoye type, our intention being to make its typography wholly subservient to Mr. Wroth's text. Like most Grolier Club publications, this book was issued in a limited edition at a fairly high price, though it is a pity that a work so valuable to students is restricted to a class of readers who seldom have occasion to make practical use of it. In contrast one may mention the illustrated *Catalogue of the Exhibited Paintings and Drawings* of the Isabella Stewart Gardner Museum, Boston, a volume in which much is to be had at a small price, and (to digress a little) the kind of book that it is interesting to arrange. There are in this country few well-printed books at moderate prices, and it is much more of a feat to produce one than it is to print limited editions at unlimited expense. If this particular catalogue is successful it is because there were limitations and these limitations were fairly well surmounted, and yet the cost of the book was kept at a moderate sum. Compare it with the thirty-dollars-a-copy limited edition of *Ellen Terry and Bernard Shaw: A Correspondence*, also printed here, and my meaning is obvious.

The outstanding book printed in 1931 was the Latin and English version of Pope Pius XI's Encyclical Letter on Christian marriage, *Casti Connubii*. This was printed from Bodoni type, with the Latin text on left-hand pages and the English version facing it on right-hand pages. The problem here was to keep the two versions parallel, this being difficult because Latin is so much more concise than English. It was solved by beginning a new page at each section of the Pope's letter and by setting the English translation in italic—a more condensed letter than roman—and leading it less than the Latin page. The volume is a very Italian affair and was purposely made as Roman as the Prayer Book is Anglican in effect.

The production of the Prayer Book was hampered by a lack of space in which to do the work conveniently, and before the book was finished this was so evident that a change of location, which we had for some time been considering, became a definite necessity. The Press had occupied its Summer Street quarters for some twenty-eight years. When we first moved into them they were considerably beyond our needs. Later we had use for all the space we had; then it became a tight fit; finally, hopelessly congested. We added half a floor to our quarters, but to little purpose, and year by year the workrooms became more crowded and inconvenient. Our workpeople complained of cramped quarters and poor light in exact ratio to the increasing praise of visitors as to the "atmosphere"—attributable chiefly (it may as well be confessed) to the smoke and grime from the South Station directly opposite. But the dirtier the place got the *more* it reminded the romanticist of "the craftsman of the Middle Ages," and the amateur of printing of "some delightful old-world workshop." Finally, after an infinite amount of wearisome search for places that would "do" and of inspection of places that would not, we found at 712 Beacon Street better and larger quarters, and the Press returned to the same street at the other end of which, more than thirty years earlier, it first started out.

Among the things I have learned from conducting a press is the importance of efficient co-operation which in industrial establishments is often hampered by a kind of hierarchy. There can be, and often is, in workshops, a table of precedence—with the result that the office snubs the proof-readers, and the proof-readers the compositors, and the compositors the pressmen, and the pressmen the shippers, and these last insult the office boy, who maltreats the cat because it is the only thing left to which he can be nasty! And, too, when an error is discovered in one department, hours are spent to show that another department is responsible—a game of industrial tag to prove who is "it." In this Press I have remedied this, or think I have done so.

I have also learned the importance of having the office of a press and its workrooms together. Offices in town and work-rooms elsewhere usually beget perpetual controversy, and points which could be easily solved by conference are relegated to correspondence. An enormous amount of time is wasted by lack of the personal contact which promotes speed in turning out work and good feeling between the work-rooms and the office. The tone of a letter or of even a telephone conversation may be very different in its effect from a face-to-face talk. Often what appears to be the fault of a worker is the result of inadequate instructions from the office or some difficulty the office has not realized, that can be explained in three minutes by the workman.

For this reason and others it becomes evident that it is best to know personally the people in one's employ. I have been told that this cannot be done in large establishments; but even there, this acquaintance can be extended more widely than is believed. If a man has a thousand employees he perhaps cannot know them all, but he can know some of them, and it is bet-ter to know a hundred than none. One reason for this lack of contact is that usually too much power is given to the different foremen, who dismiss and employ on their own initiative and are responsible only to the employer, with whom the work-people have no direct contact and, in some cases, seldom even see. With us the arrangement has been modified; neither in press-room nor in composing-room may the foreman engage help without the applicant's having been seen by Mr. Bianchi or by me, nor dismiss help without first consulting us and stat-ing a good reason for doing so. The result of such an arrangement is that the establishment is much more of a unit than when the foremen have unlimited power to engage or dismiss.

It is often as difficult for an employer to enter into the attitude of the worker as it is for the latter to enter into the employer's state of mind. But if, as is sometimes the case, an employer is better educated and has a wider outlook than the man he employs, it is discouraging to discover that when an industrial difficulty arises, and an employee states his position somewhat tactlessly, the employer—forgetting his advantages—becomes as unreasonable as his subordinate. If as a result a matter that might be adjusted ends in a state of unnecessary irritation on both sides, the employer is more at fault than the employee. But my experience has shown me that if a situation is calmly, clearly, simply, and patiently stated, the working-man—when he understands the matter—usually is entirely reasonable.

The difficulties inherent in large establishments can be remedied very simply—by having small ones. And the advantage of that is that the work then shows definite characteristics because the output is controlled by one guiding hand. A good many years ago the late Horace Hart of the Clarendon Press, Oxford, came to see the Press, and looking it over said, "Very interesting, but it will never be very big." To which I replied, "Please God, no." In current typography, the printing one likes for its individuality usually comes from small plants, in which the ideas of the proprietor have not been swamped by the size of his establishment. Small shops do not pay great dividends, but, to quote a distinguished colleague, "It is the wages of life and not the wages of the trade that reward us."

Besides learning something about printing by practising it, I have also come to perceive that even a modest success brings its penalties. One of these is the incursion of youthful applicants for positions in which they expect to learn how to help us make beautiful books, although admitting complete ignorance of the simplest operations in any department of book-making.

Some of them naïvely confess an ultimate intention—after having absorbed whatever we could teach—to set up printing offices of their own. Others, loving literature, suppose that the making of books (which may or may not contain it) leads to delightful literary associations, and an opportunity to enjoy a book while reading its proofs. As far as I can judge, the unconfessed wish of these young persons is shortly to occupy, in this or some other establishment, the places that Mr. Bianchi and I modestly strive to fill; believing, it would seem, that by a kind of benign contagion they can speedily catch the trick of designing well-made books without knowing how.

Another penalty for a slight proficiency in one's trade is that people become apologetic in presenting little jobs; and by word of mouth and by letter one is asked if one would be "willing to undertake" or "sufficiently interested to do" this or that. Now what a Press needs and wants is work, and there is no reason to appear condescending in accepting it. Over and over we have said that all kinds of work are done here and that no piece of printing, however small, is neglected—much less despised. But this is all to no purpose. "I thought that you only did beautiful work," says the applicant, thereby showing that he thinks beautiful work must look "beautiful" to him, and also incidentally suggesting that standards are being let down in his behalf! The reiterated statement that labels for biscuit boxes would be a welcome job is supposed to be the amusingly-exaggerated but unconvincing product of a whimsical mind.

As these days of labour have lengthened into years and decades it has become increasingly clear that the beauty of any piece of printing is almost always the by-product of its adaptation to its purpose, that its beauty must be a structural beauty and that ornament, if ornament there be, is only ornamental when allied to its use. In other words, the charm of good printing is something thrown off from its harmonious working. In the visible world we may find an analogy to this if we recognize that, in the charming phrase of Mozley, "all the colours of the landscape, the tints of spring and autumn, the hues of twilight and of dawn—all that might seem the superfluities of Nature, are only her most necessary operations under another view: her ornament is but another aspect of her work: and in the very act of labouring as a machine, she also sleeps as a picture."

This is the story of the Merrymount Press, and of that segment of my life pertaining thereto. The Press took its name from the fancy that one could work hard and have a good time—which was not true at its beginning, although it has sometimes been since. In no exact sense was the Press ever founded—it only began; and as to its progress—it merely continued. After any venture enjoys for a sufficient number of years a sufficient degree of success, perspective as to its beginnings is gradually lost. What was merely a venture assumes the dignity of a foundation, and its continuance appears to have been a confidently charted course. Far from being conceived at the outset with a sort of "vision," the Press was begun because of the lack of opportunity in a previous like employment, where the writer was not master but man. Had the difficulties been foreseen, and the likelihood of foundering, rather than of founding, been realized, the project might never have been undertaken at all.

The reason that it has had a measure of success is that it had a sound programme which was patiently pursued, i.e. to do the ordinary work of its day well and suitably for the purpose for which it is intended. I have never seen anything amiss with this programme, though I have often seen much the matter with the way it was carried out. Nevertheless the effort to get printing "right" led me to collect types and to study them, and to study the history of printing, and finally I began to know something about it, or (as the man said about horses) to "know more than I did." Nearly fourteen thousand pieces of printing of all sorts have been turned out here, and each one of them has had the personal supervision of my partner or myself; and not one but every page of each book has come under our inspection. This means labour, and constant labour; and to such effort—which is within the power of any man—the success of the Press is chiefly due. Add to this a love of order, a wish to make good, and, as a by-product, the desire to demonstrate that a trade can be profitably practised in the spirit of a profession, and one has the whole story. None of these characteristics or desires has, necessarily, a connection with printing; each is as applicable to other occupations. In this case, through force of circumstances, I happened to apply them to printing, for which I had little taste when I began, nor ever the kind of fervor that is stated (in improving books) to be essential to success. *"Dans toutes les carrières, il existe un conscience du métier,"* said Balzac; and if this conscience is of the New England variety, the result may easily be mistaken for an enthusiastic love of one's calling.

Here my experience as a printer and my record of the Merrymount Press come to an end together. As I cannot know when the inevitable *Finis* will be written against it—or me—instead of saying "The End," I prefer to hope that both are "To be continued." But in looking back over all these years, I still must say with John Clare, "If Life had a second edition, how I would correct the proofs!"

Notes

PUBLISHED: *Notes on the Merrymount Press and Its Work* (Cambridge, Mass.: Harvard University Press, 1934), pp. 3–57.

Updike to Cleland, 17 March 1932: "I am, when I can get the time, writing a notice of the Press, that I want you to see and criticize. It is the foreword for a bibliography of all my typographic deeds and misdeeds: and *I* think in places quite amusing. At any rate it's truthful. And Truth has the appearance of wit to those unaccustomed to deal with it!" 21 March 1934: "If the book is ever done, I think the description of its early days will amuse you—it has amused me to write it. I have purposely confined my part in it strictly *to* my part, and have said nothing about myself, except in so far as it concerned the work. One's 'self' does not belong to the public, one's work may."

1. Miss Elizabeth Bigelow Greene, a pupil of William Hunt, and still remembered by the older generation of Bostonians as an able flower painter, as well as for her unusual and charming personality. For many years she shared a studio in Mt. Vernon Street with a lifelong friend, Miss Elizabeth Bartol. [DBU]

2. This book I describe on a later page. Mr. Brown and I had already cooperated in the production of a book entitled: *On the Dedications of American Churches. An Enquiry into the Naming of Churches in the United States, some Account of English Dedications, and Suggestions for future Dedications in the American Church. Compiled by Two Laymen of the Diocese of Rhode Island* [*Fig.* 29]. This was printed under my direction at the Riverside Press in 1891 while I was still employed there. Neither Mr. Brown nor I had much in common with American Protestantism, and his position theologically was Tractarian or, as it would now be called, Anglo-Catholic, as mine has continued to be. [DBU]

3. Mr. David Pottinger, of the Harvard University Press, in an article in the *Boston Transcript*, 14 March 1931. Of the many articles about the Merrymount Press perhaps the most notable are those in the *London Times*, Printing Number of 1912; in Volume III of *The Fleuron*, London, 1924, by Mr. W. A. Dwiggins; Mr. G. P. Winship's notice in the volume entitled *The Merrymount Press of Boston*, published by Herbert Reichner, Vienna, in 1929; and the paper above quoted by Mr. Pottinger. There is also a very good account of its work in the *Encyclopaedia Britannica*, under "Books." [DBU]

4. Of these doors there must have been thirty or more. I purchased three, and Miss Amy Lowell, whom I told about them, bought, characteristically, *all* the rest. Two, possibly four, she placed in her house at Brookline; a few more she gave to her architect, who used them in one or two houses on the water side of Beacon Street, where they can still be seen. The rest Miss Lowell stored in her garage with some idea of ultimately making an "or-

angerie" of them. But this did not come to pass, for through a fire the garage, the doors, and the project went up in smoke together. [DBU]

5. See Stanley Morison, *John Bell*, 1745–1831 (Cambridge: Printed for the author at the University Press, 1930).

6. Sir John Squire. [DBU]

7. William H. Smallfield, Jr., was born at Renfrew, Ontario, in 1893, and died at Guelph, Ontario, in 1928. He was of English descent, and of the third generation of a printing family. His grandfather, Albert Smallfield, originally in the employ of the old London firm of Waterlow & Company, became on his removal to Canada the founder of the *Mercury* of Renfrew, Ontario; and his son, William Smallfield, a man of ability, conducted the paper for nearly fifty years, until its sale in 1919. After a breakdown caused by overwork in assisting his father, the son took a place with us, first as pressman, afterwards as compositor, and, later, when we began to realize his scholarship, as proof-reader and secretary. Sensitive and retiring, a born student, a great reader with a sound taste in literature, he was invaluable to me in the completion of the *Wedding Journey* for Mrs. Gordon Dexter and of my own *Printing Types*. He left us because he thought family duties called him home, but with the hope that he might again take up the position that was always open for him. It was not to be, and after a year or two of invalidism and frustration he died. I like to place beside Smallfield's name the names of two other men sometime of our force: Frank Callan and Walter Vincent Smith. To those who knew their histories, these names call up memories of faithfulness, generosity, and fortitude under circumstances in which tragedy had its part. *Lux perpetua luceat eis.* [DBU]

8. Many books described in the bibliography have been among those chosen for "Fifty Books of the Year," an annual exhibition of the outstanding book-making for each twelvemonth arranged by this organization. In the ten years since the first exhibition in 1923, this Press has contributed fifty-six books, an average of over five a year—more than have been designed and printed by any one press in this country, and more than enough to fill a year's exhibit. [DBU]

9. This type is now known to have known to have been cut by Nicholas Kis. See György Haiman, *Nicholas Kis: A Hungarian*

Punch-Cutter and Printer, 1650–1702 (San Francisco: Jack W. Stauffacher/Greenwood Press, in association with John Howell–Books, 1983).

10. See Martin Hutner, *The Making of the Book of Common Prayer of* 1928 ([Southbury, Conn.]: Chiswick Book Shop, 1990).

❦ Shorter Pieces

THE
MERRYMOUNT
PRESS

R. D. B. UPDIKE desires to call the attention of Publishers and the Trade in general to the facilities afforded for good printing at *The Merrymount Press*. He has opened a printing office of his own under this style, that he may more exactly gain the effects he desires in his work, and because under these conditions the cost is lessened. Books of all sorts which require an individual treatment—novels, volumes of poetry, genealogies, sermons—are undertaken at the *Press* under Mr. *Updike's* supervision, and the plates supplied to publishers, or the whole book produced and furnished in complete form.

The Altar Book alluded to on the following page was set up at the *Merrymount Press*, and this was followed by *The Nightingale*—both books creditable, it is believed, to the Press. The interesting collection of types and ornaments of the Press have been collected from various sources with a great deal of care, with a special view to the production of thorough and artistic work. Estimates will be furnished on application.

D. B. UPDIKE, THE MERRYMOUNT PRESS, No. 7 TREMONT PLACE, BEACON STREET, BOSTON

28   An early advertising brochure of the Merrymount Press [reduced].

Shorter Pieces

TO THE TRADE

MR. D. B. UPDIKE, for the past twelve years with Houghton, Mifflin, & Co. of Boston and of The Riverside Press, Cambridge, has now severed his connection with that firm, and has opened an office of his own at No. 6 Beacon Street, Boston.

When with Houghton, Mifflin, and Company, Mr. Updike had charge of the preparation and arrangement of the catalogues, holiday bulletins, general circulars, advertising pages, posters, and other decorative printing, as well as some of the books issued by that house. He is now prepared to undertake books for such of the trade as desire it the same class of decorative printing and book-making. Typography and design in its relation thereto have long been Mr. Updike's special study, and he has also a practical knowledge of the commercial necessities of the work in which he is engaged. The following detailed statement of the various kinds of work that he undertakes may be of interest to Publishers, Book-sellers, and Printers.

Holiday books. New books intended for a holiday sale in 1894, or old books which the Trade desire issued in attractive holiday form, will be arranged for publication in the newest styles. Catalogues of publications will be looked over, and books suggested for this treatment. The illustrations or decorations will be designed under Mr. Updike's direction, or he will advise as to the persons best fitted to make them. The style of typography will be set by him, the illustrations placed, and designs for bindings furnished. He endeavours to keep himself informed about the best English, French, and American work that he may be enabled to give books those touches which are nowadays necessary if a volume is to be a success. Mr. F. Hopkinson Smith's book, *A Day at Laguerre's*, was among those designed by him. Limited editions of attractive little books of poems or essays printed on hand-made paper, with initials and bordered title-pages in the modern aesthetic English style, he makes a specialty.

Privately printed books. Every publisher and book-seller is called upon to undertake an occasional privately printed or commission book, which, while it often has little commercial value, takes up a great deal of time and gives much trouble. Persons having such books to print, and desiring well-appointed volumes in small editions, may be referred direct to Mr. Updike; or he will do such work for publishers and book-sellers.

The above applies to genealogies and family and local histories, which are often the work of amateurs. Clear, practical arrangement is of the first importance here; and they should also be good pieces of book-making, and not "job-work." Reports of clubs, institutions, charities, libraries, etc., will be well printed in appropriate style.

Ecclesiastical printing. Mr. Updike has just completed the oversight of the decorations for *édition de luxe* of the Standard Prayer-Book of 1892, issued for the Episcopal Church. The book is from the press of Messrs. Theodore L. De Vinne & Co., New York, whose admirable work is so well known. Mr. Updike is also issuing on his own account a quarto edition of an Altar Book [*Fig.* 2] for the use of the Episcopal Church, which it is hoped will be typographically and decoratively the best piece of Church work yet produced in this country. A detailed announcement of this volume will be sent, later on, to those applying for it.

Service-Books, Books of Devotion, Memorial Sermons and Addresses, services for Christmas, Easter, etc., and all other forms of ecclesiastical printing of a rich yet simple sort, in accordance with the best traditions of such work, will be gladly undertaken.

Decorations for books. Title-pages of books which require special features will be designed, or if proofs are submitted, suggestions for ornamentation and arrangement will be made. Every sort of decoration for a book can be furnished, including colophons and "printers' marks," sets of headpieces, tailpieces, etc., in historical styles,—English, French, Italian Renaissance; Early German; the rude decorations of the New England printer; the modern English style set by Morris; and the curious revival of English work at the beginning of this century. Specimen pages of type appropriate to these decorations can also be designed if wanted.

"Practical" book-covers. Publishers or book-sellers often want attractive book-covers, with good lettering and well-designed ornament; both lettering and ornament so disposed that the cost of die-cutting will not be great; the cloth in a colour which can be easily had; to be printed in one colour of ink, or else ink and gold; and to be used on a book which will not bear a large expenditure in this respect. Mr. Updike will do his best to supply this kind of a book-cover.

Minor decorative printing. Pamphlets, circulars, catalogues, etc., intended for advertising purposes will also be prepared, for there is no class of printing to which more care and thought may be given than attractive advertising. These will be written, and suggestions made for their successful distribution, in special cases. . . .¹

Mr. Updike is at his office, No. 6 Beacon Street, Boston, between nine and five o'clock daily. Business can be transacted either by interview or correspondence.

Notes

PUBLISHED: advertising brochure (Boston, 1893). Unsigned.

Updike regularly issued brochures of this sort, later under the imprint of the Merrymount Press, and inevitably certain standard paragraphs appeared in them from year to year. This is the earliest of his brochures that I have seen. A subsequent one dated 15 October 1894 (entitled "A Few Words about Printing, Book-making, and Their Allied Arts: Being a Short Description of the Work Done by Mr. Berkeley Updike, at Number Six Beacon Street, Boston, Massachusetts") [*Fig.* 3], is worth quoting in part, because its opening paragraph offers a more generalized rationale for his activities as a book-designer:

"Among the arts and crafts in which persons of taste and cultivation have been increasingly interested during the past few years is that of printing, and design as applied thereto. The modern tendency to specialize the different portions of all work has been nowhere more apparent than in the printer's art, so that today the compositor no longer sets the styles of typography, but simply works under the direction of those who have made style in printing a special study. In other words, there are arising on every side, workers whose place is not that of the man by whom a printer's work is used, nor of the printer himself, but of one, who, by a knowledge of the requirements of clients on the one hand, and the abilities of the printer on the other, is able to produce a better result than either could do alone. This little preface answers, to a certain extent, a question that is often asked as to the precise place which one holds in relation to printer and public. Mr. Updike has for a long time past been chiefly interested in work of this kind, and he has been fitted by a very long practical experience to undertake it; but at the same time the theory that such work ought to succeed, and the actual showing that it does succeed are two very different things, and he is happy to be able to say that the successful results of a year's labour have proved the theory to be a working one."

1. The passage omitted here offers *References* and *Terms, etc.*

ON THE DECORATIONS OF THE
LIMITED EDITION OF THE STANDARD
PRAYER BOOK OF MDCCCXCII

THE HISTORY of the various steps, by which the new Standard *Book of Common Prayer* for 1892 has come into being, is too well known, and the fitness of publishing a commemorative edition is too evident, to render further words on the subject necessary. But it has been thought well to make a brief statement of the principles on which the present form of decorative treatment was adopted; and so far to interpret the symbolism as to lead the reader to examine it in its relation to the text.

In undertaking this work, the most obvious and natural method of decoration seemed to be to imitate, in a general way, the ancient books of devotion. But in endeavouring to put this idea into execution there were many drawbacks not at first apparent. In the first place the type from which this Prayer Book is printed is of modern character, and the effect of the book that of a nineteenth-century piece of printing. A book decorated in the medieval manner with borders would be very incomplete without the splendid initial letters which were a great feature of such volumes. The problem actually presented was to decorate a book practically *already printed*, without allowing for the introduction of such initials, or for any changes in typography. Again the medieval borders owed their effect largely to the use of gold and colour; and their intricacy, which gave them a part of their splendour when colour was introduced, often became an element of weakness when reduced to black and white. Again, it was almost impossible to obtain borders enough of this description, possessing sufficient variety; for, to relieve their sameness, a great deal of symbolism must be introduced, and as the number of borders is limited, this symbolism must be used over and over again, thus losing both its force and its fitness.

The method of treatment adopted, therefore, is one in conformity with the typographical requirements of the volume; and includes simply treated, flat, decorative borders in black and white of about thirty trees, flowers and plants, chosen generally with reference to their symbolism, and arranged with due regard to liturgical requirements. For the basis of this scheme of decoration the *Benedicite omnia opera Domini Domino* was selected. An analysis of the canticle shows that its verses fall naturally into certain divisions; and that these divisions lend themselves by an obvious application to portions of the *Book of Common Prayer.* The whole scheme of decoration, therefore, is based on the *Benedicite* and follows out the train of thought suggested by this hymn, by using in the borders, when possible, plants connected by some association of ideas with the seasons and offices of the Church, and by introducing verses of the *Benedicite* at certain parts of the book, which need accentuation.

It will be noticed that the verses in the borders are in Latin, adopted because of its more decorative character when printed, and that they may not be considered in any sense a part of the book itself. The greater part of the mottoes are from the *Benedicite*, but for Holy Baptism and Holy Communion, for the five chief festivals, and in one or two other places, they have been taken from the Prayer Book and the Bible. However beautiful and fitting lines from many of the old Latin hymns may seem, these have been purposely avoided, as not likely to be so generally familiar, acceptable, or suitable to the spirit of our own Church as passages from the authorized formularies, or from the Word of God.

Religious symbolism has been very sparingly employed, because in a sense all the work is symbolic; and because religious symbolism is very carelessly and irreverently used among us at the present day. No, one was ever more religious in feeling and work than were the craftsmen of the middle ages; but they were religious in spirit and in manner rather than in design. They used natural forms, but in a reverent and careful way. They usually restricted themselves to foliage, and did not carve the capitals of pillars with holy symbols and sacred monograms. A cross being primarily a symbol, and not an ornament, cannot be used carelessly if it means anything; and if it means nothing, there is no end gained by using it at all.

The amount of decoration has also been governed by liturgical considerations, and that for the services of Divine institution is finest, the Gospels for the chief festivals are next in richness, these are followed by Morning and Evening Prayer, while the remaining offices are less ornamented, and all on about the same plane. The Communion and Baptismal Offices begin with wide borders with black backgrounds, and continue with borders in outline for the remainder of the service, the words of institution being marked, in both cases, by the introduction of symbolic decorations and verses printed in a decorative form. The borders of the pages of the Lord's Supper are from designs of grapes and grapevine; those for Holy Baptism are of water-lilies, in allusion to the elements used in these Sacraments: the Baptism of Children in Houses, and the Baptism of Adults are also decorated with narrow borders of water-lilies. The first page of the Gospels is ornamented with a wide border of great richness, with a black background, and our Lord's saying, "Heaven and earth shall pass away, but my words shall not pass away," is introduced as appropriate to the opening of the Gospels, and to Advent Sunday, on which they begin.

The five festivals, for which Proper Prefaces are provided in the Communion Office,—Christmas, Easter, Ascension, Whitsunday and Trinity,—are marked by wide borders in outline, with quotations and floriated crosses of medieval design. For Christmas I have chosen the box-tree for the decorations, in allusion to a verse from the Prophet Isaiah, which forms part of the first lesson for Christmas Eve, and which has a curious application to the custom of dressing churches with garlands at Christmastide. For Easter, lilies are the flowers chosen; for Ascension, trumpet-vine; for Whitsunday, columbine, in allusion to the Holy Spirit; and at Trinity, the clover, or trefoil.

From Advent Sunday to Christmas-day, narrow borders of the trumpet-vine are used, symbolic of the warning voice of the Church at Advent, and of the Gospels, continually. From Christmas to Epiphany the box is used; at Epiphany and the Sundays after it a garland of myrrh, roses and daffodils,—typical of the Epiphany offerings of gold, frankincense and myrrh; at Septuagesima, the Old English Lent herb, tansy; on Ash Wednesday, hyssop; continued through Lent until Passion Sunday, when passion flowers are used; on Palm Sunday, palms form the borders; and in Holy Week passion flowers are used until Maundy Thursday, when a narrow border of grapes is substituted. The Gospel for Good Friday is alone, of all the pages of the book, without any adornment, plain ruled lines with verses from the Old and New Testaments marking the day. On Easter Eve, Easter lilies are used, and on Easter Day a wide border of the same flower, which continues to Ascension. For Ascension and Whitsunday, the decorations have already been mentioned; and the Sundays after Trinity are treated as Trinity itself, except that the borders are narrow and in outline. The Saints' Days are ornamented with palm branches and lilies. The gospel for All Saints' Day is ornamented with a border of divers flowers of obvious significance.

Morning and Evening Prayer open with rich wide borders with black backgrounds. For Morning Prayer, the morning-glory is used; for Evening Prayer, Canterbury-bells form the border.

For other offices which are named at random the appropriate decorations are as follows:—for Prayers and Thanksgivings the olive, typical of the peace and plenty asked or granted;

for the Litany, tansy; for Matrimony, a garland of roses and other flowers; for the Psalter, vines in leaf, flower and fruit. The borders of the Calendars are made to typify times and seasons, and also to express the cold of winter, the showers of spring, the heat of summer, and the winds of autumn. The lines from the *Benedicite* in the first of the borders surrounding the tables to find Easter Day, etc., allude to the falling of Easter being governed by the moon, while "light and darkness" and "nights and days" are used respectively for the daily morning and evening offices. The design on the cover carries out the general scheme of the book. The lining paper,—in which in a literal sense I have made "the waste places" sing—is composed of English roses and Scotch thistles with scrolls bearing the words Hosanna, Alleluia—these plants being chosen in allusion to the Scotch and English origin of the American Episcopate. Without attempting a wearisome explanation of every part of the symbolism, it will be, I think, evident that almost all the borders have some special significance. It has been my endeavour in arranging the scheme of decoration to be guided by the Prayer Book in decorating the Prayer Book—to enrich where it enriched, to abstain where it abstained, and to make its decoration an expression of itself.

It is almost impossible that the execution of any work should wholly fulfil the ideals and desires of him who plans it or those who carry it out; and if no one can be so fully aware of its difficulties, no one can be more sensible of its imperfections than myself. It is hoped, however, that the general spirit of its decorations, as suggested by the motto, *Benedicite omnia opera*, will appeal to Churchmen; and be found in harmony with that offering of devotion and praise which the Church, in her liturgy, puts before us as most justly due from the creature to the Creator, not for our own edification, but as our divine service to Almighty God.

Notes

PUBLISHED: pamphlet (New York: Printed at the De Vinne Press, 1893).
This pamphlet accompanied the large-paper edition of the Standard Prayer Book (1892) of the American Episcopal Church. Updike's essay is dated 1 November 1 1893.

TO THE CLERGY AND LAITY OF THE EPISCOPAL CHURCH

MR. D. B. UPDIKE, who has been for the past twelve years with Messrs. Houghton, Mifflin, and Company of Boston and the Riverside Press, Cambridge, has severed his connection with that house, and opened an office of his own at number six Beacon Street, Boston, where he is undertaking decorative printing of all sorts for those desiring it. He wishes to call the attention of the Clergy and others who may be interested in ecclesiastical printing to his work in this department of typography.

There seems to be a need for sober, reserved Church printing, and Mr. Updike aims to make such printing a special feature of his business. Much of the work of this kind that one now sees, is commonplace and poor in symbolism, and has often but little relation to the matter it is supposed to adorn. George Herbert's maxim as to the painting of texts—"that all be grave and reverend, not with light colours and foolish antics"—seems now forgotten. But the Church has her own spirit in such work as well as in everything else; and there is, within the limits of symbolism which she has sanctioned by custom, quite enough latitude to allow of great beauty and fitness of ecclesiastical design, when applied to printing, without running into forms of arrangement and decoration which are, in either one direction or the other, alien to her best spirit.

Mr. Updike is ready to undertake the oversight and printing of Memorial Sermons and Addresses, Books of Devotion, Services for the Festivals of the Church and for Children's Services on Christmas, Easter, and like days; also Offices for special occasions such as laying of corner-stones, consecrations of churches, ordinations, patronal and dedication festivals, etc.

In such work he aims first of all to supply good printing, on good paper, avoiding fanciful and unusual styles of type; to introduce symbolism only when appropriate and not for the sake of ornament; to have this symbolism, when used, as full of meaning and as beautiful in design as possible; and to proportion the amount and character of decoration to the importance of the particular work in which it is employed. Some kinds of liturgical printing can hardly be too splendid; and here wealth of ornament and the use of rubrication may have free play; but the minor work, like reports of guilds, societies, parish year-books, etc., should be made attractive but simple. In short, all kinds of Church work, however slight, however elaborate, will be arranged by Mr. Updike in a sober style, in accord with what he believes to be the soundest and best tradition of English and American ecclesiastical printing. He is also glad to undertake printing on vellum with illuminations introduced; and the appropriate binding of books used by the clergy in the services of the Church.

In a few cases Mr. Updike may be already known to the clergy as the joint author of a pamphlet *On the Dedications of American Churches*, the arrangement of which as a piece of printing was entirely his [*Fig.* 29]. During the past year he has furnished and arranged the scheme of decoration for the *édition de luxe* of the Standard Prayer-Book of 1892, now being printed by Messrs. Theodore L. De Vinne and Company, of New York, for the Committee appointed by the Church to take charge of this work. He is now at work on a limited edition of the Altar-Book comprising the Office for the Holy

On the Dedications of American Churches

An Enquiry into the Naming of Churches
in the United States, some Account of
English Dedications, and Suggestions for future Dedications
in the American
Church

COMPILED BY TWO LAYMEN OF
THE DIOCESE OF RHODE ISLAND

CAMBRIDGE
Printed at the Riverside Press
M DCCC XCI

29   Title-page of *On the Dedications of American
Churches* by Updike and Harold Brown (Cambridge: Printed at the Riverside Press, 1891).

Communion, and the Collects, Epistles, and Gospels for the year and for special occasions [*Fig.* 2]. This, it is hoped, will surpass anything of the kind yet printed. Special type, duly rubricated; hand-made paper; several magnificent borders and full-page plates; initial letters varying for every Gospel and embodying symbolism appropriate thereto; and the ancient plain-song at the traditional points of the Liturgy, will make a book which, while it accords with the letter and the spirit of the Church, will be a lineal descendant of her splendid service-books of past days. A detailed account of this volume, which Mr. Updike will himself publish, will be furnished, later on, to those sending in their names.

Of those to whom Mr. Updike is enabled by permission to refer may be named [*here follows a long list of names of individuals and institutions*]. . . .

Mr. Updike is at his office, at number six Beacon Street (opposite Somerset Street), Boston, between nine and five daily, except Saturdays, when he is not there after one o'clock. He will be always glad to see there the clergy and others interested in his work.

> *Besprinkle not thy Church or Book*
> *O'ermuch with Symbols. When we look*
> *At many such, we lose their sense;*
> *Honour becomes Irreverence.*

Notes

PUBLISHED: advertising brochure (Boston, 1894). Unsigned.

The full title is "To the Clergy and Laity of the Episcopal Church and to All Others Who Are Interested in Ecclesiastical Printing: Greeting."

THE BLACK ART: A HOMILY

THERE IS hardly any department of industry to which so much pains and care have of late years been devoted as to that of printing; and as one may very readily see, this improvement has come to pass in this country partly through the cultivation of taste, and partly through the demands of trade. A cultivated taste has led to a demand for fine books, and the lover of books has carried his taste into the commercial world, and has suggested an improvement in that sphere. The printer has recognized the call for artistic work, and has done his best to supply it; and then again, the advertiser has in turn depended on the printer to produce those novelties of effect which he sees and wishes to imitate. Thus it is that decorative printing has within the last few years become much more prominent as an art than ever before. Anyone who doubts it has only to compare leading illustrated magazines of today with those issued fifteen years ago, looking at text, illustrations, and, what has become a conspicuous part of magazines nowadays, the advertisements. Taking, for instance, these last into consideration for a moment, every one remembers the old form which this work always took,—a few leading lines in heavy type, and a great deal of text set in rather unreadably small type. It was plain, ugly, but usually intelligible. Now our advertisements can no longer be described as a class by any term. They are varied, ingenious, artistic, and sometimes far-fetched, vulgar, and confusing. Who is not today familiar with the riotous use and abuse of new types in large sizes with sprawling ornaments, outline vignettes, and heraldic devices surrounded with borders of all degrees of splotchy blackness? Amid this ingenious confusion, in which every one screams typographically, no one can be heard.

Then again the old-fashioned title-page of the early part of this century was not beautiful, but it told its story—often far too long a story for a title-page to tell. Today queer half-titles in the corner of the page, and title-pages which look as if we were opening into the middle of a book, mystify the reader. These are in one sense striking effects, and for such effects in printing there is a demand; but they are produced often at the expense of everything else. But because some people have managed to impress the public for a moment by very large type and very black borders, and very odd and often very bad arrangements of title-pages, it is supposed that by larger type, uglier borders, and odder effects we may get ahead, on the principle of the timeworn story of the Irishman and the two stoves, which were to save all his fuel.

In other words, a great deal of the so-called decorative printing is not decorative, and what modern printing of all kinds needs is simplicity and harmony. Very few people know any more than formerly about specific styles of type, or understand that there are any principles underling arrangement. The reason that many pieces of careful work are failures is because they have neither simplicity nor harmony. In the long run there is much more variety as well as harmony to be gained by keeping certain sets of types by themselves and using them with each other only, than by mixing them all up together. For instance, there are certain sorts of old-style types which, combined with rather bold and rough ornaments of an English style, and enclosed in panels of double rules, form a style which suggests itself naturally for reprints of old books, pamphlets, etc., and indeed anything with an antiquarian flavour. French type in roman lower case may be combined with Louis XIV ornaments, which are easily had, and when the work is done this has a certain light, graceful look which suits slight, ephemeral bits of work. The above combined with Elzevir italic type, with ornaments in black, such are often seen in volumes of French short stories, is another distinctively

French style, while a roman type with Caxton headlines and big black-letter initials is appropriate for more sober work. Thus there are four distinct and harmonious styles obtained by a careful use of types, which often appear on one page alone, and produce no effect whatever.

"This," says the reader, "is all very well; but what has a busy man to do with these finical definitions of styles, in books or in advertising? Would you wish us to have Gothic advertisements, Renaissance showbills, Old English, Modern French, Middle German, and Colonial books and pamphlets? Nobody will know whether it's correct in style or not. All we care for is the general effect,—is it intelligible and is it taking and pretty?" I suppose that in one sense, to make things "taking and pretty," is the aim of all styles, although the idea is not usually expressed in this way. It is the result of a certain logical selection of ornament, with the end to produce harmony, without which no design is either "taking or pretty" in the long run. Nothing is truer than that not one person in a hundred will know why your little book or pamphlet or advertising circular does please the eye; but it pleases, and the man who arranges it knows that it is the studied harmony of type and of ornament that makes the result pleasing. The Chicago Fair buildings please through their harmony—a harmony gained only through immense knowledge of what not to build as well as what to build. A man off a ranch, who never saw any building more ambitious than a grain elevator, admires the style without knowing what it is he is admiring, and says, "That's great"; in which opinion he agrees, I believe, with most good architects. The ranchman and the architect arrive at the same conclusions from opposite standpoints,—one because he sees that there is something which impresses him deeply, and without enough knowledge to realize what it is, admits its force; the other, because he does know all the art, restraint, and skill which have produced the harmonious and perfect whole.

But to return from the Chicago Fair to business (as most of

us have lately done), you recognize that it would not be best to advertise a millinery establishment or Huyler's candies in antique black-letter; nor the writings of the Fathers in Elzevir italic with finished rococo ornaments in pink ink. Admit that you see this, and you see all that it is necessary to see. You practically say then than one style of printing is more suitable for a given object, and others less so. Very well then. If some styles of typographical work are suitable and others are not for a given object, then some of these suitable styles are less suitable than others. Therefore, there must be some style *most suitable*, and which this most suitable style is, my beloved reader, is what you have to ascertain. But this proves at least that there must be a generally suitable and definite style for each specific case of typographical work. And when this is adopted, and the type and ornament agree throughout, then we have arrived at *harmony*.

Now, my second point is *simplicity*, and about this, in the nature of things, there is not much to say. It can be gained by using just as few different styles of type as possible, or, in other words, by reducing the styles of types used to their lowest terms. This applies, too, to sizes. If the printer puts in too many, go over the work and see where you can simplify the effect by replacing odd types by simple ones already used in the work, and by making most of the subordinate portions of text of the same size. That is simplifying it, and without knowing how it is come at, the work will slowly fall into shape, and a sober, simple, restful piece of printing will be the result.

The conclusion of the whole matter is this: Good work always tells. Good work is always harmonious and generally simple. It must be harmonious as a piece of typesetting. The style must suit the subject. The simpler it is, the better. By such work the eye of a public, wearied with crude novelties, is attracted, held, and finally made appreciative, even though the method by which these results are gained is not realized.

❧

I have given two illustrations of what seems to me (if I may say so with modesty of my own work) fairly harmonious examples of ecclesiastical printing. It will be noticed that nothing but old-style roman and Caxton are used in either. On examination, too, the number of sizes used will be seen to be comparatively few. And in the case of the title of the Order of Service they might perhaps be even more reduced in the number of sizes used without loss of effect.

Notes

PUBLISHED: *The Engraver and Printer* 5 (January 1894): 1–4. An abridged version was issued by Frederick Goudy's Camelot Press (Chicago), 1895; and a reprint of this booklet, with new prefatory matter, was published in honor of Goudy's seventy-fourth birthday (New York: Press of the Woolly Whale, 1939).

The 1895 reprint contains this prefatory note by Goudy: "In *The Engraver and Printer* for January 1894, appeared an article from the pen of Mr. D. B. Updike which so nearly voiced our own ideas as to taste and style in printing that we have endeavored to bring it (slightly abridged) to some who probably did not see it at that time."

In the 1939 reprint there is a facsimile of a letter from Updike to Melbert B. Cary, Jr., 13 February 1939, which reads in part: "I had forgotten all about my paper in the Boston 'Engraver and Printer' called 'The Black Art' until you reminded me that Mr. Goudy reprinted it in part at his Camelot Press, Chicago, in 1895. I wish it better deserved reviving now. Since it was written both Mr. Goudy and I have, perhaps gained in wisdom if not in stature, and we both probably look back on those early days hoping that our friends will think the best wine has been kept for the end of the feast. I hope that I write better now than I did then. . . ."

ANNOUNCEMENTS OF MR. BERKELEY UPDIKE, PRINTER AND PUBLISHER, SIX BEACON STREET, BOSTON, FOR THE AUTUMN OF MDCCCXCV

... THE ALTAR BOOK: CONTAINING THE OFFICE FOR THE HOLY EUCHARIST ACCORDING TO THE USE OF THE AMERICAN CHURCH.

With the Colleĉts, Epistles, and Gospels of the BOOK OF COMMON PRAYER *for Sundays and Holydays. Together with those for the Occasional Offices and from the Ordinal. Correĉted according to the Standard Prayer Book of* 1892. *With the Ancient Plain-Song (chiefly as adapted to the English Liturgy by* JOHN MERBECKE, *Organist of Windsor, for the use of the Chapel Royal under* EDWARD VI), *arranged by Sir* JOHN STAINER. *Together with seven full-page Original Illustrations from Subjeĉts in the Old and New Testaments, by a well-known English artist, surrounded and faced with fourteen elaborate Borders by* BERTRAM G. GOODHUE, *and with about two hundred and fifty different Initials by the same hand; preceded and followed by Colophons cut on Copper, by* C. W. SHERBORN, *of London. Printed from a special Font of Type on Paper made by hand for the book. With press-work by the* DE VINNE PRESS. *With text fully rubricated, and with music printed in red and black. Bound in pigskin, stamped in gold, and with metal clasps. Edition limited. Ready* 1st December 1895. *Folio,* 11×15 *inches. An announcement printed in the style of the book is in preparation.*

This book [*Fig. 2*] is the result of an endeavour to make a volume on ideal principles with satisfaĉtory praĉtical results. It has been undertaken without desire to hamper it either in the expenditure of time or of money, and it is believed that the elimination of these two faĉtors have enabled the publisher to produce a volume which shall be of lasting value. It has been aimed first to make an eminently practical book for use in Divine Service. Secondly, to make a thoroughly artistic book. Thirdly, to prove that this kind of work will reward one for the labour and time put into it. The book is meant for the use of Churches, and will be of interest to the clergy, to the book-lover and collector of liturgics. It will also appeal to the giver of memorials to churches.

Personally supervising the whole scheme of this book, Mr. Updike has arranged the details as follows:—

The text. In text this book is that portion of the *Book of Common Prayer,* in pre-Reformation days comprised chiefly in the Missal. This consists of the Collects and Epistles and Gospels for all the Sundays and Holydays of the year, the Order for the Holy Communion itself, and the Collects, Epistles, and Gospels for the Communions from the occasional Offices, and from the Ordinal. These all follow exactly the Revised Standard Book of 1892, except in typographical arrangement. The introduction of music changes this somewhat; but every point in which there could be any divergence from the Prayer Book in the matter of arrangement has been carefully weighed, always with relation to the law of the Church.

The pictures. Seven original plates are included, two of larger size than the others—one showing the lifting-up of the serpent in the wilderness, as the Old Testament type of the Crucifixion and the other the Crucifixion of our Blessed Lord. The five other pictures are devoted to the chief events of the New Testament story, commemorated by the festivals of the Church. These pictures, which are done in a bold style by an English artist whose scholarly and brilliant work is better known abroad than in this country, are, it is hoped, in their reverent and simple treatment of the subjects chosen, specially in accord with the Anglican liturgy. All the seven pictures are surrounded by elaborate and intricate borders in black and white, the work of Mr. Bertram Goodhue; and the pages opposite each plate also have borders surrounding the Gospel for the festival. All fourteen borders are different. Every Collect, Epistle, and Gospel begins with an initial letter by the same artist, and upon the large initials for each Collect there is a shield or scroll, bearing, from the first Sunday in Advent to Trinity Sunday, symbols of the seasons or saints to which the Collect is proper, and during the Sundays after Trinity the names of the four cardinal virtues, the seven gifts of the Spirit, twelve fruits of the Spirit, etc., in Latin. The initials for the Holy Communion are also richly decorated. Those in the Ordinal and occasional Offices bear the different names of our Lord upon scrolls. The symbolism of these initials was carefully arranged by Mr. Updike.

Music, and type. As the ancient ritual music of the English Church was adapted to English words by John Merbecke, for the Chapel Royal, under King Edward VI, his are the cadences which are most familiar to us at the present day in the priest's portion of Divine Service. These musical notations have been, however, somewhat elaborated and changed in the course of time; and the present music, which is introduced only in those parts intended for the priest, is the arrangement of Sir John Stainer, who kindly reads the proofs of the musical portion of this edition. In printing the music the old square notes are used, in black on a red staff, after the manner of old Anglican Office Books.

For the text of the book a Great Primer type has been chosen, which, while perfectly clear to the eye, possesses, nevertheless, great richness, solidity, and blackness. Practically but one font of type is used throughout the book, as in the volumes of the first days of printing. The press-work will be done at the De Vinne Press, New York.

Colophons, paper, binding, etc. Colophons, engraved on copper by Sherborn, of London, so much esteemed for his beautiful *ex-libris*, have been designed and cut for the book—one for the first page, the other for the last. The paper used is an antique, hand-made paper, modelled on some which was used in the

[299]

seventeenth century, and made expressly for this book. The volume is printed in folio. The binding is of pigskin, chosen for its durability, stamped in gold in a design in accord with the sumptuous character of the decorations within. The size of the book is about 15×11 inches.

Date of issue, etc. But a limited number of copies will be printed, many of which have already been taken up. After half the edition is sold the right is reserved to raise the price. It is expected that it will be ready by 1st December 1895. Those wishing to do so may put down their names for copies, or send them to the publisher, Mr. D. B. Updike, 6 Beacon Street, Boston, for information as to price, etc. *A full circular, printed in the style of the book, is now (July) in preparation. . . .*[1]

Decorative printing. Mr. Updike has for a long time past been interested in work of this kind, and has been fitted by a long, practical experience to undertake it. He is happy to be able to say that the successful results of two years' labour have proved the theory that such work ought to succeed, to be a working one.

His work consists chiefly in carrying books through the press. These books are often brought out by those who are thoroughly conversant with the effect which a book should produce when it is done, but do not know how to produce it. Mr. Updike's point of view is that of the amateur, but he endeavours to make his execution that of the professional, so that the book will show the newest and best features of decorative work, with such special touches as make each book individual and suited to its purpose. He is glad to undertake privately printed volumes of all kinds, and also minor pieces of printing which call for a specially decorative treatment, such as memorial volumes, appeals, etc., which may be presented in such a way as to render them attractive. *He has made it a rule to refuse no work, however small, that lends itself to this treatment.*

He is also interested in ecclesiastical printing of all sorts, of which he does a large amount for churches all over the country. Books with specially illuminated title-pages on vellum, inscriptions in Latin and Greek, illuminations on parchment, and single volumes bound specially for their owners with curious arrangements of ciphers, mottoes, etc., and books embroidered in velvet and gold in mediaeval fashion, are also occasionally undertaken. He is now binding the Standard Copy of the Prayer Book of the Episcopal Church, having already had charge of eleven Prayer Books on vellum bound for Mr. Pierpont Morgan for presentation to members of the Committee on the Standard Book. All this is undertaken in addition to a background of more serious work, for publishers, for large firms, and for persons who wish things done by the hundreds and thousands rather than by the single volume.

BERKELEY UPDIKE, PRINTER AND PUBLISHER, SIX BEACON STREET, [NEXT TO TREMONT PLACE], BOSTON, MASSACHUSETTS.

Notes

PUBLISHED: advertising brochure (Boston, 1895). Unsigned.
  1. The passage here omitted lists and describes three books in the press.

MERRYMOUNT: BEING A FEW WORDS ON THE DERIVATION OF THE NAME OF THE MERRYMOUNT PRESS

THE NAME of the Merrymount Press is derived from the ancient estate of a certain Thomas Morton, a sturdy Englishman, who with a company of friends emigrated to New England in 1628. Bradford, in the second book of his *History of Plymouth*, says: "Aboute some three or four years before this time, there came over one Captaine Wollastone (a man of pretie parts), and with him three or four more of some eminencie, who brought with them a great many servants, with provisions and other implaments for to begine a plantation; and pitched themselves in a place within the Massachusets, which they called, after their Captaine's name, Mount-Wollaston. Amongst whom was one Mr. Morton, who, it should seem, had some small adventure (of his owne or other mens) amongst them." Morton, with the others, settled at Wollaston, near Quincy, calling his house Ma-re Mount, or Merrymount; a name still attaching to that locality.

About the character of Morton, opinions differ. By some he is described as a roystering, worthless fellow, who made Merrymount the scene of constant carousal and the home of the idle ne'er-do-well. Others have painted the picture as that of an easy-going country gentleman, more Cavalier than Roundhead in his tendencies, whose attachment to the Church of England led to malignment by his Puritan neighbours. Probably neither one nor yet the other view is wholly true. But it is true that he made Merrymount the scene of old English sports, and that he there set up a Maypole; perhaps as a protest against the gloomy fastings of the Puritans. Morton, in that odd old book, *The New England Canaan*, says that "the Inhabitants of Pasonagessit, (having translated the name of their habitation from that ancient Salvage name to Ma-re Mount, and being resolved to have the new name confirmed for a memorial to after ages,) did devise amongst themselves to have it performed in a solemne manner, with Revels and merriment after the old English custome; [they] prepared to sett up a Maypole upon the festivall day of Philip and Jacob, and therefore brewed a barrell of excellent beare and provided a case of bottles, to be spent, with other good cheare, for all comers of that day. And because they would have it in a compleat forme, they had prepared a song fitting to the time and present occasion. And upon Mayday they brought the Maypole to the place appointed, with drumes, gunnes, pistols and other fitting instruments, for that purpose; and there erected it with the help of Salvages, that came thither of purpose to see the manner of our Revels. A goodly pine tree of 80. foote longe was reared up, and a peare of buckshorns nayled one somewhat neare the top of it; where it stood, as a faire sea marke for directions how to finde out the way to mine Host of Ma-re Mount."

As to the real Morton, the reader may suit his own prejudices, which, if adverse, may be made more so by the biographical sketch prefixed to the edition of Morton's *New English Canaan*, issued by a certain learned Society; or if more favourable, by Hawthorne's pretty web of romance spun around "The Maypole of Merrymount."[1] It is enough for the purpose of the Merrymount Press, if in disregard of any analogies or paradoxes with which curious persons bewilder themselves, we regard Morton's Maypole as a symbol of work done cheerfully and well; of happiness found in work-a-day things; of a high aim and pleasure in trying to attain it. For of this ideal the Maypole of Merrymount is an emblem [*Fig.* 1]; and to this ideal the Merrymount Press endeavours to be true.

Notes

PUBLISHED: pamphlet (Boston: Merrymount Press, [1904]). Unsigned.

1. In Hawthorne's *Twice-Told Tales* (1837).

DESIGNS TO BE USED WITH TYPE

IT MIGHT be supposed that when asked to write a few words about Mr. Dwiggins's work for *The Graphic Arts* I was pleased to have an opportunity to speak a good word for a friend; but oddly enough, I am only too glad to make use of a friend for the purpose of speaking a few words for myself, or, more properly, to call attention to a general principle of decoration which has grown upon me more and more of late years, and to use Mr. Dwiggins's work as an illustration. This principle is the necessity of a contemporaneous quality in modern decorative work. The great vice of American decorative work today, is that it is not truly contemporaneous, but too often a re-echo of other periods. There are, however, a few men who have this contemporaneous quality (if I may so call it), and whose product, if it survives, may be rightly and properly looked at as expressing American tendencies in decoration as applied to typography, at the beginning of the twentieth century.

It cannot be too often pointed out that the work of one period which is reminiscent of another is never very interesting. When it is so, it is because something of the epoch to which it belongs is left in it. This was true of the work of the Renaissance. The Renaissance people, no doubt, thought that they were very closely imitating antiquity, but the charm of Renaissance work is not in the closeness of the imitation, but in the Renaissance quality which crept into that imitation despite the best efforts of the worker. Reproductive work, therefore, is often good, precisely to the extent in which it fails, in that for which it is striving. This is the reason that in years to come people will not highly consider those very close reproductions of older decoration, which are called "working in styles"—the little decorative journeys of an artistic Rollo into the ornamentation of Italy, Germany, and France!

I am by no means saying that the work shown in the following pages is blameless of the charge which I have just formulated, but its chief interest seems to me to centre in those compositions suggested by today's activities, rather than in the decoration reminiscent of earlier styles. Even in the designs most reminiscent of earlier work, however, there is a pleasant freedom of execution and a certain distinctly Anglo-Saxon feeling, which makes them appropriate for modern Ameri-

30   Illustration by W. A. Dwiggins for a Christmas card.

can typography. I prefer the designs of which the *provenance* is more definitely English to those which are more definitely French or Italian. But as I have said, in all these designs, even if some of them appear to be (to one familiar with the history of decoration) re-echoes of earlier methods of working, there is a simplicity of attack, sobriety of design, and restraint of treatment which is in accord with the best of our modern typographical practice. In what this precise "Anglo-Saxon" spirit consists, it is difficult to say; but it is, there, and it gives us a comfortable, cozy feeling of being at home with the designer's work.

What I particularly propose for consideration in Mr. Dwiggins's drawings are those illustrations and decorations which employ for their motives features of the life of today. For instance, the two little pictures filled with figures done for "Christmas Builders" are decorative in quality, and yet they employ the costumes which we see in our daily walks about a modern town. The Christmas card showing the purveyor of Frankfort sausages extending Christmas cheer (as far as his limited menu permits) to a hungry hand-organ man [*Fig.* 30], seems to me just the kind of motive that should be taken for modern work. I suppose the charm of some of Jaques Callot's designs was not merely their delicacy and charm of execution, but the vivid representation of life as he saw it in his own period. This has always been true of good designers. That is the reason that this designer's New England country fair and the accompanying circus, the view of the sugar refinery, the sandwich merchant, and the two little pictures for "Christmas Builders" [*Fig.* 31] seem to me to point to just that part of the compass toward which a modern designer should lay his course. That this kind of work can be performed better than it is here performed, I have no doubt; but I do not know any one who, up to this moment, has done such work more decoratively, or who has shown in his performance so many indications of humour (without which all work is so dead and academic), of a cheer-

31   Illustration by W. A. Dwiggins for *Christmas Builders* by Charles Edward Jefferson (New York: Thomas Y. Crowell Company, 1909).

ful, alert, simple treatment of today's problems in design in the light of today's life, or a more nervous and sure execution, than has the modest maker of these designs.

The drawings for the Milton were originally made to be reproduced in photogravure: and in the reproduction by another process (as shown here) they suffer in effect, as the rich line of the photogravure is lost. The sketches for the advertisement of rugs were roughly done so that they might print well among the advertisements of a daily newspaper. The method of treatment is adapted for that which is to be done.

After all that is all that we want. If American design can only be characteristic of its period, adapted for the purpose for which it is intended, and then technically well performed, we have nothing further to ask. But this overture is ended, drums beat, the curtain parts, and I have, Ladies and Gentlemen, the pleasure of introducing to you Mr. William Addison Dwiggins, who now occupies the stage, and is indeed "the whole show."

Notes

PUBLISHED: *Graphic Arts* (Boston) 3 (February 1912): 110–11.
"This is the fourth of a series of exhibits presenting the work of illustrators and designs about whom those seeking information concerning the resources of the graphic arts field should be informed" (introductory note). The examples of work by W. A. Dwiggins appear on pp. 112–20 in *Graphic Arts*.

AN ADDRESS TO THE GROLIER CLUB

WHEN MR. KENT asked me to say a few words this evening upon the opening of the new building of the Grolier Club, he hinted that the future possibilities of its work might form my text. So I shall indicate a few things that I think such a Club as this might do in years to come: the kinds of books which it is most worthwhile to issue; the kind of help the Club may give to learned typography; and the kind of encouragement it can furnish to those who help fine printing, either by the doing of it or the recording of its history.

As I look over the collection of publications of the Club and the many fine books it has issued, the ones that most attract me are those that deal more directly with the history of printing. While I believe that volumes on other subjects have a place and are worth doing, they should be occasional publications rather than the norm. On the other hand, Mr. De Vinne's *Historic Printing Types*[1] and Mr. Livingston's *Franklin and His Press at Passy*[2] seem to me just the kind of volumes which ought more often to be printed. The Franklin is a volume which in its subject, the treatment of that subject, and in its typography, is almost everything that a book should be, and exemplifies the sort of volume which the Club, it seems to me, would do well to have more of. I have always hoped that it might issue that curious and whimsical volume *A Dissertation upon English Typographical Founders and Founderies*[3] by the madcap antiquarian Rowe Mores, although it must be admitted that with the orthography he used and the peculiarities of his style, it lends itself to very little in the way of treatment, other than as a reproduction of the original tractate.

I shall be sorry if, on the day when a learned press worthy of the name is founded in this country, the Grolier Club is not among its constant contributors; I mean a contributor of rare and learned types, such as Junius, tutor to Lord Arundel, and Fell, Bishop of Oxford, gave to the Clarendon Press in the seventeenth century;[4] or, in the eighteenth century, such gifts as the Greek and Hebrew type presented to Harvard College.[5] The Imprimerie Nationale of France is full of learned types which have been, many of them, cut at the expense of the Government, and collected (more Teutonico) from the press of the Propaganda Fide, and similar defenseless sources. Now these types are at the service of any printer in France who desires to avail himself of them. This custom is of very long standing, and I believe that it could be properly introduced today if we had a press in this country of sufficient means and stability to warrant it. For I must say, with all due respect to the number of University Presses which exist in this country, which are the result of the munificence and solicitude of some enlightened alumnus of the institution with which each is connected, they are very few of them learned presses. They are usually commercial presses run in connection with a University and producing work neither more nor less good than presses which are called by some less ambitious title. This is not because the persons who are in charge of these presses do not wish them to be learned, but because any press which devotes a large amount of its time to producing works of pure learning in foreign tongues, printed from rare and expensive types, cannot expect to be made to pay in the way that the average University Press is expected to pay, and is called a failure if it does not. For our Universities have, it appears to me, a tendency of late years to become commercialized, and to view from a commercial standpoint things which would be better looked at froma more idealistic point of view. I still (not being a University man myself) hold it the traditional University idea that such an institution is not intended to teach a man how to make his living but to teach him how to live and to work in a manner which is worthwhile. Meanwhile, the most learned works by American authors have been printed at Oxford, sometimes at Leipzig.

The aid which a Club of this sort may give to those who are helping on the history of typography, or are practising it, is another field of effort, and for this the future will furnish constant opportunities. It should give chances to new and promising printers and not be afraid that its standard may be lowered by letting new talent try its experiments. To employ only those whom experience and public recognition have agreed are safe persons is much like erecting tombs to the prophets. To a printer of talent, who has something typographical to say, the patronage of a Club like this is a great help and a great encouragement, and it should be generously applied, for it really enables printers to aim for a higher standard. And, too, the Club may help those who are preparing works of importance on typography or allied subjects either by grants of money, or by undertaking the expense, in whole or in part, of their publications, as Grolier did when he enabled Budé[6] to have his book *De Asse* printed by Aldus. I think now of an author who deserves well of the world for what he has done for the history of printing today, Monsieur Georges Lepreux,[7] author of *Gallia Typografica*, a work so monumental in its scope, so thorough in its accomplishments, that the parts that he has finished make one hold one's breath lest he shall be unable to complete it. Now Monsieur Lepreux was unfortunate enough to live in the north of France, and the Teutonic advance of cultivation quite swamped his modest estate. He is at present a refugee in Paris where he is working in the Ministry of War, and his great work has been stopped. There is no kinder or wiser thing to do than for any member of this Club who has not a set of *Gallia Typografica* to subscribe for it.

So much as to the future work of this Club. Let me turn from such work, which must of course be indefinite, to the definite work which lies before the Grolier Club now.

It has always been the power of the man of cultivation to take refuge in the past, whenever the time in which he lived or his own personal part therein have seemed so out of joint that its contemplation gave more pain than pleasure. We live in a moment "of distress of nations; the sea and the waves roaring; men's hearts failing them for fear,"[8] while the very powers of heaven seem shaken. In hours when we can no longer bear the tension of events about us, we turn for relaxation and help to the work of those who have gone before and seem to live calm and serene above the common affairs of life. But we are often surprised, when we know something more of their achievement, to find that these same achievements were performed under conditions scarcely less forward for such adventure than ours of today. The delightful novels of Jane Austen—which, if they have not added to the gaiety of nations, have at least added to the happiness of all English readers—were written, we must remember, in the midst of the Napoleonic struggle when England was threatened by invasion, and when the terror of Bonaparte hung over the country like a pall. Grolier, under whose name, and invocation this house is dedicated, collected books amid political conditions, personal annoyances and civic disturbances which were far from the kind of background we like to picture. We may go back indeed to the very beginnings of printing—the tragedy in the life of Gutenberg; the perplexities of Aldus; the persecution of the Estiennes; the anxieties of Plantin; the disappointment of President Le Jay; or the history of William Ged,[9] than which there is no more moving story in the records of typography, We do not know the pains Roycroft took with Walton's Polyglot[10] or the even more wonderful lexicon by Castell, which accompanied it. We forget the time spent by Ibarra over his Sallust,[11] or Bowyer in one of the greatest achievements of eighteenth-century English typography, the Works of Selden,[12] in which the types of Caslon were first adequately presented. These are a few among hundreds of instances of men who have performed so greatly that we are unable to realize with what difficulty they achieved. Like all great work, their finished products appear so simple as to be inevitable. But we forget that they were produced in times often as troubled as our own.

It is with this in mind that I feel how fine a thing it is to be assembled at this moment to celebrate the opening of this house. The arts of peace are much greater and nobler than the arts of war; but at times the arts of war are the one thing needful. We cannot all, however, take part in warlike work. It is the duty of some of us to carry on, as well as we can, the things which have always made life delightful and which always will make it so. And this I conceive to be the present duty of this Club. It is in times like these that such a society may do its best work; it is in these times that that wonderful nation, France, which exhibits in all its work such inspired practicality, is still producing exquisite and delicate books. To do this at the present moment is not altogether easy. To the most convinced believer in things of the mind and the spirit, there come moments of discouragement when fine arts or their promotion seem small affairs besides practical alleviation of immediate need and present suffering. But this light must be kept burning if only for the illumination and encouragement of those who are to come after. I shall have done something if I help justify to your own minds the worthiness of such a present aim to a Club which has always consistently borne it in mind in the past; and to dispose of the teasings of something which is a nuisance less common perhaps to New York than Boston—I allude to the New England conscience—which usually prevents us from doing many admirable things because we are afraid that later we may think of something that might have been better!

Since classical times the world of letters has been familiar with the symbol of the runner with a torch who, as he ended his race, handed it to a new and steadier hand, which today we have translated into current phraseology, and which, in the language of the trenches, is to carry on. What this Club has to carry on is merely the steady aim at knowledge and the fostering of the arts and industries connected with the making of fine books amid good and evil report, in good times and evil times. And so, however the winds of War may break on these walls, however its lengthening shadows may darken our lives, it is still meet and right for us to say: "Peace be to *this* House and to all its Works."[13]

Notes

TYPESCRIPT: Grolier Club. PUBLISHED: Martin Hutner, "Daniel Berkeley Updike at the Grolier Club," *Gazette of the Grolier Club*, n.s. No. 45 (1993): 21–27. (Since the typescript cannot now be found in the Grolier Club archives, my transcription is from a photocopy supplied by Mr. Hutner.)

This was a lecture prepared for the opening of the new Grolier Clubhouse in 1918, but, according to a note at the beginning of the typescript (which was not prepared by Updike), it was "never delivered." There was an aborted plan for the Grolier Club to publish the lecture in 1943, at which time some notes—not, of course, by Updike, who had died in 1941—were added. I have reproduced the notes (very slightly edited) below; they are identified by the initials "TS."

1. *Historic Printing Types*; a Lecture read before the Grolier Club, 25 January 1885; with Additions and new illustrations. By Theodore L. De Vinne. New York, the Grolier Club, 1886. Printed by the De Vinne Press. [TS]

2. *Franklin and his Press at Passy*; An Account of the Books, Pamphlets and Leaflets printed there . . . by Luther S. Livingston. New York, the Grolier Club, 1914. Printed by Bruce Rogers at the Riverside Press. [TS]

3. First published in London in an edition of 80 copies in 1778. A reprint with Introduction by Mr. Updike and printed by him, was published by the Grolier Club in 1924. [TS]

4. "Between 1667 and 1672 the [Clarendon] Press received some fine types imported from Holland by Dr. John Fell, Dean of Christ Church and later Bishop of Oxford. . . . A collection of Gothic, Runic, Icelandic, and Saxon characters was given also by a German, Francis Junius the younger, librarian to the Earl of Arundel."—Updike, *Printing Types*, Vol. II, pp. 95, 96. [TS]

5. "Harvard College apparently owned no types after Green's death until about 1718, when Thomas Hollis made it a present of fonts of long primer Hebrew and Greek characters." *Printing Types*, p. 150. A note in the edition of 1937 says: "Thomas Hollis was not the donor, but acted in his behalf. Who he was is not known." [TS]

6. Budé, Guillaume. *Libri V de Asse et patribus.* Venice, 1522. [TS]

7. See "George Lepreux and his 'Gallia Typographica,'" by D. B. Updike [printed in this volume] (in *The Printing Art*, Vol. 35, No. 1, March 1920, pp. 25–31). Lepreux was asphyxiated in his study in 1918, four volumes of the Departmental Series of his great work, and one of the Parisian Series having appeared. He left manuscript for further portions. [TS]

8. Luke 21:25–26.

9. "It was Thomas James who cruelly thwarted William Ged, inventor of stereotyping."—Updike's *Printing Types*, 1922, Vol. II, p. 99. [TS]

10. "The first [Polyglot Bible] was the Complutensian Polyglot of Cardinal Ximenes, printed at Alcala in 1517; followed by the Plantin Polyglot of 1645, published at Antwerp, and the Paris Polyglot of 1645, edited by Le Jay. Each succeeding work surpassed its predecessor in the number of languages employed, the London [Bishop Walton's] Polyglot containing all that were in the Paris Polyglot and adding Persian and Ethiopic. . . . It was issued between 1654 and 1657 in six folio volumes by the distinguished printer-publisher, Thomas Roycroft, who also brought out Castell's learned Heptaglot Lexicon, which supplemented it."—*Printing Types*, p. 98. [TS]

11. Sallust. *La Conjuration de Catilina v. la Guerra de Jugarta.* Madrid, 1772. Folio, in Spanish and Latin. [TS]

12. Selden, John. *Opera omnia.* London, 1762. Folio, three volumes in six. For a full description, see Updike's *Printing Types*, 1922, Vol. II, pp. 102, 136, 137. [TS]

13. Probably a paraphrase of the opening sentence ("Peace be to this house, and to all that dwell in it") of "The Order for the Visitation of the Sick" in *The Book of Common Prayer.*

THE 'LOST' CASLON SPECIMEN OF 1748

THE LIST of "specimens" issued by Caslon in the eighteenth century, given by Reed in his *History of the Old English Letter-Foundries*, states that the first showing of types cut by William Caslon II was made in two broadsides. These were devoted to roman and italic types and learned types, and appeared respectively in 1742 and 1748. Reed records them as "lost," and their existence has been hitherto known to us only through two allusions made to them by Nichols in his *Anecdotes of William Bowyer.*

A copy of the broadside of 1748 has, however, lately come into the possession of the Merrymount Press, Boston, U.S.A. Its title reads, "A Specimen by William Caslon and Son, letter-Founders, in Chiswel-Street, London, 1748," and it exhibits thirty-three fonts of "learned" types, to fourteen of which are appended the words, "W. Caslon Junior Sculp." The thirty-three fonts are arranged in four columns in the order given below, those starred being the younger Caslon's work:

Greek	* Double Pica	Two-Line English	* Two-Lines Great
* Double Pica	Hebrew	Hebrew	Primer Hebrew
* Great Primer	* Great Primer	Pica Gothick	* Double Pica Black
English	* Great Primer with	Pica Coptick	* Great Primer Black
Long Primer	points	* Pica Aethiopick	English Black
Brevier	English	English Syriac	Etruscan
* Nonpareil	English with points	English Arabick	English Saxon
Hebrew	* Pica	Pica Armenian	Pica Saxon
* Brevier	* Pica with points	Pica Samaritan	Long Primer Saxon
	Long Primer		* Brevier Saxon

The sheet belonged in the eighteenth century to Sir George Shuckburgh. A second copy was discovered not long since by Mr. Stanley Morison, and is now in the possession of the Caslon House. These appear to be the only copies known. As the companion sheet of roman and italic types of 1742 lately appeared in a book-seller's catalogue, both these specimens may now be recorded as "found."

Notes

PUBLISHED: *The Fleuron*, No. 1 (1923): 117.

Updike to Stanley Morison, 7 February 1923: "You may be interested to know that I picked up the other day, perfectly unexpectedly, Caslon's specimen of 1748, in which his son's work is first shown. There were two of these specimens: one for roman and italic, and the other for learned types; and this is the 'learned' one. The specimen is mentioned in Reed as having been lost, and the only record of it that appears is the allusion in Nichol's 'Literary Anecdotes of the Eighteenth Century.' So it would appear to be unique." Morison to Updike, 23 February 1923: "I congratulate you on having secured the 1748 Caslon Junior specimen. The allusion in Nichol is as you say the only record of it, at least that I ever found. If the opportunity presents itself I would like to include a note on it in the forthcoming *Fleuron*, should you have the time to dictate 100 words or so." (David McKitterick reports, however, that there is also a copy in the Bodleian Library.)

WHAT A PRINTER CAN DO
FOR AN ARCHITECT

I. Description and Plans of Buildings to be Erected. Architects often desire to place before Building Committees, descriptions, plans, and elevations of buildings which it is proposed to erect, and these are sometimes used by the Committees themselves to raise money for the building to be erected. Printing of this sort has been undertaken in many instances by the Press, and a brochure describing the plans for the buildings of the new Library of Boston College, of which Messrs. Maginnis & Walsh are the architects, is a recent example of work of this kind. This pamphlet, which measured 8×11 inches, was illustrated by photogravure reproductions of sketches from the architects' office, and was used to secure subscriptions from the Alumni of Boston College.

II. Description and Views of Completed Buildings. Descriptions and pictures of finished buildings are sometimes sent out by the architects, sometimes by the organizations or individuals for whom the work has been done. A recent book of this sort is the elaborately illustrated account of the First Baptist Church of Pittsburgh, built by the late Bertram Goodhue of New York. It measures $7\frac{1}{2} \times 10$ inches, and contains 102 pages with 54 half-tones, of which 19 are full-page. Another less elaborate booklet was one issued about All Saints' Chapel, Peterboro, N.H., built for Mrs. William H. Schofield in memory of her husband, by Cram & Ferguson, Boston. This pamphlet contains an account of the fittings of the building and an illustration of the exterior.

III. Announcements of New Firms, Change of Partnership, &c. The Press has printed many statements and circulars—sometimes fairly detailed—of the work which a new firm of architects intends to undertake, announcements of partnership or of change of personnel in a firm, removal of offices, etc. For such work, the aim is to make it readable, simple, dignified, avoiding the commonplace on the one hand, and eccentricity on the other.

IV. Letter-paper, Bill-heads, and Shipping Labels, for Architects. For Architects' offices, the Press prints letter-paper, bill-heads, and all kinds of material for correspondence set up in carefully selected types. Architects who have thus employed the Press have done so because it supplies simple, dignified lettering for paper, memoranda, specifications, bill-heads, etc., and for labels used in sending out packages or plans. It is desirable that all such typography be in the same style, so that the printing used by an architect's office shall have consistency throughout.

V. Book-labels for the Architect's Library. Almost every

Architect's office has its library, sometimes running to many hundreds of volumes. As a convenience for such libraries, the Press has prepared typographical book-labels printed on gummed paper, which serve all practical purposes in marking the ownership of a volume, and yet are inexpensive, attractive in appearance, and handy to use.

VI. Suggestions about Estimates. When estimates are called for, besides the specifications as to what is wanted, it is often desirable to give a general idea as to how much can be expended upon the job. This applies to books rather than to minor printing, as the latter cannot, from its nature, run into much money. If the printer can know beforehand what the customer desires to spend, he can see what is the best that can be done for that amount, and not make a scheme so elaborate as to be impracticable.

Estimates will be willingly submitted on application to D. B. Updike, The Merrymount Press, 232 Summer Street, Boston—directly opposite the South Terminal Station (Telephone, Liberty 1922).

Notes

PUBLISHED: advertising brochure (Boston: Merrymount Press, [1925?]). Unsigned.

The brochure—the full title of which is "What a Printer Can Do for an Architect, Exemplified by the Work of D. B. Updike, The Merrymount Press, Boston"—is undated, but the title and subheads are set in Poliphilus and Blado, acquired by the Press in 1925. Updike also refers to "the late Bertram Goodhue," who died in 1924.

A TRANSLATION OF THE REPORTS
OF BERLIER & SOBRY ON TYPES
OF GILLÉ FILS

AMONG French type-founders at the end of the eighteenth and in the early years of the nineteenth century, the two Gillés, *père et fils*, held a prominent place. The elder Gillé, Joseph, was a distinguished Parisian type-founder. His first specimen appeared in 1764, and in 1773 an interesting octavo specimen of his types was issued, which he presented to the king in 1774. In 1777, according to Lottin, he was nominated as typecutter and type-founder to the Crown for the material used in the Royal Lottery of France. In 1778 he printed another specimen in 16mo, entitled *Caractères de la Fonderie de J. Gillé, Graveur et Fondeur du Roi pour les Caractères de l'Imprimerie de la Loterie Royale de France, & autres. A Paris, Rue & Petit Marché Saint-Jacques. M. DCC. LXXVIII.* Gillé supplied some of the material for the foundry and printing house established by Frederick the Great and superintended by his court printer, Decker; and his types also are shown in the 1785 specimen book of Philippe Denis Pierres of Paris.

Joseph Gillé was succeeded about 1790 by Joseph Gaspard Gillé *fils*. It was he who issued the specimen sheet which is the subject of the two public addresses which are printed herewith. I have never seen a copy of this specimen, but Gillé's splendid folio specimen of 1808 shows a variety of very fine cursive types and a large number of "Didot" founts which, no doubt, were the same as those criticised in one of the addresses reprinted below. He received a medal at the Exposition du Louvre in the year 10, and in a circular in my possession (which formerly belonged to Auguste Renouard) he calls himself *Membre de l'Athenée des Arts.* He also issued a very handsome prospectus of a *Nouveau Manuel Typographique, ou Traité des moyens mécaniques qui concourent à la confection physique des Livres*, but I am not able to find that it was ever published. It is possible that had he not begun by an extensive examination of the physical means of transmitting thought employed by all peoples, whether ancient or modern, supported by quotations from the best authors, the volume might some time have seen the light! He was one of the promoters of the newer styles of ornament, and offered typographic decoration to the printers of France—in a kind of stereotype—which he felt sure—or so he asserted—was in design and method of reproduction to overthrow the superannuated woodcuts of the ancient régime.

The first of the two addresses of which Gillé *fils'* specimen sheet was the subject was made before the "Conseil des Cinq-Cents," one of the two permanent assemblies composing the *corps législatif* of the French Directory—its lower house—which continued to function until suppressed by Bonaparte. To this body it was submitted by a certain Monsieur Berlier, on 27 Prairial, year 7, whose remarks on that occasion are given below in a translation made from the minute printed as a public document at the Imprimerie Nationale.

In 1800, what appears to be this same *tableau* or specimen was submitted to the *Société Libre des Sciences, Lettres et Arts* of Paris, at which time a second address on the subject was delivered by the citizen Sobry, who was one of its members. Of this society I know nothing, though its history is no doubt ascertainable; and of Sobry I know next to nothing—merely that a printer of that name exercised his calling in the Rue du Bac, in 1797 and 1798. Sobry's paper, which was printed in a 16-page pamphlet, apparently without date or imprint, is interesting to the student of printing because it is an early example of intelligent criticism of the qualities that make for legibility in printing types, and furnishes a clear analysis of the differences between modern characters too perfect in detail and the freer forms of earlier type-designers. Furthermore, it is of importance because it is one of the evidences of that contemporary dissatisfaction with the types introduced by the Didot family which is now almost forgotten.

The account of Anisson's experiments in comparing the types of Garamond and Didot, and the conclusions thereby arrived at over a century ago, are today supported by the best authorities on typography. In the recent excellent *Report on the Legibility of Print* by R. L. Pyke (issued under the auspices of the Medical Research Council and published by His Majesty's Stationery Office in 1926), the earliest author referred to as having considered the legibility of type appears to be Hansard, who wrote in 1825. Sobry's paper antedates Hansard's criticism by about a quarter of a century.

A portion of the material of Gillé *fils* passed into the hands of the printer J. A. Pasteur, who issued a very fine specimen in folio in 1823. The larger part of it (through Laurent, an employee of Gillé's, who after Gillé's failure and death had charge of the sale of his stock in 1827) became the property of Laurent, Balzac & Barbier, a firm better known because of the novelist's partnership in it, than because it produced anything of importance to typography. The romantic association of Madame Deberny with Balzac is well known. It was to extricate Balzac from his debts that the foundry was obligingly purchased by that lady and presented—without, perhaps, too keen a sense of humour—to her son, Alexandre Deberny, who left it at his death to his associate, Tuleu. This house is now represented, if I am not mistaken, by Girard of Paris.

The Berlier discourse is from an example in the Saint Bride Foundation Institute; the Sobry address from a copy in the library at the Merrymount Press. The translations are by Mr. Paul Bloomfield.

Notes

PUBLISHED: *The Fleuron*, No. 6 (1928): 167–69.
Updike provides an introduction to a translation (which he also edited) by Paul Bloomfield.

A MERRYMOUNT EXHIBITION OF 1928

IN SHOWING this evening the recent work which we have done at the Merrymount Press, I have divided the exhibits into three classes, to show a variety of work. Much is so ephemeral that it is not often brought together, and is less known than the books we print. The first things that we show are catalogues, business cards, notices, bill-heads, note-paper, book labels and miscellaneous printing which are mounted separately and grouped so that the work, let us say, for the Club of Odd Volumes, book labels, etc. can be seen together.

In judging printing of this sort one has to take into consideration the conditions under which it was done. For instance the Club of Odd Volumes send to us their copy on a Monday or Tuesday, and we are to send out proofs by Wednesday or Thursday. The proofs are supposed to be promptly returned and the final work delivered on Friday. Under these conditions there is not much time to plan the work, and materials at hand must be used, partly because there is no time to reproduce any thing better, and for the more cogent reason that the Club won't feel able to pay for it if we could. In this sort of work there are few cases where ornamentation can be especially drawn for the purpose because of limits of time and expense. The trick, therefore (if trick it may be called), is to produce something out of material on hand that is fairly appropriate and suitable for what is wanted.

Again there are occasions where the material given us to

work with is by no means what we should select if left to ourselves. A good instance of that are the two very jazzy circulars about Crane Bond in colours. The dummy of these designs was sent to us, and Mr. Bianchi and I had to decide whether, because it was so unlike anything that we had ever handled, we should decline the work; or, accepting the designs as they were, would see what was the best we could do with them typographically. We decided (I think very sensibly) that the latter was the course to take, and we took it, turning out a large edition of a circular of which I am prouder on account of the principle it involves for the Merrymount Press, than I am of the circular itself. But, if we had been asked to do the work in types as bad as the design, we should have declined to do it. That is where I think the line should be drawn.

Thus we sometimes do work for which we may not be in sympathy; but as long as we can see a way to better it, I believe that to be the way to meet such customers. As I have said before, "The printer's part is to lead the customer into the more excellent way, by showing them what can be done to improve his work and what cannot, and by explaining the reason why. Thus we can avoid needlessly annoying a man and encourage him not only to have this particular piece of work printed well, but to have more work printed better." And the result of this is, that after one or two trials the customer, seeing that you know your way about better than he does—arrives at that happy state of mind when he leaves the whole thing to you—as most of our customers do. That is the only legitimate method of having your own way in printing.

The second class of work that we show is much like the first, except that it is a little more important—pamphlets rather than circulars, etc.—and here again the same principles have been brought into play. For instance, take the twenty-four views of Wheaton College. Now the point was in that pamphlet to make the buildings at Wheaton stand out, so that a parent or prospective students would get an idea of what it was like, and feel that it was an attractive institution. I do not like myself pictures bled as these are; but one has to ask what the views are for. If I sacrificed the interest of Wheaton College to my love of wide margins, then it seems to me we were not doing the job in the best way for Wheaton College.

One of the two piano catalogues (the one with the red and gray cover) had to be gotten up cheaply, and some cuts of pianos used in a previous catalogue were used again here. The decorations are known to those familiar with the American Type Founders specimen books, and the rest of the effect was gained by red rulings and Lutetia type. In another advertising scheme which I am grouping with the pamphlets, for Linweave French Deckle paper, we used decorative material we happened to have here, and I invented the titles, invitations, etc. to match that picture. The circular for the imaginary concert of Maria Pamphili in this piece of advertising has a singular resemblance to the initials of the Merrymount Press, and all the designs, except that one, were from blocks we already had reproduced from engravings by Pillement, an eighteenth-century engraver. In the Worthy Paper Signature all the designs were type ornaments which came with the Naudin type in which it is printed. They worked in well in this particular kind of advertising.

The third group is made up of books, of most of which I have brought duplicate copies as a more convenient way of seeing them. In some books there is an atmosphere which one has to recreate in a typographical way, while others have simple messages which have to be simply presented. Such books as the *Sulgrave Manor* volume, which is about as interesting to read as a telephone directory, nevertheless had to be dressed up in some fashion, and the situation was saved by the variety of headings which gave it typographical distinction. The book for the Latin School presented a fussy problem. This volume is shown in a glass case and a leaf turned over daily, so it had to be printed in such a way that of two pages open at a time, the right-hand page should end with the complete record of the man commemorated. The entries had to be alphabetical and no items could be omitted, which was a more difficult problem to meet in as big a book as this than at first appears.

In *West-Running Brook*, of which I am sorry that we only can show one copy, the pictures were sent to us before a line of type was set. These pictures are done in a very heavy black line, and Mr. Bianchi, who designed the book, played up to it by using a type consonant with the line of the pictures. That was not exactly the way that he preferred to go to work, but it was the way he had to go to work, and the result is, I think, a very harmonious whole.

In *Lady Louisa Stuart's Notes* not merely the text which was annotated had to be given with Lady Louisa's annotations, but notes on those annotations had to be provided for. Then again in Walton's *Complete Angler* one had to remember that there have been a hundred editions of the *Angler,* and in order to make an attractive book one must have something a little bit new to say about it typographically. The newest thing I could think of was to make the book a good reading edition which would not be so much of the seventeenth century (Walton's period) that you did not want to read it. Then again a little book that Mr. Bianchi and I particularly like, namely the *Book of Sonnets* by Mrs. Pontefract, was to be a flexible pocket book. It succeeded better in being exactly what it was meant to be than almost any volume we have ever done.

And lest it be thought it is only that kind of book that we do, there are reports such as that on Dental Education for the Carnegie Foundation of nearly 700 pages. There is an immense amount of tabulated matter which has to be managed so that it will be accurate, clear, and unobtrusive.

To overcome difficulties of this sort, and fulfill requirements, I suppose, interests us who are printers more than anything else about printing.

We are not showing these books because we are proud of

them or because we think our conception [the best or our execution of it well][1] done; but because they show, under the
limitations which each problem presents as to the wishes of
the customer, the cost of the book, the time it is to be delivered, and other like factors that come into book production,
our idea of how each book could be best made.

Notes

TYPESCRIPT: Grolier Club. PUBLISHED: Martin Hutner, "Daniel Berkeley Updike at the Grolier Club," *Gazette of the Grolier
Club*, n.s. No. 45 (1993): 27–30. (Since the typescript cannot now
be found in the Grolier Club archives, my transcription is from a
photocopy supplied by Mr. Hutner.)
  Updike's remarks were delivered at the opening of a Merrymount Press exhibition sponsored by the Grolier Club in 1928.
  1. The typescript is illegible at this point, and the conjectural
reading in brackets is suppled by Martin Hutner.

AN AUTOBIOGRAPHICAL NOTE

LIKE ALMOST all little boys who ultimately become printers, when I was a very small chap I was given a printing press,
and incidentally a very poor one it was; but unlike most little
boys in the story books, I was not in the least interested in my
small printing press, which was promptly given away to some
lad who *was*—and who afterwards became a successful pork
packer. Thus it would appear that from earliest youth I did not
do the expected of me, nor have I since done the things that I
expected. I stumbled into printing purely by accident. I had
to earn my living at the age of eighteen, and through the offices of a spinster cousin in Boston, a place was discovered for
me in a Boston publishing house. I began there in errand-boy
work, which soon turned into a primary form of clerical work,

and I hated it with varying degrees of intensity from the time I started, until years later, when I left. The position I occupied had about as much relation to printing as being in a shoe-shop has to do with taking European walking tours. After a while I was put in charge of the compilation of catalogues and advertisements, and after a still longer time I began to show considerable taste in arranging them, although much hampered by the limited type equipment at my disposal. I made, it appeared, some success of that, though I now remember chiefly the appalling amount of money I wasted by needless changes—because I did not know, and nobody thought it worth while to tell me, that type was made of metal instead of gutta percha! Now and then a handsome book came in my way, and as I have always liked well-made things in any department of art, I liked those. The only thing I remember which had any effect upon my work, was an exhibition of old books held by Quaritch of London, at the old Tremont House. I visited it many times and then tried to imitate some of this early printing in a modern way, and, as I look back upon it, anticipated by some years the scholarly essays in this direction by people who really knew something about it and discerned their objective. It should be remembered that in those days much knowledge now commonplace enough, was not available—as well as axioms which are now on everybody's lips about unity of style and "rhythm, balance and colour"—terms which to this day I only dimly understand, but the results of which (I am told by those who know) are often artlessly exhibited in my own work.

In this position, with the exception of two trips abroad which good fortune placed in my way, I remained for twelve years, which as far as I can now see, were wholly wasted. My interest in typography was so slight that when abroad I troubled myself very little to see fine books or to visit any of the places where good books were to be seen. As I look back upon it, my aim seems to have been *not* to know about printing but to forget it when I could, because the work was so full of drudgery and detail. Yet, underneath, there was a perpetual endeavour to better things, and to that perpetual endeavour I lay what little success I may have had.

During the last two years of my sojourn in this Land of Egypt, I did work at the manufacturing end of the establishment where I learned in a very half-hearted and amateur fashion to set types. The havoc I had created by not knowing anything about the mechanical processes with which I was dealing was my first "eye-opener." And about the same time I also perceived that I might go on to the end of my days and perish of dry rot if I did not get out and try my own fortunes. To do that, however, required capital, and at the moment I had none, and common sense, of which I had little. As I see it now, it appears a desperately silly adventure, and all my valour was that of ignorance. My employers thought so too, and laughing in my face, gave me six months to fail. However, an old friend was good enough and brave enough to propose an important book which he had sufficient confidence in my abilities to engage me to print, and that enabled me to start for myself. This was the Altar Book [*Fig. 2*]. With the exception of the type intended for this particular book, and one compositor—who is now my partner—I had no equipment. My innocence was such, however, that I thought I could take orders and have other printers do the composition and printing under my direction; and in order to differentiate myself from wiser colleagues, I called myself—for a short period—a "decorative printer." The result of course was that though other printers did my work, they charged prices that ordinarily should be charged to a customer, and I had to make what profit could be made over and above that. Thus my prices were higher than other people's, and higher, no doubt, than the betterment of the work warranted; and when such printing appeared to have been improved, the printers whom I employed promptly copied the feeble thing they called my "style" with varying degrees of success. So I was forced to invest in a small amount of type and ornaments, which I selected with great care and by this tortuous path I arrived where most printers start!

The reason that, in spite of all these mistakes, I did not fail, was because a simple idea had got hold of me—and this idea was to try to improve my printing and to make my work better for its purpose than had hitherto been thought worth while. Sometimes I succeeded; very often I failed. Press-work we still placed outside; and later a few books began to come in which were also done on other presses. I remember at that period having to see a Boston firm of pressmen, and after being kept waiting for a long time the foreman came out and said, "Oh, you are the feller who does the 'queer' books"; and I replied, "Yes, and it may surprise you to know, that your books appear to me as queer as mine can possibly do to you!"

These were the beginnings of the Merrymount Press, which took, its name from the fancy that one could work hard and have a good time—which was certainly not true at its beginning, although it has been since. Its programme was then, as it is now, to do the ordinary work of its day well, and suitably to its purpose—and as I have said, better than other people think worth while. I have never been able to see anything the matter with this programme, though I have often seen a great deal the matter with the way in which it was carried out. I adopted it twenty years ago, and ever since that time we have been working upon these lines. The effort to get printing "right" led me to collect types, and to study them, and to study the History of Printing, and finally I began to know something about it, or, as the man said about horses, "to know more than I did." And *through my work* perhaps I have been able to teach others. I have never cared anything about machinery, nor can I understand or run any piece of machinery in my own establishment; but I know what I want in the way of results, and because I often have not known the trouble that it made to get these results, I have demanded results *and got them* which a man who knew more about machinery would never have asked for!

I have been fortunate in always having with me a man who has felt about printing as I did, and sees values in life as I do.[1] But I never had any particular desire to be a printer; I might just as well have been something else. I have always had a desire to do things well, and that is the whole story—which is from the conventional point of view, like most real and vital situations, a bit immoral from start to finish.

The encouragement to be had from this history for little boys who do not know their own minds, is, that not one lad in a thousand does know his own mind. He is generally pushed by life into some kind of thing which he does—or does not do—to the best of his ability, and if doing things to the best of our ability we cannot be downed. I do not say that a little taste and a great deal of education isn't an enormous help; but many people who have great taste and education fail because they haven't any power of persistent application and don't trust the truth. Most people do not choose in life what they are to do. Life is more likely to choose for you, and the only way to make a success of it is like the directions given by Saint Philip Neri to be a saint. He said if you want to be a saint, be good today and be good tomorrow and be good the day after tomorrow, and by and by you will be a saint—and he might have added, you will be a saint whether you want to or not.

In other words, the kind of work one has to do in the world is not important, but in the final result it is immensely important to make a study of it, to get all there is in it out of it, and do it as well as you can, whether it be sweeping or architecture; and with this idea behind him, a man is unconquerable. Life is not as bad, or at all like what is told us in books, or even by excellent parents, Spiritual Pastors and Masters; and one of the discouraging things to a boy is to believe that it is! The work I love, and which has brought me some of the best friends in life, began in what seemed to me to be—and was at the time—a hateful necessity. It has turned out to be the thing in the world I care (perhaps) most about; though to have arrived at this conclusion surprises nobody so much, as the man who has grown from the little boy who had the printing press and gave it away.

Notes

PUBLISHED: George S. Bryan, ed., *Printing*, Merit Badge Series (New York: Boy Scouts of America, 1930), pp. 56–57. TYPE-SCRIPT (entitled "Autobiographical Note, D.B.U."): T. M. Cleland Papers, Manuscript Division, Library of Congress. (The text above is taken from the typescript.)

Updike sent a copy of the essay to Cleland, who quoted from it when he delivered a talk on Updike at a Merrymount Press exhibition sponsored by the Grolier Club in 1928. Afterwards Updike wrote to Cleland, "I heard that you read portions of my Apologia pro Vita Sua, and I was rather glad you did." Updike was probably also referring to this essay when he alluded, in a letter to Stanley Morison, 15 Feburary 1924, to "portions of an autobiography with which I regale my friends and myself. If I dared to, I would send you the autobiography, which shows that, however uninteresting a man's life is, if he tells the whole truth it always has a certain spice!"

The essay was reprinted as *Work That We Love Is Nothing More than Serious Play* (Berkeley, Calif.: Tamalpais Press, 1958).

1. John Bianchi.

BRUCE ROGERS AND THE LECTERN BIBLE

ONCE UPON a time there was a lady who lived in Fall River who somewhat bored her friends by constantly reminding them that in spite of its dingy streets, factories, and drab, polyglot population, there was a group of cultured persons, who, loving art, literature, music, and flowers, kept, in an obscure corner of that capital, the humanities alive. A second lady, more practical in temperament and less refined in speech, hearing for the one hundredth time these allusions to the cryptic culture of Fall River, said that it recalled to her what a Newport man said about the town. The refined lady asked what he did say—to which her antagonist replied: "He was on the platform of Fall River and spat upon the platform. The station-master said to him, 'Mister, you must not spit on the platform of Fall River'; to which the Newporter replied, 'If you can't spit on the platform of Fall River, where in hell can you spit?'"

Now it would appear that this (with the exception of the plural of *spat*) has nothing to do either with Mr. Rogers or his accomplishments; but I shall gently lead the audience to the realization that it *has*. Mr. Rogers has stated that the Bible tempted him and he fell. Now the Bible although energetically pushed nowadays as literature, is not as commonly found in what we call our "homes" as it used to be. In fact the only place where you may be sure of finding it is either at the Bible Society or second-rate hotels, where a benevolent and optimistic group of young men calling themselves the Sons of Gideon, place it in every bedroom—thereby hoping to protect the house-maid from the predatory instincts of the commercial traveler! Mr. Rogers' great-grandpapa undoubtedly had a Bible of less attractive but more portable form than that which his distinguished descendent has lately produced; and probably in preferring a smaller format he remembered that verse in the Good Book which informs us that "He who falls upon the Scriptures shall be broke, but he upon whom they fall will be ground into powder."

Whether Mr. Rogers reads the Bible as much as his ancestor did, I know not, but I suspect that (on some idle Sunday morning when the *Herald-Tribune* does not arrive on time) he may "Search the Scriptures" not, perhaps, for the truths they contain so much as to confound the illustrious Dr. John Johnson of the Oxford University Press, by finding a wrong font or a broken letter—and thereby thriftily obtaining the guinea which rewards those who detect such errors. I warn Mr. Rogers that in such investigations he may run across the illuminating saying, "Price goeth before a fall." This (like the inscription at Belshazzar's Feast) is one of those soul-shattering texts which may have the same devastating effect upon his career that similar discoveries had upon Ignatius Loyola, St. Teresa, John Bunyan, and Wesley! Nevertheless I beg that he will not lay it too much to heart. I hasten to assure him that whatever may be said about what occurs before a fall, nothing whatever is said about what happens after it! When Mr. Rogers regains consciousness and picks himself up, there is no possible reason why he should not be prouder than ever! In fact if a man who has made the Lectern Bible cannot be proud of it, what in hell can he be proud of?

Notes

TYPESCRIPT (photostat): Updike Collection.

Untitled and undated, but internal evidence suggests that it is a speech delivered shortly after the publication of Rogers' Oxford Lectern Bible (1935).

THE MERRYMOUNT PRESS, BOSTON

IN 1893 the Merrymount Press began its work, although it was then a press only in name; for while Mr. D. B. Updike, its proprietor, arranged its style of printing, both composition and press-work were done by other printers. Very soon, however, type was acquired and composition was undertaken at the Press, which was then at 6 Beacon Street in a building now torn down. After a few years in a pleasant old house round the corner, in Tremont Place, the Press—by that time a real one—moved to 104 Chestnut Street [*Fig. 22*], where in course of time the next house was added to it. These quarters were finally outgrown, and in 1903 larger offices at 232 Summer Street were occupied, where the Press remained for twenty-eight years. That larger, better lighted, and more convenient work-rooms might be secured and the facilities of the Press be improved, in February 1932, a move was made to 712 Beacon Street, near Kenmore Square—the other end of the same street on which the first office was located in 1893. In 1915 Mr. John Bianchi, who has been with the Press from its earliest days, was made a partner.

Its aims and methods. The press started with a simple but difficult programme: to do common work well—better, in fact, than has been generally thought worth while. Its success is perhaps to be accounted for by the conscientious and continuous efforts of its owners to carry out this idea. For, as was said by a New England philosopher, "if a man has good corn or wood or boards to sell . . . you will find a broad hard-beaten road to his house, though it be in the woods."

More than fourteen thousand pieces of printing have been turned out during the years the Press has been at work. Its style of typography is directed personally by Mr. Updike and Mr. Bianchi, who see practically every page of every book and each detail of every piece of printing that is done at the Press. An economy of means and a sort of disciplined sobriety mark its product; and this comes about, probably, through aiming at suitability—a quality which involves discarding whatever does not organically belong to the particular work in hand. For in the final analysis, printing must "not be merely good, but good for something"; and that "something" is its purpose.

Types, proof-reading and equipment. A valuable and very large collection of good types, and a stock of interesting ornaments—both of which are constantly augmented—are a feature of its Composing Room. The Caslon types are cast from the original Caslon matrices, and many of the ornaments were refitted especially for the Press. Almost all the founts employed are obtained from their original founders. The few interesting types which are special to the Press are named after it, viz., Montallegro, Mountjoye, Merrymount, etc. And the founts for machine composition have been very carefully selected chiefly from foreign sources. The Press Room is equipped with the best printing-presses, furnished with the most modern appliances. Its product is carefully looked after by trained pressmen who for many years past have consistently kept up its reputation for good work.

In proof-reading, careful, scholarly correction is aimed at, and the proof-readers' library is adequately furnished with standard dictionaries and books of reference. In general the office follows the editorial style of the University Press, Oxford, with such modifications as are called for in American work or by the special requirements of customers.

Work has been executed in Greek and Latin, and in Russian, Swedish, and most modern languages. An elaborate outfit of diacritical marks—as complete as any in this country—enables the Press to print transcripts of early manuscripts or to reproduce the characters peculiar to early typography. . . .

Notes

PUBLISHED: advertising brochure (Boston: Merrymount Press, [1937?]). Unsigned.

The brochure is undated, but the latest publications listed in it were published in 1937. Only the introductory paragraphs are reprinted here; the rest of the brochure is a list of Merrymount and Updike publications. Similar versions of this brochure were issued in 1919, 1926, and 1932.

THE UPDIKE COLLECTION OF BOOKS ON PRINTING AT THE PROVIDENCE PUBLIC LIBRARY

Mr. Chairman, Ladies and Gentlemen:

At the dinner of a certain learned Society at which I had the honour to be present not long ago, the speaker of the evening, who sat next to me, said that the most unhappy moment for a man on such occasions was when he was being introduced and, incidentally, described to his audience. I replied that Nature furnished a remedy for such discomfort by making it appear to the victim that the introducer was speaking of somebody else, and that one seldom recognized the portrait as having anything to do with oneself. So though I am able to pass over the kind things that have been said, I cannot pass over what has been done, in so generously installing this special Library in new quarters and in naming it henceforth the Updike Collection of Books on Printing. I deeply appreciate the honour the Board of Trustees has done me, and now—as a printer to printers—I want to say something about what this Library can do for them.

In the year 1753 a certain Englishwoman, Jane Collier, published a book bearing the somewhat extraordinary title *An Essay on the Art of Ingeniously Tormenting: with Proper Rules for the Exercise of that Pleasant Art.* It contained the statement that for children, one form of the Pleasant Art was to climb upon a chair "and thrust some bread and butter down the ladies' backs"—to which was added a note reading, "When the wheel of fashion shall have brought the ladies to dress themselves in the decent manner of their great-grandams; and, by that means, shall have rendered this trick of the child's impracticable; be it noted that in the year 1752 it was a general fashion for ladies to be naked *behind* almost half way down their backs." This amusing instance of the antiquity of a current fashion serves to illustrate the remark attributed to Marie Antoinette's milliner that there is nothing new except what is forgotten.

And so, many things in printing which we think of as new are either revivals of forgotten styles of type, or inventions made long ago in some other country. Such, for instance, is the American point-system of measurement in typography, adopted in this country about 1886, but formulated by Simon-Pierre Fournier in Paris, as early as 1737, perfeſted by him in 1742, still further clarified in his well-known *Manuel Typographique* of 1764, and improved and superseded by the Didot point system at the end of the eighteenth and beginning of the nineteenth century. The English, if I am not mistaken, adopted the point-system after we did in the United States, and in a sense derived it from America, though it long before existed in France—not forty miles off! Again what is called "labour-saving furniture," in which hollow metal appliances take the place of wood in locking up a forme in a chase, is generally thought of as a modern contrivance. As a matter of faſt, it was invented by the Parisian printer Molé in 1815, who received a medal for it at the Exposition du Louvre held in Paris in 1819. Many of the excessively black-faced types temporarily popular for advertising, though, alas, sometimes appearing in books, are mere survivals of English and American types produced a hundred years ago, which grieved the judicious then as they do now.

The value of knowing these unimportant and very unrelated faſts is that it gives us perspeſtive and puts in its place much so-called "modern" typography, and enables us to know what the best types are—both old and new—and how to use them. There is no way to develop such knowledge except by studying the printing of the past and present, by reading books on printing, lives of printers, and, in particular, by consulting collections of printers' type-specimens, ancient and modern, which are enlightening and incidentally show, as I have pointed out, how old most new things are.

Many men think that studying printing all by themselves is a dull and lonely business and may be better accomplished in groups or associations, apparently feeling (as Mrs. Wharton once said of members of women's clubs) like "one of the ladies who pursue Culture in bands as though it were dangerous to meet alone." Hence we have companies of Book Builders, Book Clinics, and what not, which are supposed to impart knowledge with a minimum of suffering to the patient. I am not so sure that much is accomplished by such gatherings, for "good work means *tête-à-tête* with what you are doing and is incompatible with the spirit of picnics."

If a printer does not care how his work looks, this Library will not only be wasted on him, but its implications will make him uncomfortable. If he is filled with a desire to improve his output, such a collection will be of help not merely in the production of individual pieces of work, but in broadening and improving the mental outlook which he brings to his work as a whole. To accomplish this is what the Library is for. It may be said that Providence already has libraries where the masterpieces of printing can be studied, like the Annmary Brown, the John Carter Brown, and the John Hay libraries; but appreciation of the finest books in these collections requires considerable knowledge. This Printing Collection can of course be used to supply it; but its primary purpose is for workers in the printing trade and for that reason a public library, open to all on equal terms, is its proper home.

Industrial life today, and the distractions outside it, do not encourage taking time for study, and I realize that many of us, who go into printing as a business, have not had the advantages of a thorough education; but any person of moderate intelligence can make the most of his advantages—the trick being to make the most of one's disadvantages. That, in one way or another, is what we all have to do, for Life confronts us with a rickety table, a bad pencil, imperfect light, and personal handicaps, and under these conditions, a respectable design in living must somehow be made.

This Library was begun more than twenty-five years ago. Its nucleus was a collection of about 1,000 duplicates bought in 1911 from the St. Bride Foundation Technical Reference Library on Printing and the Allied Arts, of London. These books were devoted to typography, book illustration, and like topics in English, French, German, Italian, and other languages, many of them having been part of the collections of Passmore Edwards, Talbot Baines Reed, author of *A History of the Old English Letter Foundries*, and William Blades, the biographer of William Caxton. Finding that these books were for sale, a group of persons interested in the formation of a library on printing in Providence raised the money for its purchase. The original subscribers to the undertaking were: Isaac C. Bates, Daniel Beckwith, then librarian of the Providence Athenaeum, Mrs. William Binney, Mrs. Harold Brown, Mrs. John Nicholas Brown, Walter R. Callender, William Carroll, Dr. Frank L. Day, Stephen O. Edwards, William E. Foster, then librarian of this Library, Arthur L. Kelley, Dr. Eugene P. King, Frederick Roy Martin, Mrs. Stephen O. Metcalf, Mrs. Jesse H. Metcalf, Samuel L. Nicholson, Mrs. Gustav Radeke, Miss Ellen D. Sharpe, Henry Dexter Sharpe, Nicholas Sheldon, Miss Anna T. White, George Parker Winship, then of the John Carter Brown Library, a group of printers in the office of the Providence *Journal* and *Evening Bulletin*, "A Journal Reader," two unknown friends represented by the initials N.D.A. and H.P.W., besides myself and four other donors who are still to be identified.

Perhaps the most effective help was given by Mr. Frederick Roy Martin of the Providence *Journal* who, by published appeals and by printing from day to day the names of contributors, aroused and sustained interest in the scheme. To him, and to Mr. Foster and Mr. Winship's efforts its success was largely due. Beginning, as I have said, with one thousand volumes, since that time through purchase and gift the Library numbers nearly thirty-five hundred titles. Now owing to the effective generosity of Mr. William Davis Miller and the Board of Trustees, with the interest and constant co-operation of Mr. Sherman, new and convenient quarters are arranged for consultation and quiet study. I am naturally greatly pleased if anything that I have done seems to make the new name given this Collection fitting.

I did not have the benefit of such a library when I began my work, otherwise many false routes would have been avoided. But I shall say nothing more about myself remembering too well some verses called "The Hero's Return." It is the story of a man who, absent a long time from the village where he was born, on his return was driven from the railway station to his parents' farm by an old schoolmate, who seemed neither sympathetic nor communicative. After telling a good deal about his own doings, to which the driver responded merely "yes" and "no," the returning native—no longer able to contain himself—said, "Well! I guess I surprised you all a good deal these past years. What did the boys say when they heard I was in Congress?" "Oh," the reply was, "they just laughed!"

I too am a "returned native" but I hope of another sort. It has not been my fortune to live in Rhode Island. But in this city where the first twenty years of my life were spent, I always feel more at home than I can ever feel elsewhere. No streets are so familiar, no houses so full of happy association or of dear ghosts, as they are here. And "the South County" where my family has held land for nearly three hundred years is to me full of memories. "Home is the place where when you have to go there, they have to take you in," said Robert Frost in one of his poems.¹ I do not like that definition—it is too full of duty and too empty of feeling. I would rather say that "home is the place where when you wish to go there, they want to take you in." That better describes my thoughts in being here tonight; while for the kindly welcome you have given me, I am more grateful than I can say.

Notes

PUBLISHED: *Address by Daniel Berkeley Updike at the Official Opening of the New Installation of the Updike Collection of Books on Printing at the Providence Public Library, Providence, Rhode Island, December Sixteenth,* 1937 (Boston: Merrymount Press, [1937]).

After Updike's death, the Collection acquired the reference library of the Merrymount Press, and it now contains more than 7,500 volumes.

1. Frost's "The Death of the Hired Man."

RECOLLECTIONS OF THE ATHENAEUM, 1878 AND 1879

MR. STEERE has asked me to contribute a few paragraphs for the *Bulletin* giving my recollections of the Athenaeum during the short period—from November 1878 to September of the following year—in which I filled a temporary place there. Though I cannot agree with his belief that anything I can say would be "tremendously interesting to the shareholders," I am glad to render any service I can to a library to which my love of books is largely due.

I cannot remember when I first came to know the Athenaeum, but it was no doubt when my father moved from a house on Benefit Street, the garden of which overlooked St. John's churchyard, to 14 George Street, a house built by the Carlile family and bought from them by my grandfather, Seth

Adams, Jr.—the site of which is occupied by the newer part of the Hope Club. This house was scarcely five minutes walk from the Athenaeum, and as I had no liking for school, there were many days when headaches or other ills, real or pretended, occurred in morning hours, effectively providing an escape from it. Usually I recovered early enough to frequent the Athenaeum later in the day, where various members of my father's and mother's family owned shares.

At that time, or perhaps earlier, there was behind the delivery desk a wall enclosing a "stack," later thrown into the main reading room, and the present entrance from College Street did not then exist, nor, of course, the annex to the right of the original building. The Directors' Room (now used for cataloguing) was then at the right of the entrance, and contained glazed book-cases where the most valuable books were kept. The room at the left, now occupied by Miss Leonard, took to some extent the place of the Art Room now over the entrance. It was at that time a kind of sacred spot in which Reynolds' lovely portrait of his niece Theophila Palmer hung above a carved wooden case enclosing Malbone's famous miniature *The Hours.* The Reynolds picture, as well as portraits of John Hampden and of a cavalier (attributed to Van Dyck) were gifts from Mr. Ethelbert Billings in 1863. An immense round table of brilliant green malachite was also lent by Mr. Billings, who I believe purchased it in Russia, and it had been part of the contents of a rather fine brown-stone house which stood, if I mistake not, near Aborn Street, in a part of Providence now devoted to business. The ultimate fate of this gilded and imposing piece of furniture, I do not know, but a page of the *Bulletin* might well be devoted to the history of Mr. Billings and his benefactions. I have the impression that either the table or the window seat of the room supported three marble reproductions, in miniature, of columns in the Roman Forum. One or two other pictures hung on the walls, among them a portrait of Cyrus Butler, founder of the Butler Hospital and builder of the Arcade in Westminster Street. This picture was the gift of his son-in-law, Alexander Duncan, and I remember seeing a replica, of it in Mr. Duncan's London house many years later. A portion of the Arcade for which Mr. Butler was responsible appeared in the corner of these portraits. In those days the basement, a somewhat damp and musty chamber, was used as a reading-room where magazines and newspapers were displayed on tables. Its dinginess did not prevent it from being the meeting-place of many young people whose conversation and laughter had sometimes to be checked by the librarian.

It was because of my assiduous loitering at the Athenaeum that the then librarian, Mr. J. Dunham Hedge, brother to a well-known Unitarian clergyman in Cambridge, asked me if I was willing to be on duty there a few evenings a week. Mr. Hedge (who lived in one of the three wooden houses still standing on the right-hand side of Benefit Street, nearly opposite the foot of Charles Field Street) was even then somewhat of an invalid—tortured by attacks of asthma, the inroads of which allowed him to be less and less at the Athenaeum, and in consequence obliged me to be there more and more. So to evenings were added afternoons, and when Mr. Hedge became quite incapacitated, mornings as well; and what began as an occasional, became a daily, duty. At that moment the assistant librarian was Miss Mary M. Angell, a bright-eyed, diminutive, maiden lady, somewhat of a martinet and not particularly easy to get on with. She was a person of "liberal" theological views, which, however, did not prevent her from highly disapproving of what theological opinions I then had, and she was equally unsympathetic with (what would now be termed) my "social contacts"! As I look back on it, she ruled me pretty rigorously, but only, I am sure, in the interests of the Athenaeum, to the efficiency of which she was thoroughly and conscientiously devoted.

I am at a loss to recall, save in a few instances, the chief habitués of the Athenaeum at that time. Mr. William Gammell

[344]

was then president of the Board of Directors, the vice-president being Mr. Alexander Farnum. Professor William Whitman Bailey was a constant visitor—an ardent botanist and, as I remember, a somewhat peppery person. His cousin William M. Bailey, Jr. was for fifteen years secretary to the Board of Directors. The Reverend C. A. L. Richards, rector of St. John's Church and a Director, was also much at the library, as was Dr. George Collins, Mr. Abraham Payne, his clever son, my schoolmate Charles Hart Payne, Mr. Stephen Arnold, Mr. Howard Rice; and a retired Lutheran clergyman, a certain Carl Ernst who wrote articles for the Providence *Journal* and much concerned himself, as in the manner of his race, with the plans and duties of other people. Among the women who were interested in the library and the books therein, were Mrs. James Coggeshall, Mrs. Arthur Dexter, Miss Anne Morse and her sisters, Mrs. Elizabeth Shepard and Miss Charlotte Dailey, a person of great cultivation and charm. While I well remember Mrs. Sarah Helen Whitman, I do not recall her as a reader at the Athenaeum, though she presented it at just that period with Malbone's fine miniature of her ancestor Nicholas Power. Mr. Marshall Woods, outstanding as the proprietor of more shares than anyone else—he had five—generally "took out" French books; and he and my mother were devoted readers of Balzac—then considered a very loose, immoral writer. Years afterwards in Paris, my mother sent a generous subscription to the erection of a monument to Balzac by the *Societé de Gens-des-Lettres* in gratitude for the many hours of pleasure she had gained through his books. One incident stands out in my memory—the request of a student for Gray's *Elegy*; when given two volumes of Gray's poems to find it for himself, he handed back the second volume saying "One volume of the *Elegy* will, I think, be enough for the present." But why blame the poor lad, when only a few months since I received a bill from a well-known book-seller "for one copy of Hardy's *Far from the Mad Dining Crowd*"!

In the interim between Mr. Hedge's death in August 1879, which completed a term of service lasting for twenty-five years, and the appointment of a new librarian, Miss Angell took full charge and I acted as her assistant. She hoped that the place left vacant might fall to her; but this did not come to pass. In September 1879, the Directors selected Mr. Daniel Beckwith for the position—a cultivated man admirably fitted for the post. On the news of this appointment, Miss Angell retired for a day to her lodgings; and thus for a short moment, alone and unadmonished, I presided over the destinies of the institution. She continued as assistant librarian up to the summer of 1895, having served in that post for twenty-four years, giving to her work unstinted labor and devotion.

With Mr. Beckwith's appointment my term of service was over, and it was but a year after, that I left Providence. But in all the intervening years, I have never lost my interest in libraries in general nor in the Athenaeum in particular. My service there taught me to feel at home among books and, to a slight degree, to understand the workings of libraries. I have had the good fortune since to continue a more or less intimate association with them—in Boston thrice as official visitor to the Public Library, on the Library Committee of the Museum of Fine Arts, and trustee of the Boston Athenaeum; and in Providence as a member of the Board of Management of the John Carter Brown Library and adviser on purchases for the Collection of Books on Printing at the Public Library. Probably this would not have come about had it not been for those early days when I played truant from school and thereby gained what school did not supply—a familiarity with books which has stood me in good stead all my life.

Notes

PUBLISHED: *The Athenaeum Bulletin* ("published occasionally by the Providence Athenaeum") 10 (April 1938), unpaginated.

NOTA BENE

BUT TWO kinds of printing exist in the world—good and bad; and all that I have to say about the Merrymount Press is that it has endeavoured to print well rather than print badly. Printing is a trade and not an art, but it has frontiers on the arts. Printing is a trade and not a profession, but it can be practised in the spirit of a profession. When I say in the spirit of a profession, it means that excellence of work comes first and rewards in money, second. If practised as a trade, rewards in money come first and excellence of work is like the way Lady Mary Rooney drove—"as God willed." That distinguished (but in spots, second-rate) man, Benjamin Franklin, had a trick of suggesting low reasons for effecting high results. When he said "honesty is the best policy" he was talking like a tradesman; but the saying that "the difference between honesty and honour is, that honour is seldom the best policy," and that "he who is honest from policy is not an honest man," represents the professional point of view.

There is a great deal of misleading writing about printing based on loose thought. There is much loose talk about printing based on such writing; and I have noticed that people who practise printing as a trade in private are the most likely to talk about it as an art in public! The solution for this difficulty is to talk less and think more. This should bear fruit in more serious work—which is merely applying our best thought to the needs of the customer and then supplying those needs in the best way we know how. The result of this effort may be imperfect because the printer directing the work is but a human being; though with this aim in view he will go farther than by other roads and farther than other printers. "The chief want in life," says Emerson, "is to have someone who will make us

[347]

do what we can." An alternative is to make ourselves "do what we can"! If I were a parson (which God forbid!) I should call this "A Message to my Fellow Craftsmen."

Notes

PUBLISHED: pamphlet (Boston: Merrymount Press, 1938).

The pamphlet contains a photograph of Updike and explains that "Mr. Updike was enrolled as Honorary Life Member of the Boston Club of Printing House Craftsmen in 1936." Updike's note is dated July 1938.

METROPOLITAN MUSEUM PRINTING

THERE IS an old-fashioned word in the dictionary—so old-fashioned that it went out of common use a hundred years ago—that I have never before had occasion to use; but it is a word connected with a city and the manners that life in, and associated with, great cities promotes. That word is *urbane*, and I use it because I can think of no word that so accurately or better describes the man whom we have met affectionately to honour. Now urbaneness or urbanity may be defined as kindness, civility, politeness—in short, gentle manners; but it also connotes one who is at home in the ways of cities and whose life has been formed by the best that cities have to give.

It is such a man that our friend is, and no one has more reason to know it than the citizens of New York—or in particular, that group of intelligent and cultivated persons who make up the artistic and intellectual life of the town, to whom the administration of this great Library where I now speak has been so constantly hospitable. Mr. Kent as Secretary of The Metropolitan Museum of Art has unceasingly promoted the advancement and jealously guarded the interests of that institution. One of his minor activities at the Museum has been the care he has given to its printing, where he has set a standard for all such institutional typography, as this exhibition so convincingly illustrates. In fact the Museum Press, inaugurated by Mr. Kent, is Kent himself, and most of the practical things the Museum works with—its labels, forms, announcements, posters, resolutions, booklets, and some of its books—are mainly designed by him. This in turn has been but a part or offshoot of his general interest in good printing, manifested by his influence on the publications of the Grolier Club in past years, as his like influence as president of The American Institute of Graphic Arts is evidenced today. In many other ways Mr. Kent has helped—in public by his thoughtful care that the public should know and have what is best, as this present exhibition witnesses; in private by patient counsel, and by teaching individuals what the best is and how to attain it—and that testimony too is here. To all these official and personal activities he has sacrificed, under a smiling and courteous demeanour, his strength, his time, his convenience, his inclinations—in other words, himself—far more than many of us care to realize. Asking no rewards, he has stood before us in good times and in evil times, the same helpful, cheerful, cultivated, urbane man. And it is because he has so often laughingly disclaimed to me in private the possession of any of these virtues, that I make bold to say in public now what he prevented me from saying then.

We hear nowadays a great deal about the cleansing and calming influence of nature, and it is hopefully supposed that aimless, thoughtless, and selfish people will, in the leisure of rural (or even suburban) surroundings, somehow develop interesting and generous traits hitherto smothered by urban activities. But many celebrated figures have loved towns and been town-minded, and some of them—in this quite unlike Kent, who loves the country—have breathed freely only in the atmosphere of great centres. Madame de Staël in the seclusion of Coppet sighed for the gutters of the Rue du Bac. Sidney

Smith called the country "a kind of healthy grave." A daughter of Rufus Choate, one of the most cultivated and brilliant women that New England ever produced, is credited with saying, "If you are going to the country and see a tree, kick it for me." Thus it is not rural delights that can always be depended upon to produce the thoughtful or well-rounded man.

And so, among many other accomplishments, Mr. Kent has proved in the sight of all men what a delightful character a town can form. He is an example of true townliness—true urbanity. And this civilized awareness of values, this delicate consideration of the interests of others have made him not only the loved and effective citizen of a great community, but a charming and distinguished citizen of the world.

Notes

PUBLISHED: *Addresses Given at the Opening of the Exhibition of Metropolitan Museum Printing Held in the Pierpont Morgan Library on* 24 *October* 1938, Keepsake No. 58 (New York: American Institute of Graphic Arts, 1939), pp. 1–3. Untitled. TYPESCRIPT: Updike Collection.

"In appreciation of the work initiated and furthered by Mr. Kent, in raising the standard of institutional printing to that of one of the Fine Arts, the Trustees of The Pierpont Morgan Library arranged that an *Exhibition of Printing done by and for The Metropolitan Museum of Art, under the Supervision of Henry Watson Kent* should be held in that Library from October 26 to November 12, 1938. The following addresses were delivered on the evening of October 24 at the private view, held for the members of The American Institute of Graphic Arts" (prefatory note by Belle da Costa Greene).

A NOTE ON BRUCE ROGERS

IN WRITING anything worth while about an exhibition of the work of the most distinguished American designer of books in our time, it is not for me to give a description of what has been so adequately described in many quarters, or to praise further what has already been discriminatingly praised both here and abroad. The task that I propose to myself is to consider—very briefly—what appear to me to be the reasons for this work being what it is, and how far it reflects the personality of the man who produced it.

One of the remarkable things about Mr. Rogers' work is that, without the preliminary trial-by-error which afflicts most would-be designers of fine books, his first book issued by the Riverside Press was the production of an accomplished master of his art. Thus one is unable to see retrogression or progression in the books shown in this exhibition, and although at first glance this seems a dubious compliment, on consideration it will be seen to be very high praise. Of course certain books have properly and inevitably lent themselves to a kind of magnificence in typography and design that makes them automatically "exhibition pieces." But others, demanding more sober treatment, show no less success in arriving at what their designer intended them to be. In short, Rogers at the first step "got into his stride" and there was no learning to walk by distressing tumbles. So without the intermediate stages that many of us have to travel, he arrived *per saltum* at the goal where most men would be content to finish. This ability may to some degree account for, if it does not explain, the fact that his earliest reactions were no less admirable than his latest, and this surprisingly sustained excellence is but one instance of his varied talents.

Again, certain circumstances, which in the case of ordinary men might be supposed to retard progress—early years passed far from the great centres of artistic cultivation, such as London, Paris, or Rome—were not liabilities but actually assets in his career. With mind and eye unusually sensitive to beauty, the impact of great examples of design in printing or in decoration came upon him with a fresh and vivifying shock that produced immediate fruition; and (if I am not mistaken) became a source of strength. Thus he sensed certain possibilities which the more sophisticated native of England, France, or Italy might have passed by.

Viewing these books from another angle, we also recognize an enormous versatility; and this versatility appears to make Rogers not so much at home in any one style, as in many a delightful if somewhat disconcertingly clever guest. That, too, to my mind, has its reason. Rogers has never been deeply attached, as many are, to particular localities. He has been eclectic in his mode of living, in the variety of places where he has lived, in the different friends that he has made, and in his varied business associations; and it would be hard to say whether the land or the sea claims his special affection. Just as one cannot feel that in these respects he has marked predilection, neither can one see marked predilection for any particular style in printing. He has worked in many styles and successfully in all, but it would not be easy to say which style he, at heart, preferred—to say, "This *is* Rogers." These books are all "Rogers" and no one but he could make them; but which book he liked best—that is his secret—and if he liked one best today, tomorrow?—perhaps tomorrow he might like his model of a ship better and the ship would be as charming as the book! Thus the diversities of his work are somewhat a characterization of the man.

Rogers once said to me, "I have no originality; I am only an imitator"—one of those exaggerations illustrating the French apothegm that we can say of ourselves what we should not like

[352]

others to say of us because we know where to put the accent. At the moment I replied, "Nonsense," and as a matter of fact, what he said was not true. Certain books assuredly demand a treatment that is imitative—but the originality in such work lay in his ability to see possibilities of adaptation to which others were blind. And some of his minor and more ephemeral work exhibits qualities of ingenuity and originality in the use of type and ornament that are unsurpassed.

It is here that he is truly American—for an American can always make one thing "do" for another. An Englishman opens a bottle with a corkscrew, and without a corkscrew no respectable British bottle will allow itself to be opened. The more passionate Latin breaks the neck of the bottle, though he may die, perchance, from imbibing bits of glass with his wine. A Yankee will use pin, scissors, poker, pitchfork—'tis all one to him if the bottle gets uncorked!—he is not bound by convention, takes anything that comes to hand, and sees useful possibilities in the most unlikely quarters. In that, Rogers is a thoroughgoing Yankee, and has made gorgeous the poop of a model seventeenth-century ship with bits of tawdry gilt comb bought at a ten-cent store.

Perhaps the only possible criticism of Rogers' printing was that made long ago by Mr. Alfred Pollard in his paper *Modern Fine Printing in England and Mr. Bruce Rogers.* "Can Mr. Rogers," he asks, "develop a style exclusively his own and can he (bibliographies and verse are a little anaemic) print a full-blooded modern book? . . . Hitherto, like all the other experimenters, we have always found him looking around for a hint. By this method he has achieved all but the very highest success. I am eager to see him aim at the very highest and produce an individual and characteristic book with no antiquarian flavour." Since then Mr. Pollard's challenge has been ably met; but when he made this criticism he forgot the elusive personality of the man he was writing about. This extraordinary versatility made Pollard a bit uncomfortable; he wished to force

Rogers into a pigeon-hole—then he could be classified and all would be neat and tidy. But if Rogers was to be thus classified, he would not be Rogers—nor the man in whose honour and for the pleasure of others this collection has been assembled, the most exquisitely sensitive designer of books that this country, or perhaps any country, possesses, whose praise of late is in all the churches and who has something more than that "infinite capacity for taking pains" which—so inadequately—defines genius; that something far higher and finer, which partakes of genius itself.

Notes

PUBLISHED: *The Work of Bruce Rogers, Jack of All Trades, Master of One: A Catalogue* (New York: Oxford University Press, 1939), pp. xi–xv.

The contribution by Updike is entitled "Introductory Note" and dated November 1938; the volume is a catalogue of a Rogers exhibition sponsored by the American Institute of Graphic Arts and the Grolier Club.

Rudolph Ruzicka's memories of the occasion offer a slightly different perspective: "[In 1938] there was being planned a big Bruce Rogers show, and I was given the task of getting Updike to write something for the catalogue that was to commemorate it. Updike and Rogers were not very friendly. So, it was quite a task to persuade Updike. But, finally, he did it, wrote the statement; and I delivered it" (*Rudolph Ruzicka: Speaking Reminiscently*, p. 107). (There are further details about this episode in the Updike–Ruzicka correspondence, Chap. 12.) Updike's personal relationship with Rogers was generally cordial, but he had misgivings about Rogers' more flamboyant style of book-making, and he was acutely aware that many saw them as rivals.

STANLEY MORISON

THE WRITER of a preface is much like the manager of an excursion who, when he has conducted his party to the sight to be seen, finds his duty done. But there are different ways of doing this duty. One way is to take his sight-seers by the most direct route, however travel-worn and dusty it may be. Another is to choose a pleasanter, though more circuitous route which—since an element of surprise should exist in every work of art—at first seems to lead in a direction contrary to the point to be reached. By various wooded curves, however, a nearer approach to the end of the jaunt is achieved than is realized; soon objects seem to indicate its neighbourhood; at last glimpses of what we are to see actually are disclosed, and after skirting its demesne at new angles, the object of our search lies before us. This is the better sort of approach, for it may put the traveller—even the reader of a preface—in a kindly humour.

If all knowledge, like some diseases, were contagious, it would be an interesting speculation to consider the results of such benign phenomena. And yet I often think that many gatherings of those who seek, rather than possess, knowledge, are held on some such supposition. It is supposed, vaguely, that a number of not particularly well-informed units may, by association or combination, make a well-informed whole; and thus we see many earnest persons encourage "getting together" when a more exact perception of their own intellectual needs would counsel getting apart. As was cleverly said by a modern writer, people form bands for culture, as if they feared to meet it alone. It is commonly forgotten that special knowledge can be had only at the price of what has been termed "selective ignorance"; and for that reason, evenings devoted to learning to distinguish vegetables from wild-flowers should be sedulously

[355]

avoided by the serious student of astronomy!

Now solitude, of itself, produces no more fruitful intellectual results than mixing with one's fellows. If we desire to be alone, there must be a conscious purpose in so doing, or else vacuity and boredom will ensue. Isolation, in this instance, is simply a means to an end, and this end, I suppose, is an opportunity to think out by ourselves what we cannot seriously consider amid noisy companionship. A difficulty, however, is that we have come to depend upon other people's thoughts; we stop to think, and find our minds empty. "To a man not accustomed to thinking," says Trollope in one of his novels, "there is nothing in the world so difficult as to think. After some loose fashion we turn over things in our mind and ultimately reach some decision, guided probably by our feelings at the last moment rather than by any process of ratiocination;—and then we think we have thought. But to follow out one argument to an end, and then to found on the base so reached the commencement of another, is not common to us." Conscious of such inability, most persons turn to books. There they are met by a further dilemma—whether to read books that do their thinking for them, or books that demand undivided attention and that so stimulate and exercise the mind that it may be surprised into thinking itself.

The present volume falls into the second of these two classes. No one of late years has done more constructive thinking on subjects connected with typography than Mr. Stanley Morison. I do not always agree with him. He appears to me now and then a bit fanciful, and his theories perhaps cannot always be soundly supported. But no student of [*one or more illegible words*] or typography can pass him by. He has obliged me to reconsider several high-sounding but hasty generalizations; to revise some too readily accepted opinions; and he has told me—which was easy—many things I did not know. No papers about types and printing have been more useful and fruitful. "Mr. Morison," says a recent critic, "trusts his instincts, but he is always testing them by the light of reason. He is impatient of mere antiquarianism, and insists that the history of printing should be studied 'not as an end in itself, but as an inspiration towards the typographical task before us'. This is the spirit of the modern revival, and it is the right spirit. It has enabled us to shake off that idolatry of the fifteenth century which, as Mr. Morison sees, made the work of the Kelmscott Press and its imitators 'an anachronism'—the product of a dilettantism remote from the real world, which left the ordinary printer where it found him. Producers of books are now learning to study the tradition of the art as a whole, and to apply its lessons without surrendering their independence."

Morison is, in short, a "whet-stone of witte." What he writes is worth serious attention: and his stimulating pages are an admirable exercise for rusty minds. I recommend them to those who wish to learn, still more to those who would like to learn and be made to think at the same time. We must all begin by acquiring facts: by orderly arrangement, these facts may become information, and this accumulated information, thoughtfully applied, as Mr. Morison applies it, becomes knowledge. We may even now and then transmute our knowledge into wisdom, a feat, however, *consciously* unattainable; for the wise man alone knows how foolish he can still be!

Printers and lovers of good printing in these United States are now and then told that typographically England had little to teach us. I dare not attempt to meet to wide an indictment nor echo so sounding a phrase. Like the Psalmist, I can but "sit astonied" at it. Apart from all the admirable, restrained and considered printing that has always come to us from British presses, a further rebuttal to such statements is a book like this—perfected under amazingly [*illegible word*] difficulties—one of the many thoughtful books which modest English students year by year have produced and we may be sure will give us in the years to come.

Now gentlemen—and ladies, if there be any in the party

[357]

—our omnibus has arrived. You will find Mr. Morison waiting to guide you further on.

Notes

TYPESCRIPT: Updike Collection.

This document, entitled "Omnibus," was a preface to a book by Stanley Morison that was abandoned when his London flat was bombed in 1941. Morison recalled that in 1939, during his last meeting with Updike, "I promised to proceed as quickly as possible with the work, already begun, upon a volume of my collected papers, to which he was to contribute an introduction" (Beilenson, p. 66). The typescript is heavily (and somewhat illegibly) revised in Updike's hand; it is annotated "In final form," and is dated successively September 1926 and 1940.

The relationship between Morison and Updike is discussed in the introduction to David McKitterick's edition of their correspondence and in Morison's essay "Recollections and Perspectives" (Beilenson, pp. 16–66).

A MERRYMOUNT EXHIBITION OF 1940

A DISTINGUISHED member of the teaching staff of Harvard University once said to me, that as he looked back on his life, it seemed to him nothing more than a confused getting ready to begin. It seems so to me, as I look at the books shown in this exhibition, and realize that they are the result of a lifetime of work. Sometimes I ask myself, "Is this all that we at the Merrymount Press have accomplished? If we could have begun with the knowledge that we have now!" For I am not one of those who consider long life necessarily a matter for congratulation. It may be that it is allotted chiefly to those who have been slow in learning their lesson—like the dull pupil kept after school. Alas, by the time we get our training in life and in work, we are whisked away to some other part of the universe for which we faintly hope that our experiences here may have prepared us. That all this discipline cannot be pure waste is, perhaps, a convincing argument for immortality. How often I have said to myself, "I write illegibly; this time I will do better," only to find that, after my best effort, the written characters differ but little from those of every day. This seems to suggest that our limitations are inexorable, that we can only do what we can, and it is no use to try to be more than we are. So this exhibition shows the best that Mr. Bianchi, our associates, and I can do.

These reflections, however, may be the reverberations of a New England conscience. A New England conscience does not prevent one from doing wrong, but it takes away any possible pleasure there may be in so doing. If you behave in a manner consonant with its suggestions, you not only make yourself miserable, but do not even attain what it requires. The only personal consolation that has ever been suggested to me on this score came from an unexpected quarter. The Merrymount Press employed, many years ago, a rather shiftless Irish errand boy, who after a time disappeared into that limbo from which errand boys seldom return. About eight years after this disappearance we received a letter from him. He asked if we remembered a young man such as I have described. He announced that he intended to enter the Roman Catholic priesthood. Into that priesthood he entered, by way of a religious Order. After many years of training he came to see me. I was discoursing to him much as I am to you, about how little one fulfilled one's ideals in life or in work. He replied, with a grin, "Did it ever occur to you, Mr. Updike, that if you were what you wanted to be, the Lord could not stand you?" So perhaps if I were what I wanted to be, you could not stand me either!

But let me speak seriously for a moment. "When we consider," said an English writer, "the many races of man, their starts, their fortunes, their mutual alienation, their conflicts, their aimless courses, their random achievements and acquirements, the impotent conclusion of long-standing facts, the tokens so faint and broken, of a superintending design . . . the greatness and littleness of man, his far-reaching aims, his short duration, the curtain hung over his futurity, the dis-appointments of life, the defeat of good, the success of evil, physical pain, mental anguish, the prevalence and intensity of sin—all this is a vision to dizzy and appall; and inflicts upon the mind the sense of a profound mystery, which is absolutely beyond human solution."

This was written nearly a hundred years ago. Can we say that the problems the writer presented have as yet attained any solution? The world we live in is more distracted than when he wrote—though the echoes of the guns of Waterloo were still resounding in the world in which he lived. These periods of disorder have seldom been beneficent to literature or the arts. Yet, at the gloomiest periods of the world's history there have been many men and women, who, amid distress and uncer-tainty from which there seemed no happy issue, continued pa-tiently their daily tasks in arts and letters. "History harbors an optical illusion," a recent writer reminds us. "Looking back-ward we know how the exciting adventure turned out; but they did not. When we read of the past we are as beings who can see into the future, since that future is the present and we are living in it; but do we pause to reflect what courage it took to live in the past and not know how it turned out? Beethoven's deafness is a perfect example. To read his letters at the age of thirty when he began to lose his hearing is to wonder at his despair. Did he not live to become one of the world's greatest composers? Yes, but he had no guarantee of that." Nor have we any better guarantee than he had. So perhaps the best remedy for most of us in these our present discontents is to be found in a very old formula. That formula is "to learn and labour truly to earn our own living, and to do our duty in that state of life to which it shall please God to call us." [1]

"How old-fashioned," you may say, "and what a feeble light

to guide us in anxious days when skies seem falling and we are teased by problems that we cannot solve." In the past, though skies were falling they never fell! If mankind fell, it recovered and went on. It is because of this, that civilization has survived every disaster, as it does today, and will tomorrow. To those who insist that everything worth while is going down to defeat, I venture to say: Fear nothing but Fear.

It is to aid men working in the arts and belonging to what the eighteenth century termed the Republic of Letters that organizations like the Institute of Graphic Arts and The Grolier Club exist. The lengthening shadows of war may darken our lives, but they remain cities of refuge—protected not by artillery but by a civilized conception of life. It is to them that the promotion of this exhibition is due. I am most grateful to them for it, to Mr. Kent and his Committee, Messrs. Adams, Archer, Küp, Lydenberg, McCombs, Ruzicka, and Silve, who have laboured so long and generously to show the work of the Merrymount Press to the best advantage; and to Mr. McKay and many others who helped them. I am equally in debt to my old friends Mr. Cortissoz, Mr. Wroth, and Mr. Pottinger, who have found such kind words to say tonight. Although I cannot find as graceful words with which to thank you all, none the less you will know that they come from my heart.

Notes

PUBLISHED: *Daniel Berkeley Updike and the Merrymount Press*, Keepsake No. 61 (New York: American Institute of Graphic Arts, 1940), pp. 39–42.
The booklet contains addresses delivered at the opening of a Merrymount Press exhibition, held at the Grolier Club in 1940. Updike's remarks are entitled "Address by Mr. Updike."
1. The Catechism in *The Book of Common Prayer.*

A LAST WORD

It was, I think, Talleyrand who said that one could have no conception of the charm of life—*la douceur de vivre*—who had not lived before the French Revolution; though those who read Arthur Young's *Travels in France* written before that upheaval suspect that the charm was confined to the class to which Talleyrand belonged. Today it might be even more plausibly said that no one who has not lived before the Great War has any idea of that sense of enveloping security and that belief in the upward progress of humanity that was felt then. Meanwhile, a generation has grown up which learns of such peaceful beliefs and happy surroundings merely by hearsay. It knows, for itself, only a distracted world where large bodies of men have dared to deny by word and deed the old basic concepts of law, order, liberty, and progress. All this is disturbing and, disconcerted, we begin to wonder what is our place and part in such a world and how we who "have seen better days" are to carry on.

To me the answer is simple. To whatever generation we belong, we cannot, either individually or corporately, do much to right what seems to go so terribly askew in the world about us—or in politics or in printing. But a knowledge of history and the teaching of experience suggest that we have still a contribution to make. This is to put into our job, whatever it may be, the order, integrity, and decency which we may feel is lacking elsewhere; to work calmly, intelligently, persistently at what we are about. Just now various social, political, and economic upheavals have produced in us a vivid awareness of problems which prosperity concealed. While these problems are real they need not paralyze us. In the aspect of the world, here and now, there is nothing to despair of about which thoughtful persons, at various periods of history, have not *always* been puzzled and perhaps despairing. We forget that these same individuals, however, still carried on, that they ate their three meals a day, and took pains to avoid damp sheets, wet shoes, and draughts. We forget that Jane Austen wrote her placid masterpieces in the days of the French Revolution and amid the fears of French invasion. We forget that some of the best work which has been done in the world, in music, in literature, and in art, was undertaken despite "the slings and arrows of outrageous fortune." In these troubled days that same refuge is ours.

I do not intend to conclude with words that seem to suggest a hiding-place from impending and universal disaster. There are those who feel that everything of value in the world is cracking about our heads. I do not believe that. *Our* world may crack but not *the* world. "New ideas in their violence," says the philosopher, "and new needs in their urgency pass like a storm; and then the old earth, scarred and enriched by those trials, finds itself still under the same sky, unscarred and pure as before." For life, in nature and in human nature, after each cosmic disaster or phase of man's folly, is renewed again and again.

Notes

PUBLISHED: *Some Aspects of Printing*, pp. 72–73.
This essay was written at the beginning of the Second World War, shortly before Updike's death.

Index

Index

de Staël, Madame (Germaine de), 349

De Vinne, Theodore Low, 4, 40, 217, 227, 309, 314
  quoted, 39

De Vinne Press, 4, 218, 232, 280, 289, 297, 299

Dibdin, Thomas Frognall, 137

Dickey, Adam H., 264

dictionaries, 213

Didot family, 38, 50, 54, 81, 86, 135, 203, 208–10, 215–16, 322, 338

Ditson, Oliver, Co., 241

Doane, Bishop William C., 227

Dolphin, 109

Dorr, George, 219

Doubleday, Page & Co., 237

Doves Press, 82, 140–41, 207–08, 218, 243

Drevet, Pierre-Imbert, *le jeune*, 205

Dryden, John, 205

Ducarel, Andrew, 112

Dumas, Alexandre, 84

Duncan, Alexander, 344

Dupré, Louis, 210

Durand, 73

Dürer, Albrecht, 130, 252

Du Cerceau family, 241

Dwiggins, William Addison, 79, 92, 252, 253, 256, 265, 274, 303–08

Eaton, Walter Pritchard, 255

École des Beaux Arts, 21

Eddy, Mary Baker, 264

Edelinck, Gerard, 207

Edwards, Passmore, 340

Edwards, Stephen O., 340

Edward VI, King, 297, 299

eighteenth century, 16, 26, 42, 47, 54, 75, 82, 85, 90, 96, 103, 111, 138, 171, 174, 177, 212, 230, 241, 249, 255, 309

Einstein, Lewis, 246

electrotyping, 49

Elizabeth, Queen, 29

Elstob, Elizabeth, 119–20

Elzevir family, 46

Emerson, Ellen, 225

Emerson, Ralph Waldo, 21, 170, 225
  quoted, 91, 173, 232, 347

em quads, 32, 33

end-papers, 39, 237–38, 253

English literature, 221

Engraver and Printer, 296

engraving, 136

Enschedé Foundry, 215, 263

Episcopal Church, 221, 231, 236, 238, 249, 266–67, 274, 280, 288–91, 301

Eragny Press, 87

Ernst, Carl, 345

Estienne family, 25, 81, 86, 208, 215, 312

Evening Prayer, 285–86

extracts, 39

Eyre & Spottiswoode, 103

Faber, John, 205

facsimiles, 87, 239, 256

Falkland, Lucius Cary, 2nd Viscount of, Lord Carye
  quoted, 185

Farnsworth Art School, 243

Farnum, Alexander, 345

Farrand, Mrs. Max, 212

Fell, Bishop John, 101, 104, 130, 196, 217, 309, 314

Fezandat, Michel, 85

Fick family, 83, 85

Fields, Annie, 225

fifteenth century, 23

fine printing, 90

Fittles, James, 208

Flaxman, John, 208

Fleischman, J. M., 215

Fleuron, 22, 54, 79, 92, 274, 317

Florence, 80, 84

Florio, John, 213

footnotes, xvi

format, 39, 45–46, 49

Foster, William E., 340

Fothergill, Thomas, 130

Foulis family, 87